W9-BVK-901

SAN FRANCISCO FLAVORS

San Francisco
FLAVORS

favorite recipes from

THE JUNIOR LEAGUE *of* SAN FRANCISCO

PHOTOGRAPHS BY JONELLE WEAVER ✳ ILLUSTRATIONS BY KELLI BAILEY

CHRONICLE BOOKS

SAN FRANCISCO

Text copyright © 1999
by the Junior League of San Francisco
Photographs copyright © 1999
by Jonelle Weaver
Illustrations copyright © 1999
by Kelli Bailey
All rights reserved.
No part of this book
may be reproduced in any form
without written permission
from the publisher.

Library of Congress Cataloging-in-Publication Data:
San Francisco Flavors: favorite recipes from the Junior League of San Francisco/
by the Junior League of San Francisco; photography by Jonelle Weaver.
      p.   cm.
  ISBN-10: 0-8118-2342-3   ISBN-13: 978-0-8118-2342-5
  1. Cookery, International. 2. Cookery—California—San Francisco.
  I. Junior League of San Francisco.
  TX725.A1S345 1999
  641.59—DC21   98-55731
                      CIP

Printed in Canada.

Designed by Deborah Bowman
Typesetting by Deborah Bowman

Distributed in Canada by Raincoast Books
9050 Shaughnessy Street
Vancouver, British Columbia V6P 6E5

10 9 8 7 6 5 4 3

Chronicle Books LLC
680 Second Street
San Francisco, CA 94107

www.chroniclebooks.com

Contents

ACKNOWLEDGMENTS

The Junior League of San Francisco thanks the following committees, who have worked on the planning, developing, recipe testing, manuscript editing and production, marketing, and sales of this cookbook:

COOKBOOK DEVELOPMENT AND PRODUCTION CO-CHAIRS: Sally James and Michele Meany

COMMITTEE MEMBERS: Sheila Addiego, Lorijon Bacchi, Susie Baker, Julie Banks, Anne Baxter, Linette Boudreaux, Melissa Brown-Hansen, Catherine Campbell, Sondra Carmody, Laura Cocozziello, Shelby Coffman, Karen Forsstrom, Suzanne Galuszka, Melanie Garner, Stephanie Gleason, Tammy Grady, Pamela Linke, Susan Llewellyn, Reynolds Martin, Lee Monozon, Elizabeth Monti, Nita Moore, Denise Nowell, Kristin Palma, Phoebe Pluchar, Wendy Riley, Sonia Tajirian, Marit Taylor, Beth Wagner, Eve Wirth, Holly York

COOKBOOK MARKETING AND SALES CHAIR: Holly York

COMMITTEE MEMBERS: Lorijon Bacchi, Susie Baker, Julie Banks, Lisa Barnes, Sara Donlon, Genie Donnelly, Heather Fairfull, Mary Fenton, Suzanne Galuszka, Melanie Garner, Tammy Grady, Kimberly Hooker, Susan Llewellyn, Jennifer Matfiak, Diana Miller, Starla Navis, Erin Nelson, Kristin Palma, Carol Rachwald, Beth Saunders, Lisa Schneider, Alexia Smith, Hayley Swift, Frances Szeto, Marit Taylor, Eve Wirth, Victoria Wright, Heidi Wurtele, Amanda Wyse, Katherine Young

COOKBOOK RESEARCH AND DEVELOPMENT CHAIRS: Angela Gyetvan 1995–97
Jan Halper 1995–96

We also thank our families, friends, co-workers, and neighbors who submitted recipes, tested recipes, and supported our efforts in producing this book.

About the Junior League of San Francisco

FOUNDED IN 1911, THE JUNIOR LEAGUE OF SAN FRANCISCO (JLSF) is an organization of women committed to promoting voluntarism, developing the potential of women, and improving the community through the effective action and leadership of trained volunteers. The purpose of the organization is purely educational and charitable.

The League reaches out to all women, regardless of race, color, religion, sexual orientation, handicapped status, or national origin, who possess an interest and commitment to voluntarism.

The League focuses its efforts on the preservation of the family. It supports programs and collaborative efforts for parent education, support groups, life-skills instruction, after-school programs, health-awareness education, child care, and family activities. Additionally, the League believes that the cycle of violence must be broken, and thus it supports domestic violence programs as well as programs that help battered women make the transition to economic self-sufficiency.

For more information about JLSF, write to:

THE JUNIOR LEAGUE OF SAN FRANCISCO

2226A FILLMORE STREET

SAN FRANCISCO, CALIFORNIA 94115

or visit our Web site at: WWW.JLSF.ORG.

This cookbook celebrates the honest virtues of homemade cuisine and dining at home. So, why should a restaurateur introduce it? Well, this restaurateur's proudest moments have been when I've allowed myself to be persuaded that the food we serve at Chez Panisse may have actually inspired people to eat family meals together.

The ritual of the family meal is among the keys to humane and peaceable civilization. In the words of Francine du Plessix Gray, "The family meal is not only the core curriculum in the school of civilization discourse; it is also a set of protocols that curb our natural savagery and our animal greed, and cultivate a capacity for sharing and thoughtfulness." Children learn the art of human companionship by sitting down and eating with others; without this experience, they may never acquire the fellowship and empathy necessary for creating and sustaining compassionate communities. It is true that it takes time and effort to do the shopping and cooking and cleaning up—like any ritual, the family meal requires sacrifices—but making these sacrifices nurtures us all.

Shopping and cooking require us to make choices. If we choose food with rich colors, irresistible aromas, and varied flavors, our senses are stimulated in ways that can improve our ability to communicate. And if we choose to buy fresh, organically grown food directly from the people who produce it, we are supporting an agricultural economy that enriches the soil, preserves the land for future generations, and spawns vibrant communities of producers and consumers.

On the other hand, if we settle for food that's denatured, processed, shrink-wrapped, and frozen, we are dulling our senses and depriving ourselves of a wealth of information. And if we choose to buy only commodified, mass-produced, and heavily advertised foods, we are supporting an unnatural agriculture that depletes natural resources and destroys communities.

The right to choose has to be made available to everyone. At Chez Panisse, we are proud to be part of the demand for real food that is helping bring back farmers' markets all over the country. Here in the Bay Area, we have had a part in the creation of a network of scores of small-scale suppliers—gardeners, farmers, ranchers, fishermen, foragers, millers, bakers—all of whom share our vision of a future in which fresh local seasonal food is a right, not a privilege.

The home cook can hasten the day: Head for the market; buy the finest, freshest produce that can be found; and use cookbooks like this one for inspiration and guidance. When you sit down with your family, be grateful for the bounty of nature, and for the farmers and farm workers whose labor makes our nourishment possible. Give thanks to the Junior League for making our communities better places to live, and take pride in supporting a sustainable future for yourself, your family, and the generations to come.

—ALICE WATERS, CHEZ PANISSE

INTRODUCTION

We welcome you to the pages of San Francisco Flavors, *a cookbook that pairs the international culinary experience of our unique city with fine, fresh ingredients from the San Francisco Bay Area. San Francisco's cuisine includes the flavors of Asia, Latin America, and Europe. Ingredients for almost any type of cuisine can be found locally, and the Bay Area provides everything from fruits, vegetables, and herbs to meats, cheeses, and wine. More and more Northern California growers and producers are growing organic foods and heirloom varietals. San Francisco also enjoys a supply of seafood from the Pacific Ocean. The professional chef and the home cook have plentiful resources from which to create flavorful, yet simple dishes. ✳ San Francisco chefs are known for their trend-setting, award-winning cuisine. We have captured some of these trends in our recipes for appetizers and drinks, brunch dishes, entrées, pastas, salads and side dishes, soups, and desserts. Over the past few years, hundreds of Junior League volunteers have worked together to develop recipes from their own culinary experiences. This book is the product of much work and experimentation to bring you the ultimate San Francisco dining experience. ✳ We hope* San Francisco Flavors *will inspire you to explore and enjoy the vast world of food by visiting your local farmers' markets and experimenting with different styles of cuisine and unusual ingredients. Our book recommends wine selections to enjoy with many of the dishes, offers tips on how to prepare or use particular ingredients, provides a culinary glossary, and includes a resource guide for ingredients. Read through the pages of* San Francisco Flavors *and indulge in a wider world of preparing, cooking, and enjoying good, fresh food with your family and friends. Enjoy a little bit of San Francisco in your own home.*

APPETIZERS AND FIRST COURSES

Greek Salad Salsa with Toasted Pita Chips

Toasted Walnut and Ginger-Garlic Dip

Muhammara

Eggplant and Yellow Pepper Dip

Spinach Hummus

Cheese Platters

Cambazola Apricots

Brie and Papaya Quesadillas

Leek and Artichoke Quesadillas with Cherry Tomato Salad

Onion Confit Crostini

Mozzarella and Olive Tapenade Bruschetta

Bruschetta with Flageolet Puree and Wilted Greens

Fig and Pâté Bruschetta

Leek, Pancetta, and Feta Cheese Tart

Artichoke and Cherry Tomato Tart

Caramelized Onion Tart

Asparagus and Goat Cheese Tart

Smoked Salmon and Onion Tart

Delicata and Cotswold Pizzas

Salsa Verde and Tomato Pizzas

Wild Mushroom and Teleme Pizzas

Corn Cakes with Chipotle-Tomato Sauce

Roasted Heirloom Tomatoes

Butternut Squash Ravioli with Sage Butter

Scallops with Cider, Riesling, and Sage

Pancetta-Wrapped Scallops and Papaya

Thai Minced Chicken in Lettuce Leaves

Grilled Sesame-Garlic Beef Skewers

Skewered Orange-Ginger Chicken

Spiced Lamb Triangles

Chicken Empanadas with Mango Salsa

East-Meets-Southwest Salmon Sushi Wrap

Grilled Five-Spice Duck on Pear Chips with Pear Chutney

Spicy Jumbo Shrimp with Tomatillo Sauce

Beef and Asparagus Wraps

Greek Salad Salsa with Toasted Pita Chips

This zesty blend of feta cheese, olives, tomatoes, cucumber, and parsley is a wonderful alternative to guacamole and chips. If, by chance, there is any left over, pulse it in a blender or food processor and use as a sauce for grilled fish. (See photograph, page 65.)

8 ounces feta cheese, crumbled
  (1½ cups)

1 large ripe tomato, seeded and
  chopped (see page 40)

3 scallions, thinly sliced,
  including green portions

½ cucumber, peeled, seeded, and
  coarsely chopped

½ cup black olives, pitted and
  sliced

¼ cup minced fresh flat-leaf
  parsley

2 tablespoons minced fresh
  oregano

2 tablespoons snipped fresh dill

Juice of ½ lemon

⅓ cup olive oil

Freshly ground pepper to taste

Toasted Pita Chips (recipe follows)

1. In a medium bowl, combine all the ingredients except the pita chips and gently mix.

2. Cover and refrigerate for at least 2 hours or up to one day.

toasted pita chips

You might want to double this recipe—these chips disappear quickly! Make them
the night before you plan to serve them, and leave them in the turned-off oven overnight.

1. Preheat the oven to 300°F. Cut the pita rounds in half. Cut each half again into thirds, then separate each piece to make two bite-sized chips. Using a pastry brush, lightly coat each chip with the melted butter.

2. Lay the chips in a single layer on a large baking sheet. Dust with the garlic powder, dill, and paprika. Place in the oven and turn the oven off. Do not open the oven door until the oven is completely cool and chips are crisp, about 4 hours or overnight. If the chips are still soft, repeat cooking process, preheating oven to 200°F.

1 package mini pita breads
½ cup (1 stick) unsalted butter, melted
Garlic powder, dried
Dill, and paprika to taste

CHEF'S TIP HUBERT KELLER, FLEUR DE LYS: *To coat food lightly with olive oil or butter, instead of using a pastry brush, fill a plastic squeeze-trigger bottle with oil or warm melted butter; hold 12 to 18 inches from the food and give a couple of quick squeezes to provide a light, even coat.*

Toasted Walnut and Ginger-Garlic Dip

MAKES 2 CUPS

This aïoli-like dip has a nutty, aromatic flavor with a garlic bite that everyone will enjoy.
Make it a day ahead to allow the flavors to meld. Serve it with crudité such as blanched asparagus
and green beans. You can also use it as a spread for chicken or turkey sandwiches.

1 ½ cups good-quality
mayonnaise

¼ cup walnuts, toasted, and finely
chopped (see page 18)

2 garlic cloves, minced

1 tablespoon finely grated fresh
ginger

½ teaspoon salt

1 teaspoon ground pepper

1 ½ tablespoons fresh lemon juice

Pinch of saffron dissolved in 1
tablespoon hot water (optional)

1. In a medium bowl, combine all ingredients and mix well. Taste and adjust the seasoning with salt or lemon juice. Cover and refrigerate overnight. Serve as a dip with vegetables.

ARNOLD WONG, EOS RESTAURANT: *Always store nuts in an airtight container in the freezer to prolong freshness.*

Muhammara

A rich red pepper spread with walnuts and a hint of spiciness.
Make this the day before serving to allow the flavors of the spices to mix.
The olive oil may separate slightly, so stir well before serving.

1. In a blender or food processor, combine the peppers and all the remaining ingredients except the oil. With the machine running, gradually add the olive oil. Serve with the pita triangles.

NOTE: To roast and peel peppers, preheat the broiler. Cut the peppers in half lengthwise. Stem, seed, and devein the peppers. Place them skin-side up on a broiler pan lined with aluminum foil. Broil until completely blackened, 12 to 15 minutes. Transfer the peppers to a paper bag, close the bag, and let cool for about 15 minutes. Remove blackened skin.

6 red bell peppers, roasted, peeled, and chopped (see note)

⅔ cup fresh bread crumbs

⅓ cup walnuts, toasted and finely chopped (see page 18)

3 garlic cloves, minced

½ teaspoon salt

1 tablespoon fresh lemon juice or to taste

2 teaspoons clover honey

1 teaspoon ground cumin

½ teaspoon red pepper flakes

¾ cup extra-virgin olive oil

Toasted Pita Triangles (recipe follows)

---

toasted pita triangles

1. Preheat the oven to 350°F. Toss the pita triangles in a bowl with the paprika and oil. Place on a baking sheet and bake for about 10 minutes, or until crisp.

5 mini pita breads, cut into quarters

½ teaspoon paprika

2 tablespoons olive oil

Eggplant and Yellow Pepper Dip

SERVES 10 TO 12 AS AN APPETIZER

When choosing eggplant for this colorful vegetarian dip, look for a shiny texture, which is an indication of freshness. The consistency of the dip is better if made the day before.

One 1½-pound globe eggplant, halved and stemmed

2 teaspoons olive oil

1 onion, finely chopped

4 garlic cloves, minced

1 yellow, red or green bell pepper, seeded, deveined, and chopped

1 large tomato, chopped

½ teaspoon salt

1 teaspoon ground pepper

1 tablespoon balsamic vinegar

1 tablespoon capers, rinsed and drained

¼ cup pine nuts, toasted (see note)

2 tablespoons minced fresh flat-leaf parsley

Warm pita triangles, toasted pumpernickel bread, crackers, or crostini for serving

1. Preheat the oven to 450°F. Put peeled eggplant on a baking sheet and bake for 25 to 30 minutes, or until tender when pierced with a sharp knife. Let cool to the touch and cut into small cubes.

2. In a medium, heavy saucepan over medium heat, heat the oil and sauté the onion for 4 to 5 minutes, or until lightly browned. Add the garlic and cook for 1 minute. Add the pepper and cook for 4 minutes. Add the eggplant, tomato, salt, and pepper and cook for 8 to 10 minutes, or until the vegetables are soft. Add the vinegar and cook for 2 to 3 minutes, or until thick and jam-like. Add the capers, pine nuts, and parsley and cook for 2 minutes. Taste and adjust the seasoning. Cover and refrigerate for at least 24 hours or up to 2 days. Serve with pita triangles, toasted bread, crackers, or crostini.

ARNOLD WONG, EOS RESTAURANT: *When preparing eggplant for a salad or stir-fry, try lightly oiling it then roasting it in a very hot oven. This will allow you to use less oil.*

NOTE: To toast nuts and sunflower seeds spread the nuts or seeds in a single layer in a shallow pan. Bake in a preheated 350°F oven, stirring occasionally, until lightly toasted, 5 to 8 minutes, depending on the size of the nut. Very small amounts may be stirred in a dry skillet over medium heat until fragrant and lightly toasted.

Spinach Hummus

Garbanzo beans, also known as chickpeas, are a great source of protein.
Fresh spinach adds flavor and texture to a traditional hummus
and is available prewashed and packaged for your convenience.

1. If using dried beans, pick over them and rinse. Soak the beans overnight in a large saucepan of water to cover by 2 inches. Drain. Return the beans to the same pan and add water to cover by 2 inches.

2. Bring the beans almost to a boil. Reduce heat to low and simmer, uncovered, for 45 minutes, or until tender. Drain and let cool.

3. In a blender or food processor, combine the garbanzo beans and garlic and puree until smooth. Add the spinach, lemon juice, spices, salt, and pepper. Blend thoroughly. With the machine running, gradually add the olive oil. Taste for seasoning. Serve with toasted pita bread triangles or crudités.

2 cups dried garbanzo beans, or
   8 ounces canned garbanzo
   beans, drained

1 garlic clove

1 cup packed spinach leaves

1 tablespoon fresh lemon juice

½ teaspoon garam masala

½ teaspoon ground cumin

1 teaspoon salt

½ teaspoon ground pepper

¼ cup olive oil

Toasted Pita Triangles (page 17)
   or crudités for serving

Cheese Platters

Selecting cheeses can be a mind-boggling experience with so many choices
and variations available today. Following are suggestions for putting together interesting
combinations of cheeses. Be creative in arranging the platters. Use unusual trays lined
with maple or lemon leaves, or purple basil. Scatter dried red currants or apricots around the platter.
Garnish with bunches of grapes, slices of apples, or a ramekin of large marinated olives.

THREE-CHEESE PLATTERS

Explorateur, Gorgonzola, Morbier

or

Roquefort, Montrachet, Aged English Cheshire

FIVE-CHEESE PLATTERS

Brie, Brillat-Savarin, Stilton, Tomme de Savoie, Emmantaler

or

St. Andre, Morbier, Crottin de Chavignol, Maytag Blue, Aged Mimolette

Cambazola Apricots

Cambazola is a rich cheese combining the texture of Brie and the tanginess of
blue cheese. Dried apricots and toasted pecans nicely balance the robust cheese flavor.
If you find fresh apricots at your local farmers' market, use them instead of dried.

1. In a dry large skillet over medium-high heat, toast the pecans,
stirring constantly, for 4 to 5 minutes, or until browned. Pour into a
bowl and let cool.

2. In a medium bowl, mix the Cambazola and cream cheese together
until blended. Place a dollop of the cheese mixture on each apricot and
top with a pecan. Refrigerate for 30 minutes. Serve.

32 dried apricots

32 pecan halves

*½ cup room-temperature
Cambazola cheese*

*3 ounces cream cheese at room
temperature*

Brie and Papaya Quesadillas

SERVES 4

This winning combination will bring raves. The quesadillas are also fabulous grilled.
If just making a couple, cook them in butter and oil in a cast-iron skillet.
This is a great last-minute appetizer when friends drop by to watch the big game.

1 red onion, thinly sliced

1 papaya, peeled, seeded and
   diced

1 jalapeño chili, seeded and
   minced

½ bunch cilantro, stemmed and
   minced

Juice of 2 Mexican or regular
   limes, plus lime wedges for
   garnish

4 large flour tortillas

10 ounces Brie cheese, rind
   removed, thinly sliced

2 tablespoons butter

2 tablespoons olive oil

1. Soak the onion in a small bowl of ice water for 20 minutes. Drain well and pat dry. In a medium bowl, combine the onion, papaya, chili, and cilantro. Add the lime juice and gently stir.

2. Preheat the oven to 400°F. Lay the tortillas on baking sheet. Place slices of Brie on one half of each tortilla. Evenly divide the papaya mixture over the Brie slices. Fold each tortilla in half.

3. In a small saucepan, melt the butter and combine with the olive oil. Brush the top of each quesadilla with the butter mixture. Bake for 5 to 7 minutes. Turn the quesadillas over and brush the other side with butter mixture. Bake 5 to 7 minutes longer, or until the cheese is melted and the tortillas are lightly browned. Cut each quesadilla into 3 pieces and serve warm, garnished with lime wedges.

Leek and Artichoke Quesadillas with Cherry Tomato Salad

SERVES 12 AS AN APPETIZER, 6 AS A LUNCH ENTRÉE

Northern California is the world's largest producer of artichokes, so you'll
find them on the menus of many San Francisco restaurants in a variety of dishes.
These quesadillas can serve as a simple summer appetizer or a light lunch. Fresh artichoke
hearts are preferred for both flavor and texture, but canned hearts may be substituted.

WINE SUGGESTION BY KRIS HARRIMAN: SAINTSBURY CARNEROS PINOT NOIR

1. To prepare fresh artichoke hearts, fill a bowl with water and add the lemon juice. Cut two-thirds off the top of each artichoke and break off the tough outer leaves. Cut off the stem and all of the dark green parts of the base. Rub the freshly cut areas with the cut lemon half. Cut the artichokes into quarters and, using a paring knife, cut out the choke. Cut each piece of heart in half and soak in the lemon water for several minutes; drain. Chop the fresh or canned artichoke hearts.

2. In a large skillet over medium-high, heat the 2 tablespoons olive oil. Add the garlic and sauté for 1 or 2 minutes, then add the bay leaf and thyme. Add the leeks, lower heat to medium, and cook until soft but not browned, about 8 minutes. Add the artichoke hearts and cook until tender, about 8 minutes. Remove and discard the bay leaf. Add the salt and pepper. Stir in the mustard. Set aside and let cool.

3. In a small bowl, combine the bell pepper, parsley, tomatoes, and red onion. Season with salt and pepper to taste and mix well. Set aside.

4. Heat a large cast-iron skillet over medium-high heat. Lightly coat the pan with olive oil and put a tortilla in the pan. Spread about ¼ cup of the leek mixture over the tortilla. Cover with some crumbled goat cheese, top with a second tortilla, and press down. Cook for about 1 minute, or until the bottom is browned, then turn and cook until the second side is browned. Remove and keep warm in a low oven. Repeat with the remaining ingredients, using more olive oil as needed.

5. Cut the quesadillas into wedges and place on a large warm serving platter. Garnish each wedge with a large spoonful of the bell pepper and tomato mixture and serve at once.

3 large artichokes, or 1 cup
   canned artichoke hearts

Juice of 1 lemon, plus 1 lemon
   half

2 tablespoons extra-virgin olive
   oil, plus oil for cooking

2 garlic cloves, minced

1 bay leaf

2½ tablespoons minced fresh
   thyme

3 large leeks, white part only,
   washed and thinly sliced

Salt and freshly ground pepper to
   taste

1 tablespoon Dijon mustard

½ cup chopped yellow bell pepper

1 tablespoon minced fresh
   flat-leaf (Italian) parsley

2 cups cherry tomatoes, halved

1 tablespoon minced red onion

12 flour tortillas

5 ounces fresh goat cheese,
   crumbled (1 cup)

Onion Confit Crostini

MAKES 30 APPETIZERS

Onion confit is made by slowly cooking onions until they caramelize to a jamlike consistency. Look for Vidalia or Walla Walla onions because they produce a sweeter confit. This confit can be made up to 2 days ahead and is a delicious accompaniment to pork or chicken.

WINE SUGGESTION BY KRIS HARRIMAN: NEWTON UNFILTERED CHARDONNAY

ONION CONFIT:

5 tablespoons butter

2 pounds sweet onions, such as
    Vidalia, Walla Walla, or Maui,
    thinly sliced (about 8 cups)

½ cup sugar

1 teaspoon salt

1 teaspoon ground pepper

1 cup Cabernet or other dry red
    wine

6 tablespoons balsamic vinegar

CROSTINI:

1 French baguette cut into
    ¼-inch-thick slices

Extra-virgin olive oil for brushing

1. TO MAKE THE CONFIT: In a large skillet, melt the butter over medium heat. Add the onions, sugar, salt, and pepper and cook, stirring occasionally, until very soft and lightly browned, about 35 minutes. Add the wine and vinegar and simmer, uncovered, for 25 minutes, stirring often. Taste for seasoning. Let cool. If making ahead, store in an airtight container in the refrigerator for up to 2 days. Bring to room temperature before serving.

2. TO MAKE THE CROSTINI: Preheat the oven to 400°F. Brush one side of each baguette slice with a little olive oil and arrange on a large baking sheet. Bake until lightly browned, about 8 minutes. Turn over and lightly brown on other side, about 8 minutes. Let cool on a wire rack. The crostini can be prepared several days ahead and kept in an airtight container.

3. To serve, spread 1 tablespoon onion confit on each toast.

Mozzarella and Olive Tapenade Bruschetta

MAKES 24 APPETIZERS

Tapenade is a delicious olive spread available in gourmet markets and many supermarkets. Keep a jar in your pantry, and you can whip up this appetizer at a moment's notice. The arugula garnish gives this hors d'oeuvre a peppery finish.

1. Preheat the oven to 400°F. Brush the bread slices lightly with oil. Place the slices on a baking sheet and bake until browned, about 15 minutes, turning once halfway through.

2. Preheat the broiler. Spread 1 tablespoon tapenade on each slice. Place equal amounts of cheese on top. Place under the broiler until melted and slightly bubbling, about 2 minutes. Remove from the oven and sprinkle with the arugula. Serve at once.

½-inch slices from a French baguette

Olive oil for brushing

8 ounces (1 cup) fresh mozzarella cheese, sliced

½ cup olive tapenade

½ cup arugula leaves, chopped

Bruschetta with Flageolet Puree and Wilted Greens

SERVES 6

A simple appetizer to serve before a barbecue or an informal
Italian dinner. Dried flageolets are immature kidney beans
with a delicate flavor similar to that of fresh beans.

1 cup dried flageolets or other
   white beans

4 garlic cloves, minced

1 tablespoon minced fresh thyme,
   or 1 teaspoon dried thyme

8 tablespoons olive oil, plus more
   for brushing

Salt and freshly ground pepper to
   taste

1 baguette, cut into 18 ½-inch-
   thick diagonal slices

6 cups coarsely chopped stemmed
   bitter greens, such as Swiss
   chard, dandelion, or arugula

1 tablespoon Cabernet or other
   red wine vinegar

1 tablespoon balsamic vinegar

1. Pick over and rinse the beans. Put the beans in a medium saucepan and add water to cover by 2 inches. Soak overnight. Drain. Add water to cover the beans by 2 inches and bring to a boil. Reduce heat and simmer, uncovered, until tender, about 2 hours, stirring occasionally. Drain.

2. In a blender or food processor, pulse the beans, half of the garlic, and the thyme. Add 6 tablespoons of the olive oil and puree. Add salt and pepper. Use now, or cover and refrigerate for up to 2 days.

3. Preheat the oven 400°F. Brush the bread slices with olive oil and place on a baking sheet. Bake for 8 minutes, or until lightly browned. Turn over and bake until lightly browned on the second side, about 3 to 4 minutes. Let cool. Use now, or store in an airtight container for up to 2 days.

4. In a large saucepan over medium-high heat, heat the remaining 2 tablespoons olive oil and sauté the bitter greens for 3 minutes. Add the vinegars, the remaining garlic, and salt and pepper to taste and continue to cook until wilted. Remove from heat.

5. Spread the bean puree on the croutons. Place 3 on a plate and top with the warm wilted greens. Serve at once.

Fig and Pâté Bruschetta

These appetizers can be passed on a tray or served at the table
to accompany a salad as a first course. Choose large ripe figs when they
come to market in the summer months. (See photograph, page 66.)

1. In a small skillet, melt the butter over medium heat. Add the sliced
shallots and sauté until golden and caramelized, about 6 minutes.
Set aside.

2. In a small saucepan, combine the minced shallots, port, bay leaf, peppercorns, and zest. Bring the mixture to a boil, reduce heat and simmer
until the liquid has reduced to a thick syrup, 20 to 30 minutes. Remove
from heat and strain into a medium saucepan. Add the figs, salt, pepper,
and thyme. Cook over medium heat until the figs soften, about 5 minutes. Remove from heat. This can be made the day before.

3. Preheat the oven to 400°F. Place the bread slices on a baking sheet
and lightly brush both sides with oil. Toast until golden brown, 4 to 5
minutes on each side. Remove from the oven. Spread each slice of bread
with pâté. Spoon the fig mixture over the pâté and garnish with the sliced
shallots. Serve at once.

 Maria Helm, PlumpJack Café: *Grilled figs that have
been marinated in balsamic vinegar and a touch of olive oil are
a great accompaniment to pork, duck, game hens, or blue cheese.*

1 tablespoon butter

4 shallots, 2 thinly sliced, 2
    minced

1 cup port or Madeira

2 bay leaves

4 whole peppercorns

1 teaspoon orange zest

16 Mission or other large figs,
    quartered, or 2 cups dried figs,
    coarsely chopped

Salt and freshly ground pepper to
    taste

1 tablespoon minced fresh thyme,
    or 1 teaspoon dried thyme

Eight ¼-inch-thick slices
    whole-grain walnut bread or
    diagonal slices of baguette

Olive oil for brushing

12 ounces smooth pâté, such as
    foie gras or chicken liver pâté

Leek, Pancetta, and Feta Cheese Tart

SERVES 6

A flavorful, savory tart that can be made earlier in the
day and reheated or served at room temperature.

Pastry Dough (recipe follows)

4 ounces pancetta or bacon, thinly
   sliced and cut into medium dice

4 tablespoons butter

6 leeks, white part only, washed
   and thinly sliced

Kosher salt and freshly ground
   pepper to taste

½ cup heavy cream

1 egg at room temperature

2 teaspoons coarse-grained
   Dijon mustard

¼ teaspoon Madras curry powder

4 ounces feta cheese crumbled
   (¾ cup)

Mixed salad greens or frisée leaves
   for serving

1. Preheat the oven to 450°F. On a lightly floured board, roll the pastry dough into a 13-inch circle, and place in a 12-inch tart pan with a removable bottom. Roll the rolling pin over the top of the pan to trim the dough even with the edges. Transfer the pan to a baking sheet. Cover with plastic wrap and refrigerate.

2. In a large skillet over medium-high heat, cook the pancetta or bacon until lightly browned, 5 to 8 minutes. With a slotted spatula, transfer to paper towels to drain. In the same skillet, melt the butter over medium-high heat. Add the leeks, salt, and pepper. Cook, stirring occasionally, until the leeks are lightly browned, 12 to 15 minutes. Set aside to cool.

3. In a small bowl, whisk the cream, egg, mustard, and curry powder. Add half of the feta cheese and gently mix. Add salt and pepper to taste.

4. Remove the pastry from the refrigerator and scatter the cooled leeks over it. Pour the cream mixture over the leeks and scatter the pancetta on top. Sprinkle the remaining feta cheese over. Bake for 10 to 12 minutes, or until the cheese has melted and the crust is golden brown. Serve warm or at room temperature, cut into wedges placed on top of lettuce or frisée.

pastry dough

1. In a food processor, combine the flour, sugar, and salt. Add the butter and quickly pulse until the butter is the size of small peas. Add 2½ tablespoons of the ice water and pulse just until the pastry comes together and almost forms a ball. Add more water if necessary. To make by hand, in a medium bowl, stir the flour, salt, and sugar together. Cut in the butter using a pastry cutter or 2 knives, until the mixture resembles coarse meal. Gradually stir in the water with a fork until all the dry ingredients are moistened.

2. Turn the dough out on a lightly floured board, gather it into a ball, and shape it into a disk. Wrap in plastic and refrigerate for about 30 minutes.

1 cup all-purpose flour

¼ teaspoon sugar

½ teaspoon salt

6 tablespoons cold unsalted butter, cut into small cubes

2½ to 3½ tablespoons ice water

Artichoke and Cherry Tomato Tart

SERVES 6

The beautiful colors of red, yellow, and orange cherry tomatoes make this a great first course.
Look for red Sweet 100s and yellow Sungold cherry tomatoes for the most flavor.

Pastry Dough (page 29)

2 eggs at room temperature

½ cup crème fraîche or sour cream

2 teaspoons minced fresh thyme,
   or ¾ teaspoon dried thyme

Salt and freshly ground pepper to
   taste

1½ cups marinated artichoke
   hearts, drained and cut into
   quarters

1 small red onion, thinly sliced

20 cherry tomatoes, a mixture of
   red, yellow, and orange, halved

1. Preheat the oven to 450°F. On a lightly floured board, roll the dough out into a 13-inch circle. Transfer to a 12-inch tart pan with a removable bottom. Roll the rolling pin over the top of the pan to trim the pastry even with the edges. Put the pan on a baking sheet.

2. In a small bowl, whisk the eggs, crème fraîche or sour cream, thyme, salt, and pepper together until blended. Spoon one-fourth of the egg mixture over the dough. Distribute the artichoke hearts over the dough and scatter the onion slices. Arrange the tomatoes, cut-side up, on the dough and spoon the remaining egg mixture over. Bake for 10 to 12 minutes, or until the pastry is lightly browned. Let cool to room temperature. Cut into wedges to serve.

Caramelized Onion Tart

Vadalia, Walla Walla, and Maui onions are sweeter varieties of white onions and are well suited for an onion tart. Look for them in the early summer months. Blue cheese adds a flavorful dimension to the onions but the tart can also be made without the cheese. (See photograph, page 67.)

1. In a large, heavy skillet over medium heat, cook the bacon until golden, about 8 minutes. Reduce heat to low and add the butter, onions, salt, and pepper. Cook the onions, stirring occasionally, for 45 to 55 minutes, or until deep golden brown and jamlike. Taste for seasoning. Use now or cover and refrigerate for up to 1 day.

2. Put the 2 pastry sheets side by side on a lightly floured board. Press the edges of the sheets together and lightly crimp. To create a circular pastry, cut 2 inches dough from one long end of the rectangle and attach to the top, crimping the edges together to seal them. Gently roll the dough to smooth it out. Place it in an 11-inch round tart pan with a removable bottom. Trim off the excess dough. Freeze for 20 to 30 minutes.

3. Preheat the oven to 425°F. Fill the crust with the caramelized onions and the optional blue cheese. Bake until the crust is golden, about 25 minutes. Let cool slightly and serve warm, or serve at room temperature.

4 bacon slices, chopped

3 tablespoons butter

4 pounds sweet white onions such as Vidalia, Walla Walla, or Maui, thinly sliced

1 teaspoon salt

1 teaspoon ground pepper

One 17-ounce box frozen puff pastry, thawed

¼ cup crumbled blue cheese, such as Maytag blue (optional)

Asparagus and Goat Cheese Tart

Tender asparagus is one of the delights of springtime, and its sweet flavor is the perfect companion to fresh goat cheese. Several producers of goat cheese in the Bay Area distribute to markets around the country. Serve this free-form tart on top of mixed salad greens.

Pastry Dough (page 29)

8 ounces fresh white goat cheese at room temperature

12 asparagus stalks, trimmed and cut into 1-inch diagonal slides

2 teaspoons extra-virgin olive oil

1 small red bell pepper, roasted, peeled, seeded, and cut into matchsticks (see page 17)

1 tablespoon minced fresh oregano, or 1 teaspoon dried oregano

Kosher salt and freshly ground pepper to taste

1 large egg yolk beaten with ½ teaspoon water

4 ounces thinly sliced prosciutto, chopped

Mixed salad greens for serving

1. Preheat the oven to 450°F. On a lightly floured board, roll the dough out into a 13-inch circle. Transfer to a baking sheet.

2. Spread the goat cheese over the pastry, leaving a 1-inch border. In a small bowl, combine the asparagus and olive oil and quickly toss. Arrange the asparagus on the pastry with the pepper strips and scatter the oregano over. Season with salt and pepper. Fold 1 inch of the pastry over the topping, pleating as you go, and brush the rim with the egg mixture. Bake for about 20 minutes, or until the pastry is golden brown. Remove from the oven and let cool slightly. Scatter the prosciutto on top and serve warm, cut into wedges and placed over salad greens.

Smoked Salmon and Onion Tart

SERVES 6 AS AN APPETIZER, 4 AS AN ENTRÉE

Crème fraîche gives a lovely finish to this free-form tart,
which can be served as an entrée or as an appetizer.

1. Preheat the oven to 450°F. On a lightly floured board, roll the dough out into a 13-inch circle. Transfer to a baking sheet.

2. Scatter the onion slices over the pastry in a single layer, leaving a 1-inch border. Season with salt and pepper. Fold 1 inch of the pastry over onto the onion, pleating as you go, and brush the edges with the egg mixture. Bake for about 20 minutes, or until the pastry is golden. Let cool completely.

3. Arrange the salmon and capers on the tart. In a small bowl, blend the crème fraîche or sour cream, dill, chives, and lemon juice together. Drizzle the mixture over the tart and serve.

Pastry Dough (page 29)

1 large red onion, thinly sliced

Kosher salt and freshly ground
   pepper to taste

1 large egg yolk beaten with
   ½ teaspoon water

5 ounces thinly sliced smoked
   salmon, cut into thin strips

2 teaspoons capers, drained and
   chopped

3 tablespoons crème fraîche or
   sour cream

1 teaspoon snipped fresh dill

1 teaspoon snipped fresh chives

Juice of ½ lemon

Delicata and Cotswold Pizzas

MAKES TWO 8-INCH PIZZAS; SERVES 4

The substitution of roasted squash for tomato sauce and the
sharpness of Cotswold cheese makes a simple but unusual pizza.

1 Delicata or butternut squash,
 halved and seeded

Kosher salt and freshly ground
 pepper to taste

2 partially baked and oiled Pizza
 Dough rounds (recipe follows)

1 cup (4 ounces) shredded
 Cotswold or sharp Cheddar
 cheese

1. Preheat the oven to 350°F. Sprinkle the squash with salt and pepper.
Place on a baking sheet and bake until tender when pierced with a knife,
about 30 minutes. Remove from the oven and scoop out the flesh. Mash
the flesh. Taste and adjust the seasoning. Increase the oven temperature
to 500°F.

2. Spread the squash on the pizza rounds and top with the grated cheese.
Bake until the crust is golden brown and the cheese is melted, about
5 minutes. Serve at once.

MARIA HELM, PLUMPJACK CAFÉ: *Never wrap cheese in
plastic. Store it instead wrapped loosely in waxed paper.*

pizza dough

MAKES DOUGH FOR TWO 8-INCH PIZZAS

1. In a food processor, combine the yeast, 1½ cups of the flour, and the salt and pulse for 5 seconds. Pour in the olive oil. With the machine running, pour in the hot water and process for 10 seconds. Add the remaining ½ cup flour and process until the dough forms a ball. Continue processing for 15 seconds. Remove the warm dough from the processor. Place the dough in a plastic bag and refrigerate for 1 hour.

2. Preheat the oven to 500°F with a baking stone inside, if you have one. Remove the dough from the refrigerator. Turn out onto a lightly floured board and divide into 2 balls. Flatten each ball and stretch, turn, and push the dough into an 8-inch circle with the edges slightly thicker than the rest. If using a baking stone, sprinkle some cornmeal on a baker's peel or a flat-edged baking sheet. Put one of the dough rounds on the peel or pan and slide the dough onto the stone. Repeat with the remaining round. Without a stone, sprinkle the cornmeal on a baking sheet and add the 2 rounds. Bake for 3 minutes. Brush each round with olive oil. Use as directed in Delicata and Cotswold Pizzas or another pizza recipe (see pages 34–37) or add a topping of your choice and bake for 5 to 10 minutes, or until the crust is golden brown. Serve at once.

1 package active dry yeast

2 cups (1 pound) bread flour

1 teaspoon salt

½ cup extra-virgin olive oil, plus oil for brushing

1¼ cups very hot water (130°F)

Cornmeal for sprinkling

REED HEARON, ROSE PISTOLA RESTAURANT: *A favorite baking secret is to use quarry tile stones on the racks of a home oven. They make a tremendous difference for all sorts of baking, not just for pizzas and flat breads.*

Salsa Verde and Tomato Pizzas

An Italian rendition of green salsa uses parsley instead of tomatillos
which is appropriate when topped with true robust garden tomatoes. Italian parsley
is the flat version of parsley and boasts a stronger flavor than its curly cousin.

1 bunch flat-leaf parsley

2 garlic cloves

2 tablespoons fresh lemon juice

1 cup extra-virgin olive oil

2 partially baked and oiled Pizza
   Dough rounds (page 35)

2 large tomatoes, thinly sliced

Kosher salt and freshly ground
   pepper to taste

1. Preheat the oven to 500°F. In a blender or food processor, puree the parsley, garlic, and lemon juice until smooth. With the machine running, drizzle in the olive oil. Spread the salsa verde on the pizza rounds and top with tomato slices. Sprinkle with salt and pepper. Bake until the crusts are golden brown and the tomatoes are cooked, 5 to 7 minutes.

THOMAS KELLER, THE FRENCH LAUNDRY RESTAURANT:
When cutting tomatoes, use a serrated bread knife to make even, thick slices. This way you won't squash the tomato and lose all the delicious juice.

Wild Mushroom and Teleme Pizza

Teleme is a tangy, soft ripened cheese that blends well with the hardy flavor of mushrooms. Keep the cheese very cold to make slicing or grating easier.

1. Preheat the oven to 350°F. In a large skillet, melt the butter over medium heat and sauté the mushrooms with the thyme until the mushrooms are lightly browned and their liquid has evaporated, 5 to 8 minutes. Season with salt and pepper.

2. Increase the oven temperature to 500°F. Spoon the mushroom mixture over the pizzas. Arrange slices of the cheese on top. Bake until the crusts are golden brown and the cheese is melted, 8 to 10 minutes.

3 tablespoons unsalted butter

1 pound wild mushrooms such as chanterelles, stemmed shiitakes, and porcini, sliced

2 teaspoons minced fresh thyme, chopped, or ¾ teaspoon dried thyme

Kosher salt and freshly ground pepper to taste

2 partially baked and oiled Pizza Dough rounds (page 35)

1 pound Teleme or fresh mozzarella cheese, sliced

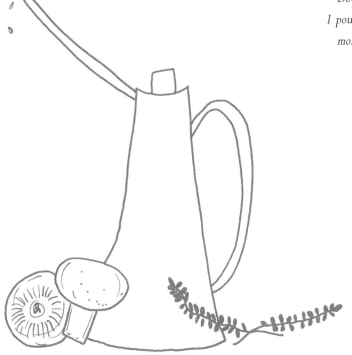

Corn Cakes with Chipotle-Tomato Sauce

Chipotle chilies in adobo sauce have a marvelous smoky flavor. Make the tomato sauce the same day as serving, as it will become hotter the longer it sits.

1 tablespoon extra-virgin olive oil

2 cups fresh white or yellow corn
  kernels (about 4 ears)

2 green onions, including green
  tops, finely chopped

½ cup yellow cornmeal

½ cup all-purpose flour

1 teaspoon salt

1 teaspoon sugar

½ teaspoon baking powder

¼ teaspoon cayenne pepper

1 large egg, lightly beaten

¾ cup buttermilk

3 tablespoons butter, melted and
  cooled

1 teaspoon canola oil

Chipotle-Tomato Sauce (recipe
  follows)

1 cup crème fraîche or sour cream

¼ cup minced fresh cilantro

1. In a large skillet over medium-high heat, heat the oil and cook the corn and green onions, stirring constantly, until golden brown. Remove from heat and mash lightly with a fork. Set aside.

2. In a small bowl, combine the cornmeal, flour, salt, sugar, baking powder, and cayenne. Mix well and set aside. In another bowl, whisk the egg, buttermilk, and melted butter together. Add to the dry ingredients and stir just until blended. Fold in the corn and green onions.

3. In a large skillet over medium heat, heat the oil. Pour ⅓-cup portions of batter into the skillet and cook until golden on each side, about 2 minutes per side. Place on a baking sheet covered with waxed paper and keep warm in a low oven until ready to serve. Repeat until all the batter is used.

4. To serve, place 2 corn cakes on each plate. Spoon the sauce over and top with a dollop of crème fraîche or sour cream and a sprinkling of cilantro.

chipotle-tomato sauce

MAKES 2 CUPS

1. Preheat the broiler. Line a broiler pan with aluminum foil. Put the tomatoes and bell pepper on the pan and broil 3 to 4 minutes, or until the skins are blackened.

2. Peel, seed, stem, and chop the roasted pepper. In a large saucepan, combine the roasted tomatoes with their skins, the garlic, shallots, and roasted pepper. Cook over medium heat for 45 minutes, stirring occasionally. Add the chilies and cook an additional 45 minutes. Strain or pass through a food mill. Discard the solids. Return the sauce to the pan and simmer until thickened, about 10 minutes.

3 pounds ripe tomatoes

1 red bell pepper

2 garlic cloves, sliced

2 shallots, thinly sliced

¼ cup canned chipotle chilies in adobo sauce, chopped (available in Latino markets and many supermarkets)

Roasted Heirloom Tomatoes

SERVES 4

In this rendition of Italian bruschetta, the tomatoes are roasted whole instead of chopped and served atop golden croutons as a first course. Look for vine-ripened heirloom or hybrid tomatoes, grown by local farms. In the height of summer, the San Francisco farmers' market yields over nineteen varieties of home-grown tomatoes in a myriad of colors. Don't be put off if they are cracked or bruised; the intense true tomato flavor will overcome any doubts you may have.

WINE SUGGESTION BY KRIS HARRIMAN: BYRON PINOT NOIR

8 assorted heirloom or hybrid
    tomatoes, such as Early Girl,
    Green Zebra, Sungold, and Ace,
    peeled (see note)
8 garlic cloves
1 bunch fresh basil, stemmed
1 cup extra-virgin olive oil
Kosher salt and freshly ground
    pepper to taste
Eight ½-inch slices from a French
    bâtard (short thick loaf)

1. Preheat the oven to 400°F. Scatter the garlic cloves and basil leaves in an 8-inch square baking dish. Place the tomatoes in the dish as tightly as possible in one layer. Pour in the olive oil. Sprinkle with salt and pepper. Bake for 45 minutes to 1 hour, or until the tomatoes are roasted and soft.

2. Meanwhile, place the bread slices on a baking sheet. Bake in the 400°F oven for 5 minutes, or until lightly brown. Turn and bake another 5 minutes, or until lightly browned.

3. To serve, place 2 pieces of bread on each plate. Spoon the roasted tomatoes, basil, and garlic over the bread and serve.

NOTE: To peel and seed tomatoes bring a pot of water to a boil. Using a sharp knife, cut out the stem and cut a small X on the bottom of the tomatoes. Drop the tomatoes in boiling water for about 10 seconds, or until the skins split. Transfer to a bowl of ice-cold water. Drain. Peel and discard the skins. To seed, cut the tomatoes in half crosswise. Hold each half upside down over the sink and gently squeeze and shake it to release the seeds.

Butternut Squash Ravioli with Sage Butter

SERVES 6

For your autumn or Thanksgiving entertaining, try this attractive first-course ravioli made with wonton wrappers instead of pasta. Look for the wrappers in the freezer section of your market. The sage leaves are lightly browned in butter and served on top of the ravioli for an impressive presentation.

WINE SUGGESTION BY DAVID PAULEY: HONIG SAUVIGNON BLANC

1. Preheat the oven to 400°F. Brush the olive oil over the cut sides of the squash. Sprinkle with salt and pepper and place, cut-side down, in a glass baking dish. Bake for about 45 minutes, or until soft. Let cool. Scoop the squash out of the skin and puree in a blender or food processor until smooth.

2. In a large skillet, melt 1 tablespoon of the butter over medium-high heat and sauté the leek until browned, about 7 minutes. Add the squash, cheese, and parsley and stir until just heated through. Season with salt and pepper to taste.

3. Place 1 tablespoon filling on a wonton wrapper. Brush the edges of the wrapper with water, fold, and seal shut around the filling. Repeat until all the filling is used.

4. In a large pot of salted slowly boiling water, cook the ravioli until they float to the top, about 4 minutes. Using a slotted spoon, transfer to serving bowls.

5. While the ravioli are cooking, melt the remaining 2 tablespoons butter in a small saucepan over medium heat. Brown the sage leaves in the butter for 3 to 4 minutes. Pour over the ravioli and serve at once.

1 butternut squash (about 1½ pounds), halved and seeded

2 tablespoons extra-virgin olive oil

Salt and freshly ground pepper to taste

3 tablespoons butter

1 large leek, white part only, halved lengthwise and cut into ¼-inch pieces

½ cup (2 ounces) grated Parmesan cheese

1 tablespoon minced fresh flat-leaf parsley

1 package square wonton wrappers

12 sage leaves

Scallops with Cider, Riesling, and Sage

Sea scallops are the larger scallops known for their rich, succulent flavor and texture. Be careful not to overcook the scallops, as they may become rubbery. Instead, allow the sauce to gently poach the scallops. Riesling is a slightly sweet German white wine with apple and citric flavors. Here it is paired with apples and sage to create a delicate sauce for scallops. Serve over fettuccine for a light dinner.

WINE SUGGESTION BY KRIS HARRIMAN: CAYMUS "CONUNDRUM"

1 cup fresh apple cider

½ cup Riesling wine

6 tablespoons butter

1 pound sea scallops, rinsed and
    patted dry

Salt and freshly ground pepper to
    taste

1 unpeeled Fuji apple, cored and
    cut into matchsticks

1 shallot, minced

18 fresh sage leaves, minced

2 tablespoons fresh lemon juice

1. In a large, heavy skillet, combine the cider and Riesling. Bring to a boil over high heat and cook until reduced to about ¼ cup. Pour into a bowl and set aside.

2. To the same skillet, add 2 tablespoons of the butter and melt over medium-high heat. Add the scallops, season with salt and pepper, and cook until lightly browned, about 2 minutes on each side. Transfer the scallops to a serving plate and loosely cover with aluminum foil.

3. Add the remaining 4 tablespoons butter to the skillet. Add the cider mixture, apple, shallot, sage, and lemon juice. Cook over medium heat until the apple is tender, about 3 to 4 minutes. Season with salt and pepper to taste. Drizzle the sauce over the scallops and serve.

Pancetta-Wrapped Scallops and Papaya

MAKES 30 APPETIZERS

In North Beach, the Italian section of town, world-class imported pancetta is readily available, but lean bacon may be substituted. The saltiness of pancetta, the sweetness of papaya, and delicate scallops create a dazzling combination. Prepare the wraps a day in advance and refrigerate. Just before broiling, brush with the mustard cream sauce.

1. Lay about half of the pancetta or bacon on a cutting board. Place a scallop half on the end of each pancetta slice. Lay a few pieces of papaya and some green onions on top of the scallop and roll up in the pancetta. Skewer the pancetta through the scallop to secure the insides. Repeat with the remaining pancetta.

2. TO MAKE THE SAUCE: In a small bowl, combine all the ingredients and mix to blend.

3. Preheat the broiler. With a pastry brush, coat the pancetta pieces with the cream mixture. Line a baking sheet with aluminum foil and set a wire rack on top of the foil. Place pancetta pieces on the rack and broil for 8 to 10 minutes, or until lightly browned. Serve.

8 ounces pancetta, thinly sliced and halved lengthwise

15 sea scallops, halved crosswise

½ ripe papaya, peeled, seeded, and diced

3 green onions, including green tops, halved lengthwise and cut into 1-inch slices

MUSTARD CREAM SAUCE:

½ cup heavy cream

2 tablespoons Dijon mustard

1 tablespoon minced fresh dill, or 1 teaspoon dried dill

½ teaspoon ground pepper

Thai Minced Chicken in Lettuce Leaves

Lemongrass, cilantro, and fish sauce are staples of Thai cooking and
are readily available in San Francisco's Chinatown and many supermarkets
across the country. Traditionally, the minced chicken is served rolled up
in lettuce leaves, but endive leaves or tartlet shells are better for passing.

WINE SUGGESTION BY DAVID PAULEY: CAYMUS SAUVIGNON BLANC

MINCED CHICKEN FILLING:

3 boneless, skinless chicken breast
   halves

2 teaspoons olive oil

3 garlic cloves, crushed

¼ cup minced fresh cilantro or
   basil

1 teaspoon ground pepper

¼ cup soy sauce

¼ cup fish sauce (nam pla or
   nuoc mam)

3 tablespoons fresh lime juice

2 tablespoons sugar

½ to 1 teaspoon cayenne pepper

2 stalks lemongrass, white part
   only, finely chopped

2 teaspoons grated fresh ginger

¼ cup finely diced red onion

30 small butter or red oak lettuce
   leaves, endive leaves, or tartlet
   shells

Fresh mint sprigs for garnish
   (optional)

1. TO MAKE THE FILLING: In a food processor or using a large chef's knife, finely chop the chicken. In a small skillet over medium-high heat, heat the oil and sauté the chicken for 5 to 8 minutes, or until opaque throughout.

2. In a medium bowl, combine the cooked chicken and all the remaining filling ingredients. Cover and refrigerate for at least 30 minutes or overnight. Taste and adjust the seasoning with lime juice, fish sauce, and/or cayenne.

3. To serve, spoon 1 heaping tablespoon filling into each lettuce or endive leaf or tartlet shell. Garnish with a mint sprig and serve.

Grilled Sesame-Garlic Beef Skewers

MAKES 8 SKEWERS

Delicious served as appetizers or as part of a mixed-grill buffet. The meat can also be taken off the skewers and rolled up in lettuce leaves with shredded carrots and a few mint sprigs.

1. In a shallow glass baking dish, combine the Worcestershire, sherry, peanut oil, sesame oil, garlic, and ginger. Alternately thread the beef strips and snow peas on twelve 10-inch bamboo skewers. Place the skewers in the baking dish and turn to coat with the marinade. Cover and refrigerate for at least 1 hour or up to 4 hours, turning the skewers several times.

2. Remove the skewers from the refrigerator 30 minutes before cooking. Light a fire in a charcoal grill or preheat a gas grill or broiler. Grill or broil the skewers for 4 to 6 minutes on each side. Serve immediately.

½ cup Worcestershire sauce

2 tablespoons dry sherry

1 tablespoon peanut oil

1 tablespoon Asian sesame oil

1 garlic clove, minced

1 teaspoon minced fresh ginger

1 pound beef top round steak, cut into ¼-by-3-inch strips

24 snow peas, trimmed and strings removed

Skewered Orange-Ginger Chicken

MAKES 24 APPETIZERS

The addition of orange and ginger updates this appetizer with an Asian bent.
You can substitute any marmalade for a different fruit flavor. Assemble as much
as 1 day before cooking and refrigerate. These will be the hit of the party.

1 boneless, skinless whole chicken
breast, about 12 ounces

¼ cup orange marmalade

1 teaspoon grated orange zest

2 tablespoons fresh orange juice

2 tablespoons soy sauce

1½ teaspoons grated fresh ginger

2 garlic cloves, minced

1 teaspoon ground pepper

12 slices apple-smoked or regular
bacon

8 ounces canned water chestnuts,
drained and cut into fourths

Flowering kale or ornamental
cabbage leaves for serving

1. Cut the chicken into twenty-four 1-inch pieces. In a medium bowl, combine the marmalade, zest, orange juice, soy sauce, ginger, garlic, and pepper. Add the chicken pieces and toss to coat. Cover and refrigerate for 30 minutes or overnight.

2. Drain the chicken and let sit at room temperature for 30 minutes. Preheat the broiler. On a cutting board, lay out the bacon slices. Put 1 chicken piece and 1 water chestnut piece on one end of each bacon slice and roll up. Secure with a wooden toothpick.

3. Line a broiler pan with aluminum foil. Put the bacon rolls on the rack and broil 4 to 5 inches from the heat source for 5 to 8 minutes, or until the bacon is cooked, turning once. Drain on paper towels.

4. To serve, line a serving platter with flowering kale or ornamental cabbage leaves and top with the appetizers.

Spiced Lamb Triangles

SERVES 8

These triangles will be a favorite at any party. The lamb filling can be prepared
ahead and refrigerated for up to 2 days, or the triangles can be baked
1 day ahead, then reheated. Serve with a jarred plum sauce or an Indian chutney.

WINE SUGGESTION BY KRIS HARRIMAN: SEGHESIO OLD VINE ZINFANDEL

LAMB FILLING:

½ cup golden raisins, chopped

2 teaspoons olive oil

1 onion, finely chopped

2 garlic cloves, minced

8 ounces lean ground lamb

2 teaspoons ground cumin

1 teaspoon ground cinnamon

¾ teaspoon ground allspice

¼ cup Chicken Stock (page 61)
  or canned low-salt chicken broth

2 tablespoons pine nuts, toasted
  and chopped (see page 18)

¼ cup minced fresh flat-leaf
  parsley

1½ tablespoons fresh lemon juice

Salt and freshly ground pepper to
  taste

8 sheets frozen phyllo dough,
  thawed

⅓ cup melted butter

1 teaspoon sesame seeds

Chinese plum sauce for serving

1. TO MAKE THE FILLING: Soak the raisins in hot water to cover for 5 minutes; drain and set aside. In a large skillet over medium heat, heat the oil and sauté the onion and garlic until beginning to color, 5 to 10 minutes. Add the lamb, cumin, cinnamon, and allspice. Cook, stirring, until the lamb is no longer pink, 5 to 7 minutes. Transfer to a colander and drain. Return the lamb mixture to the skillet and add the broth or stock, raisins, pine nuts, parsley, and lemon juice. Cook until the liquid is absorbed, about 3 minutes. Season with salt and pepper. Let cool. Use now, or cover and refrigerate for up to 2 days.

2. Preheat the oven to 350°F. Lightly coat a baking sheet with vegetable-oil cooking spray and line with parchment paper.

3. Lay a sheet of phyllo on a work surface with the short side toward you. Cut the sheet lengthwise into thirds. Brush the lengthwise half of each strip lightly with the melted butter. Place 1 tablespoon lamb filling at the bottom of the strip and fold one corner of the strip over the filling diagonally to the opposite edge to form a triangle. Continue to fold the triangle into itself, as you would fold a flag. Place on the prepared pan. Repeat with the remaining phyllo and filling.

4. Brush the triangles lightly with the remaining melted butter and sprinkle with the sesame seeds. Bake for 20 to 25 minutes, or until golden. Let cool for 5 minutes. Serve hot, with the plum sauce alongside. To make ahead, let cool completely, wrap the triangles and baking sheet with plastic wrap, and refrigerate for up to 24 hours. Reheat in a preheated 350°F oven for 12 minutes.

Chicken Empanadas with Mango Salsa

MAKES 20 MINI EMPANADAS

Peppered cheese spices up these chicken turnovers for a festive
Mexican appetizer. Offer chilled Sangría (see page 257) to cool the palate.
Keep some turnovers in your freezer for impromptu gatherings.

WINE SUGGESTION BY DEBBIE ZACHAREAS: RABBIT RIDGE MARSANNE

EMPANADA DOUGH:

2¾ cups all-purpose flour

2 teaspoons salt

1¾ cups (3¼ sticks) cold unsalted
   butter, cut into small pieces

½ cup ice water

FILLING:

2 boneless, skinless whole chicken
   breasts

2 red onions, chopped

8 garlic cloves, 4 crushed and
   4 minced

2 bunches cilantro, stemmed and
   coarsely chopped

1 bay leaf

1 tablespoon salt, plus salt to taste

1 tablespoon ground pepper, plus
   freshly ground pepper to taste

1½ cups shredded Havarti, or
   peppered Monterey jack cheese

2 teaspoons ground cumin

1 cup sour cream

1 egg, beaten

Mango Salsa (recipe follows)

1. TO MAKE THE DOUGH: In a food processor, combine the flour and salt and pulse several times. Add the butter and pulse until the butter pieces are pea sized. With the machine running, gradually add the water and process until the dough forms a ball. To make by hand, combine the flour and salt in a medium bowl. Cut in the butter with a pastry cutter or 2 knives until the mixture resembles coarse meal. Gradually stir in the water with a fork until the dough comes together. Turn the dough out onto a lightly floured board and form into a disk. Cover with plastic wrap and refrigerate for 1 hour.

2. TO MAKE THE FILLING: In a large saucepan, combine the chicken, half of the onions, the crushed garlic, half of the cilantro, the bay leaf, the 1 tablespoon salt, and the 1 tablespoon pepper. Add water to cover. Bring to a boil, then reduce heat and simmer for 10 minutes, or until the chicken is tender when pierced with a knife. Remove the chicken and let cool, then shred. In a large bowl, combine the shredded chicken, cheese, the remaining onion, the minced garlic, the remaining cilantro, the cumin, sour cream, and salt and pepper to taste. Refrigerate for at least 1 hour.

3. Roll the dough out to thickness of ⅛ inch. Cut into rounds with a 3-inch cookie cutter. Brush one half of each round with the beaten egg and place 2 tablespoons filling on the other side. Fold each round in half, press to seal, and crimp the edges with the tines of a fork. Refrigerate for 30 minutes.

4. Preheat the oven to 350°F. Brush the empanadas lightly with the remaining beaten egg and bake until golden, about 10 minutes. Serve at once, with the mango salsa.

mango salsa

MAKES 2 CUPS

1. In a food processor or blender, combine the onion, garlic, jalapeño, salt, lemon juice, and lime juice. Pulse to coarsely chop. Add the cilantro and mango and pulse to a chunky consistency. Stir in the sugar to taste. This can be made 1 day before serving and refrigerated.

½ onion, chopped

2 garlic cloves, chopped

Juice of ½ lemon

Juice of ½ lime

½ jalapeño chili, seeded and
    minced

Salt to taste

½ bunch cilantro, stemmed

3 mangos, peeled, pitted, and
    chopped

Pinch of sugar

East-Meets-Southwest Salmon Sushi Wrap

MAKES 24 APPETIZERS

This appetizer embodies a meeting of great tastes. Fermented black beans are used frequently in Asian cooking. Due to their pungent flavor, they are used in small quantities to add a unique flavor. Serve as an hors d'oeuvre accompanied with a bowl of sauce for dipping, or serve wraps end-up in a pool of soy-ginger sauce on each individual plate.

2 cups water

1 cup basmati rice

3 tablespoons rice vinegar

1 teaspoon sugar

1 cup canned black beans, drained
  and rinsed

1½ teaspoons Chinese fermented
  black beans

1 teaspoon wasabi powder

1 teaspoon water

1 avocado, peeled and pitted

1 garlic clove, minced

1 teaspoon fresh lemon juice

1 bunch cilantro, stemmed

6 large flour tortillas

1 jicama, peeled and shredded

8 ounces smoked salmon

Soy-Ginger Sauce (recipe follows)

1. In a medium saucepan, bring the water to a boil and gradually stir in the rice. Reduce heat to a simmer, cover, and cook for 15 minutes or until all the water is absorbed. Set aside.

2. In a small bowl, combine the rice vinegar and sugar and stir to dissolve the sugar. Pour over the hot rice. Mix together and let cool. In a blender, puree both types of black beans together and set aside.

3. In a small bowl, combine the wasabi powder and water and mix to form a paste. Mash the avocado with the lemon juice and garlic. Add the wasabi paste. Coarsely chop half of the cilantro.

4. To assemble, place a tortilla on a flat surface. Spread the bottom third of the tortilla with the black bean mixture, then spread the rice mixture on top, followed by the avocado mixture. Sprinkle with jicama. Line the center of the tortilla with smoked salmon. Sprinkle some of the chopped cilantro on top. Roll the tortilla tightly and wrap in plastic wrap. Repeat to use the remaining tortillas and filling. Refrigerate the wraps for at least 1 hour or as long as overnight. Cut into 1-inch slices. Garnish with the remaining cilantro sprigs and serve with the soy-ginger sauce.

soy-ginger sauce

1. In a medium bowl, combine all the ingredients and mix well. To store, refrigerate in an airtight container for up to 1 week.

¼ cup soy sauce

¼ cup water

½ cup balsamic vinegar

2 tablespoons olive oil

1 tablespoon minced fresh ginger

1 tablespoon minced fresh cilantro

1 tablespoon minced red onion

1 tablespoon minced jalapeño
   chili

1 teaspoon sugar

Grilled Five-Spice Duck on Pear Chips with Pear Chutney

SERVES 10 TO 12

While Chinatown is the place to buy the freshest duck in San Francisco, most butchers and supermarkets carry locally grown duck. In this elegant appetizer, the duck is marinated in ginger, oranges, five-spice powder, and soy sauce, giving it an intense flavor. The pear chutney complements the marinade. The chutney and the pear chips may be made the day before.

1-inch piece fresh ginger, grated

1 tablespoon grated blood orange or naval orange zest

1 cup blood orange or naval orange juice

¼ cup packed light brown sugar

½ cup soy sauce

1 teaspoon Chinese five-spice powder

2 green onions, including green tops, chopped

1 whole boneless duck breast, about 1 pound, skinned and halved

1 tablespoon peanut oil

Salt and freshly ground pepper to taste

1 bunch basil, stemmed

Pear Chips (recipe follows)

Pear Chutney (recipe follows)

1. In a small bowl, combine the ginger, zest, juice, brown sugar, soy sauce, five-spice powder, and green onions. Stir to blend. Place the duck breasts and marinade in a heavy self-sealing plastic bag. Refrigerate for at least 2 hours or as long as overnight, turning several times.

2. Remove the duck from the refrigerator 30 minutes before cooking and drain. In a large cast-iron skillet over medium-high heat, heat the oil. Season the duck with salt and pepper and cook until barely pink inside, 5 to 6 minutes on each side. Remove to a cutting board and let rest for 15 minutes.

3. Cut the duck breast into ⅛-inch-thick slices. Place 1 basil leaf on each pear chip and top with a duck slice and a dollop of pear chutney.

pear chips

MAKES ABOUT 30 CHIPS

1. Preheat the oven to 200°F. Line 2 baking pans with parchment paper. In medium saucepan, combine the sugar, water, cinnamon stick, and anise. Bring to a boil, reduce heat, and simmer for about 10 minutes to thicken.

2. Add the pears to the simmering syrup and cook for 1½ minutes. Using a slotted spoon, transfer the slices to a baking sheet. Repeat with the remaining slices.

3. Bake the pear slices for about 3 hours, or until dry and crisp but not browned, checking them regularly. Let cool on wire racks. Use now, or store in an airtight container for up to 2 days.

1 cup sugar

1 cup water

1 cinnamon stick

1 star anise pod

5 unripe Bosc or Comice pears, peeled, cored, and cut into ⅛-inch-thick lengthwise slices

pear chutney

MAKES 1½ CUPS

1. In a large skillet, melt the butter over medium heat. Add the shallots and cook until lightly browned. Sprinkle with sugar and cook for 5 minutes. Add the pears, dried fruit, and five-spice powder. Season with salt and pepper. Increase the heat to medium high and cook until the pears have softened, about 5 minutes. Add the vinegars and cook to reduce, stirring constantly, for about 4 minutes. Use now, or cover and refrigerate for up to 1 week. Bring to room temperature before serving.

1½ tablespoons butter

2 large shallots, thinly sliced

2 teaspoons sugar

2 ripe but firm Bartlett pears, peeled, cored, and cubed

¼ cup dried cherries or cranberries

1 teaspoon Chinese five-spice powder

Salt and freshly ground pepper to taste

1 tablespoon balsamic vinegar

2 teaspoons pear vinegar or sherry vinegar

Spicy Jumbo Shrimp with Tomatillo Sauce

MAKES 36 APPETIZERS; SERVES 6 AS FIRST COURSE

This colorful dish is a delightful summer starter. To cook on the grill,
squeeze the lemon over the shrimp as they cook.

36 jumbo shrimp, shelled and
  deveined

1 teaspoon kosher salt

2 teaspoons mustard seeds

2 teaspoons peppercorns

3 tablespoons chopped fresh
  cilantro

¾ teaspoon red pepper flakes

½ teaspoon cayenne pepper

2 teaspoons cumin seeds, toasted
  (see note)

2 bay leaves, crushed

3 tablespoons extra-virgin olive
  oil

Juice of ½ lemon

⅓ cup Sauvignon Blanc or other
  dry white wine (optional)

Red oakleaf lettuce for garnish

Tomatillo Sauce (recipe follows)

Lemon or lime wedges for garnish
  (optional)

1. In a glass bowl, combine the shrimp, salt, mustard seeds, pepper-corns, cilantro, pepper flakes, cayenne, cumin seeds, and bay leaves and stir to coat. Let sit for 15 minutes.

2. In a large skillet over medium heat, heat the oil. Increase heat to high and add the shrimp. Add the lemon juice and white wine and sauté until all the shrimp are a bright pink (3 to 4 minutes). To grill, put the shrimp on a screen or small grid and cook, sprinkling them with lemon juice, about 2 minutes on each side. Do not use the wine. Transfer the shrimp to a baking sheet and let cool. Cover the shrimp with plastic wrap and refrigerate.

3. Serve the chilled shrimp on a bed of lettuce leaves with a bowl of sauce alongside for dipping. As a first course, arrange lettuce leaves on each plate. Place 6 shrimp around the plate and spoon some tomatillo sauce over the shrimp. Garnish with lemon or lime wedges.

NOTE: To toast seeds, place them in a small dry skillet. Cook over medium heat, stirring constantly, until fragrant, 1 or 2 minutes.

tomatillo sauce

1. Cook the tomatillos in a pot of salted boiling water for 2 minutes. Using a slotted spoon, transfer the tomatillos to a bowl of ice water. Let cool. Drain and chop the tomatillos. In a blender or food processor, pulse the tomatillos until coarsely chopped. Add the remaining ingredients and process until minced but not pureed.

1 pound tomatillos, husked

2 teaspoons white wine vinegar

½ cup chopped fresh cilantro

1 tablespoon olive oil

2 serrano chilies, seeded and
  chopped

1 teaspoon salt

Beef and Asparagus Wraps

MAKES 24 APPETIZERS

An elegant hors d'oeuvre for a cocktail party. Serve warm, on a platter
of radicchio. A horseradish cream or aïoli is a nice accompaniment.

12 pencil-thin asparagus stalks,
   trimmed to 3 inches

½ cup soy sauce

¼ cup packed light brown sugar

1 teaspoon rice vinegar

1 tablespoon Asian sesame oil

¼ teaspoon red pepper flakes

1 bunch scallions, green parts
   only

1 small beef tenderloin, about 1½
   pounds

Freshly ground pepper to taste

Radicchio leaves for serving

1. Cut the asparagus tips in half lengthwise. Blanch the tips in salted boiling water for 1 minute and immediately transfer to a bowl of ice water for 5 minutes. Drain and set aside.

2. In a small bowl, mix the soy sauce and sugar until the sugar is dissolved. Add the rice vinegar, sesame oil, and red pepper flakes. Mix well. Cut the scallion leaves into 3-inch lengths and cut again in half lengthwise.

3. Preheat the broiler. With a very sharp knife, cut the beef into ¼-inch slices. Place the slices between sheets of waxed paper and pound flat to make a 2-by-5-inch rectangle. Dip each piece of beef into the soy sauce mixture and season with pepper. At one end of the beef, place 2 asparagus tips and a piece of scallion so that they extend beyond the beef rectangle. Roll the beef around the vegetables and place on a grill pan lined with aluminum foil. Broil until just seared, about 2 minutes. Turn, brush with the soy sauce mixture, and sear for about 2 minutes on the second side.

4. Serve warm.

SOUPS

Corn Bisque

Cool Cucumber Soup

Spanish-Style Lentil Soup

Cioppino

Moroccan-Style Carrot Soup

Red Lentil Soup with Orzo

Roasted–Red Pepper Soup with Grilled Polenta

Roasted-Vegetable and Chicken Soup

Smoked Salmon and Rosemary Bisque

Burmese-Style Chicken Soup

Thai Spicy Prawn Soup

Summer Squash Soup with Basil Crème Fraîche

Strawberry Soup with Basalmic Vinegar

Tuscan Bean Soup

Spring Veal Ragout with Vegetables

Beef-Zinfandel Stew

White Bean and Chicken Stew

Roasted-Tomato Soup

Fresh Pea and Arborio Soup

Beef Stock

Roasting the bones makes a darker, richer stock. Red wine and tomato paste
add color as well as flavor. Splurge on a good-quality wine; you will taste the difference.

6 pounds beef, lamb, or veal shank
  bones

¼ cup tomato paste

2 large yellow onions, cut into
  quarters

1 leek, white and light green
  parts only, washed and coarsely
  chopped

1 celery stalk, cut into 2-inch
  pieces

1 carrot, peeled and cut into
  2-inch pieces

3 garlic cloves, crushed

10 peppercorns

1 bay leaf

5 fresh parsley sprigs

2 fresh thyme sprigs

1 cup California Cabernet or
  other dry red wine

1. Preheat the oven to 400°F. Put the bones in a large roasting pan and roast for 20 minutes. Coat the bones with the tomato paste and bake for 15 to 20 minutes longer, or until lightly browned. Remove from the oven, leaving the oven on. Place the bones in a large stockpot and add cold water to cover by 4 inches. Bring to a boil and reduce heat to a simmer. Skim off the foam.

2. While the stock is simmering, add all the remaining ingredients except the wine to the roasting pan. Stir to coat with the pan drippings and roast, stirring occasionally, for 30 to 40 minutes, or until the vegetables are golden brown. Add the contents of the roasting pan to the stockpot.

3. Place the roasting pan over medium to high heat. Add the red wine and stir to scrape up the pan drippings from the bottom of the pan. Cook to reduce the liquid for about 5 minutes. Add the liquid to the stockpot and continue simmering, uncovered, for 3 hours, skimming as needed. Strain through a fine meshed sieve lined with paper towels. Let cool.

4. Cover and refrigerate overnight. Remove and discard the congealed fat. Store in the refrigerator for up to 3 days. To keep longer, bring to a boil every 3 days, or freeze for up to 3 months.

Chicken Stock

Homemade stock is so much better than canned broth, it's worth the time
to make your own. Save any cooked carcasses, parts, and bones to make stock,
or purchase backs, necks, and wings, rinsing well before cooking them.

1. Put the carcasses or bones and parts in a large stockpot and add cold
water to cover by 4 inches. Bring to a boil over high heat, reduce heat
to a simmer, and skim the foam from the top. Add the celery, carrots,
onion, leek, peppercorns, bay leaf, parsley, and thyme. Simmer for
4 hours, occasionally skimming off the foam. Strain through a fine-meshed
sieve lined with paper towels. Let cool, cover, and refrigerate overnight.
Remove and discard the congealed fat. Store in the refrigerator for up
to 3 days. To keep longer, bring to a boil every 3 days or freeze for up to
3 months.

2 whole chicken carcasses, or 4
    pounds chicken bones, backs,
    necks, and wings, rinsed well
4 celery stalks, chopped into
    2-inch pieces
4 carrots, peeled and chopped into
    2-inch pieces
1 large yellow onion, cut into
    8 pieces
1 leek, white and light green
    parts, washed and coarsely
    chopped
12 peppercorns
1 bay leaf
5 fresh parsley sprigs
2 fresh thyme sprigs

Vegetable Stock

Start with the best ingredients to make the most flavorful stock. Keep some on hand in the freezer.

2 tablespoons olive oil

1 onion, chopped

1 large leek or 2 small leeks,
   including pale green part,
   washed and chopped

1 zucchini, chopped

2 carrots, peeled and chopped

2 celery stalks with leaves,
   chopped

3 garlic cloves, minced

1 tablespoon minced fresh
   tarragon, 1 tablespoon minced,
   fresh thyme, or 1 teaspoon
   dried thyme

5 fresh flat-leaf parsley sprigs

5 peppercorns

2 bay leaves

Salt to taste

8 cups water

1. In a large stockpot over medium heat, heat the oil and sauté the onion and leeks for 3 minutes, or until the onion is translucent. Add all the remaining ingredients except the water. Cook for 10 to 12 minutes. Add ½ cup of the water if mixture becomes too dry.

2. Pour in the remaining water. Bring to a boil, then reduce heat and simmer covered for at least 40 minutes. Strain into a large bowl through a fine-meshed sieve. Discard the cooked vegetables. Let cool, then cover and refrigerate for up to 3 days (to store longer, bring to a boil every 3 days) or freeze for up to 3 months.

Chilled Avocado-Cilantro Soup

SERVES 6

This wonderful soup has a fresh citrus flavor that is perfect for a summer fiesta.

1. In a blender or food processor, combine 2 of the avocados, the stock or broth, lime juice, yogurt, and sour cream. Blend until smooth. Add the tomato and cilantro. Pulse until the tomato is coarsely chopped, not puree. Pour into a bowl and season with salt. Coarsely chop the remaining avocado half and stir it into the soup. Refrigerate for at least 2 hours. Ladle into bowls and serve with a dash of hot sauce.

2½ large ripe Haas avocados, peeled and pitted

3 cups Chicken Stock (page 61) or canned low-salt chicken broth

1 tablespoon fresh lime juice

⅔ cup plain yogurt

⅓ cup sour cream

1 large tomato, peeled and seeded (see page 40)

¼ cup chopped fresh cilantro

Salt to taste

Tabasco or other hot sauce, for serving

Asparagus-Crab Soup

SERVES 6

A bright green asparagus soup with the added pleasure of sweet crabmeat makes an elegant first course.

WINE SUGGESTION BY DEBBIE ZACHAREAS: RABBIT RIDGE VIOGNIER

2 tablespoons unsalted butter

2 tablespoons olive oil

1 pound asparagus, trimmed and
chopped

1 leek, white part only, washed
and chopped

2 cups Chicken Stock (page 61)
or canned low-salt chicken
broth

1 cup milk or half-and-half

8 ounces fresh lump Dungeness
crabmeat

Salt and freshly ground pepper to
taste

Lemon wedges for garnish

1. In a large, heavy saucepan, melt the butter with the olive oil over medium heat. Add the asparagus and leek and sauté until tender, about 7 minutes. Add the salt, pepper, and stock or broth. Reduce heat and simmer, uncovered, for about 7 minutes.

2. Transfer the mixture to a blender or food processor and puree until smooth. Return to the saucepan and add the milk or half-and-half. Bring to a simmer and cook for 10 minutes; do not boil. Stir in the crabmeat and cook for 2 to 3 minutes. Serve hot, with lemon wedges.

THOMAS KELLER, THE FRENCH LAUNDRY RESTAURANT:
We use a lot of fresh stock in the restaurant every day, but when I'm cooking at home, I like to keep small amounts handy. I suggest freezing your homemade stocks in ice cube trays. Once they have frozen hard, pop them out of the trays and place them in clearly marked plastic bags in the freezer. This way you have convenient portions to add to a quick sauce or sautéed vegetables.

GREEK SALAD SALSA WITH TOASTED PITA CHIPS, *pages 14–15*

FIG AND PÂTÉ BRUSCHETTA, *page 27*

CARAMELIZED ONION TART, *page 31*

ROASTED–RED PEPPER SOUP WITH GRILLED POLENTA, *page 82*

THAI SPICY PRAWN SOUP, *page 86*

TUSCAN BEAN SOUP, *page 89*

ASIAN TRI-CABBAGE COLESLAW, *page 101*

BEET SALAD WITH ORANGE AND TARRAGON VINAIGRETTE, *page 102*

Butternut Squash and Apple Harvest Soup

SERVES 6

This simple yet hearty soup is a Thanksgiving favorite. The squash provides a beautiful color, while the apples add texture and sweetness. Sugar (pie) pumpkin can be used in place of squash.

WINE SUGGESTION BY DEBBIE ZACHAREAS: BONNY DOON PACIFIC RIM RIESLING

1. Preheat the oven to 400°F. Place the squash, cut-sides down, on a baking sheet. Roast until tender, about 1 hour. Let cool slightly. Spoon out the flesh and put in a medium bowl.

2. In a soup pot over medium heat, heat the oil and sauté the onions and sage until tender, about 5 minutes. Add the stock or broth, apple cider, squash, apples, salt, and pepper. Simmer covered for 20 minutes, or until the apples are soft. In batches, if necessary, puree the soup in a blender or food processor. Return to the pot to heat through. Serve garnished with dollop of crème fraîche or sour cream.

4 pounds butternut squash or acorn squash, halved and seeded

3 tablespoons hazelnut oil

1 large yellow onion, chopped

6 fresh sage leaves

4 cups Chicken Stock (page 61) or canned low-salt chicken broth

1 cup apple cider

5 Granny Smith apples, peeled, cored, and chopped

2 teaspoons salt

1 teaspoon ground pepper

Crème fraîche or sour cream for garnish

California Minestrone with Olives

SERVES 6

Olive production in Northern California is growing rapidly and rivals that of Spain. Experiment with different styles of olives for varied accent flavor. Double the recipe and freeze half for another easy dinner.

WINE SUGGESTION BY DEBBIE ZACHAREAS: ATLAS PEAK SANGIOVESE

1 onion, chopped

2 large garlic cloves, minced

12 ounces lean ground beef

1 small globe eggplant, diced

1 carrot, peeled and sliced into
  ½-inch pieces

15 ounces canned tomato puree

4 cups Beef Stock (page 60)
  or canned low-fat broth

3 cups water

½ teaspoon ground pepper

1½ cups pitted kalamata olives,
  coarsely chopped

1 cup shell pasta

¼ cup minced fresh flat-leaf
  parsley

1 tablespoon chopped fresh basil

Salt to taste

¼ cup grated Parmesan cheese

1. In a soup pot over medium heat, cook the onion, garlic, and ground beef until the beef is browned, 5 to 7 minutes. Add the eggplant, carrot, tomato puree, stock or broth, water, and pepper. Cover and simmer for 15 minutes, or until the vegetables are tender. Add the olives, pasta, parsley, and basil and simmer for 10 more minutes. Add salt. Serve garnished with Parmesan cheese.

Thai Cold Melon Soup

SERVES 8

A unique and refreshing summer soup that can be made with a variety of fresh melons.
The farmers' market is the place to find the most variety and the sweetest melons, as they have
been allowed to ripen on the vine longer. Also try Crenshaw and Casaba melon in this recipe.

1. In a blender or food processor, puree the honeydew, cantaloupe, and watermelon. Add the coconut milk, lime juice, chili sauce, ginger, cilantro, basil, and chopped mint. Cover and refrigerate for at least 1 hour or overnight. Serve garnished with the minced mint and peanuts.

2 cups diced honeydew melon

2 cups diced cantaloupe

2 cups seeded, diced watermelon

1 cup unsweetened coconut milk

¼ cup fresh lime juice (about 3 limes)

½ tablespoon Asian chili sauce

1 tablespoon grated fresh ginger

2 tablespoons coarsely chopped fresh cilantro

1 tablespoon coarsely chopped fresh basil

3 tablespoons coarsely chopped fresh mint, plus 1 tablespoon minced mint for garnish

1 tablespoon peanuts, toasted and finely chopped (see page 18)

Corn Bisque

SERVES 6

Choose sweet white corn for this flavorful soup.
The water used to cook the corn enhances the taste of the broth.

3 cups water

4 ears fresh white corn, husks and
   silk removed

½ cup (1 stick) butter

1 large leek, including some light
   green portions, washed,
   quartered lengthwise and
   thinly sliced

3 Yukon Gold potatoes, cut into
   1-inch cubes

¼ cup minced fresh flat-leaf
   parsley

1 ½ cups Chicken Stock (page 61)
   or canned low-salt chicken
   broth

½ cup milk or half-and-half

¼ cup chopped fresh basil

Tabasco sauce for garnish

1. In a large stockpot, bring the water to a boil. Add the corn, cover, and cook for 2 minutes. Drain and cut the kernels from the cobs; set the kernels aside. Put the cobs back into the hot water, bring to a boil, and cook for 20 minutes. Discard the cobs, then strain the cooking water into a bowl.

2. In a soup pot, melt the butter over medium heat and sauté the leek and potatoes, stirring frequently, until the potatoes are slightly soft, about 10 minutes. Add the corn and parsley and cook for 3 minutes. Add the stock or broth and the reserved cooking water and simmer for 5 minutes; do not boil. Add the milk and basil. Simmer for 3 to 5 minutes. Add salt and pepper. Serve with a drop of Tabasco sauce swirled on top of the soup.

Cool Cucumber Soup

A refreshing soup of cucumbers, sour cream, and herbs makes a lovely
first course for a summer lunch or dinner party. Seek out the more unusual
varieties of cucumbers, which tend to have less water and more flavor.
Try the long Japanese cucumber or yellow lemon cucumber.

1. In a blender or food processor, combine all the ingredients except
the garnish and puree until smooth. Pour into large bowl and refrigerate
for at least 2 hours or overnight. Taste for seasoning. Serve garnished
with a dollop of sour cream or yogurt and a sprig of dill.

4 cucumbers, peeled, seeded,
   and coarsely chopped
1½ cups sour cream or yogurt
3 coarsely chopped scallions,
   including green portions
1½ teaspoons snipped fresh dill
1 tablespoon Worcestershire sauce
1 tablespoon fresh lemon juice
½ teaspoon salt
¼ teaspoon ground white pepper
¼ cup sour cream or yogurt,
   for garnish
6 fresh dill sprigs, for garnish

Spanish-Style Lentil Soup

SERVES 6

Serve a salad and bread with this nutritious soup and you have a hearty meal.
Sweet paprika and wine vinegar add another layer of taste to the soup.

WINE SUGGESTION BY DEBBIE ZACHAREAS: JOSEPH PHELPS PASTICHE

2 cups dried lentils

2 bay leaves

2 to 3 fresh flat-leaf parsley
   sprigs

4 ounces bacon, cut into 1-inch
   pieces

3 tablespoons olive oil

2 onions, chopped

1 leek, white part only, washed
   and chopped

2 carrots, peeled and finely
   chopped

4 garlic cloves, minced

2 teaspoons sweet Hungarian
   paprika

Salt and freshly ground pepper to
   taste

¼ cup red wine vinegar

2 Yukon Gold potatoes, peeled and
   cut into 2-inch pieces

1. Pick over and rinse lentils. Put the lentils in a pot and add cold water to cover by 4 inches. Add the bay leaves, parsley, and bacon. Bring to a boil. Cover and simmer for 45 minutes.

2. Meanwhile, in a medium skillet, heat the olive oil over medium heat and sauté the onions, leek, carrots, and garlic until the onions are translucent, about 3 minutes. Remove from heat and stir in the paprika.

3. After the lentils have cooked for 45 minutes, add the onion mixture. Add the salt, pepper, vinegar, and potatoes. Cover and cook an additional 30 minutes, or just until the potatoes are tender. If the soup becomes too thick, add additional water.

Cioppino

SERVES 6

Traditionally served on Friday nights in North Beach's Italian restaurants,
this fish soup is loaded with the catch of the day in a rich tomato stock.
Crusty sourdough bread is essential for soaking up all the delicious broth.

WINE SUGGESTION BY KRIS HARRIMAN: VOSS SAUVIGNON BLANC

1. In a soup pot over medium heat, heat the olive oil and sauté the onion, leek, shallot, garlic, fennel, bay leaf, saffron, and parsley for 8 to 10 minutes, or until the vegetables are tender. Add the salt and pepper. Add the tomatoes and cook for 3 minutes. Add the fish stock or clam broth and wine. Simmer for 15 minutes. Add the fish and shellfish and simmer for 5 to 10 minutes, or until the shrimp is pink, the fish is firm, and mussels and clams have opened. Do not overcook, or the fish will be tough. Discard any clams or mussels that do not open.

¼ cup olive oil

1 large red onion, thinly sliced

1 large leek, white part only,
    washed and chopped

1 shallot, minced

3 garlic cloves, minced

1 fennel bulb, trimmed and thinly
    sliced

1 bay leaf

⅛ teaspoon saffron threads

3 tablespoons minced flat-leaf
    parsley

Salt and freshly ground pepper to
    taste

6 tomatoes, peeled, seeded, and
    chopped (see page 40)

1 cup fish stock or clam broth

1 cup dry white wine

2 pounds fresh white fish, such as
    sea bass or monkfish

8 ounces shrimp

1 live Dungeness crab, cleaned,
    and sectioned (see page 127)

8 ounces bay scallops

8 ounces mussels, scrubbed and
    debearded or cherrystone clams

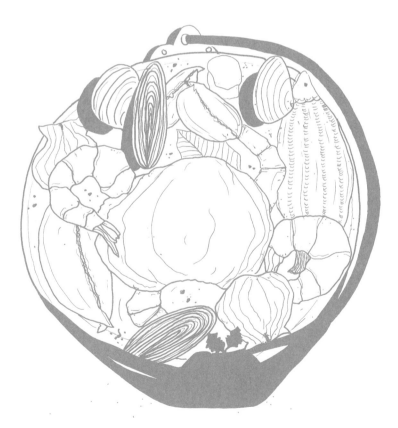

Moroccan-Style Carrot Soup

SERVES 8

This recipe evolved from several carrot soup recipes.
The hint of orange and cumin gives it a Moroccan flair.

¼ cup olive oil

1 small onion, thinly sliced

2 russet potatoes, peeled and diced

1 celery stalk, sliced

1 pound carrots, peeled and cut
  into ½-inch slices

½ cup fresh orange juice

1 teaspoon ground cumin

¼ teaspoon dry mustard

5½ cups Chicken Stock (page 61)
  or canned low-salt chicken broth

1. In a large soup pot over medium heat, heat the oil and add the onions, potatoes, celery, and carrots. Cover, reduce heat, and simmer for 15 minutes, or until the celery and onion are limp; do not allow the vegetables to brown.

2. In a small bowl, mix the orange juice, cumin, and mustard together until smooth.

3. Add the stock or broth and the orange juice mixture to the vegetables. Bring to a boil, cover, and simmer for 30 minutes. Remove from heat and let cool. In a blender or food processor, in batches if necessary, process the soup until smooth. Return to the pot and reheat.

Red Lentil Soup with Orzo

SERVES 4

Here's a variation on a red beans and rice dish, using orzo and
lamb sausage. Many meat markets prepare house-made sausage, or you can
order them from Aidell's or through the Williams-Sonoma catalogue.

1. In a medium skillet over medium heat, heat 2 tablespoons of the olive
oil. Add the sausages and brown on all sides. Remove from the pan, then
slice into ½-inch pieces. Set aside. Add the remaining 2 tablespoons olive
oil to the pan and sauté the leek, onion, garlic, carrots, bay leaf, parsley,
salt, and pepper for 3 to 5 minutes, or until the onion has wilted and
carrots are soft. Add the lentils and stir constantly for 2 to 3 minutes.
Add the stock or broth, reduce heat to a simmer and cook for 15
minutes. Add the cooked sausage and simmer for 10 minutes.

2. Meanwhile, cook the orzo in a large saucepan of salted boiling water
until al dente, about 10 minutes; drain. Divide the orzo among serving
bowls and ladle the soup over. Garnish with a lemon wedge and serve.

4 tablespoons olive oil

1 pound lamb sausages

1 leek, white part only, washed
   and chopped

1 yellow onion, chopped

2 garlic cloves, minced

2 carrots, peeled and finely diced

1 bay leaf

3 tablespoons minced fresh
   flat-leaf parsley

Salt and freshly ground pepper to
   taste

1 cup dried red or green lentils

4 cups Chicken Stock (page 61),
   canned low salt chicken broth
   or Vegetable Stock (page 62)

1 cup orzo pasta

6 lemon wedges for garnish

Roasted—Red Pepper Soup with Grilled Polenta

SERVES 6

This soup is best in late summer, when peppers are fully ripe and plentiful.
When choosing peppers, look for firm skin without wrinkles. The grilled polenta garnish
adds a little taste of Italy to this fragrant soup. (See photograph, page 68.)

2 cups milk or water

1 tablespoon butter

½ teaspoon sugar

¼ teaspoon salt, plus salt to taste

⅔ cup polenta or stone-ground
   yellow cornmeal

1 cup fresh corn kernels (about 2
   ears)

4 tablespoons butter

4 garlic cloves, minced

1 onion, chopped

4 red bell peppers, roasted,
   peeled, and coarsely chopped
   (see page 17)

3 cups Chicken Stock (page 61)
   or canned low-salt chicken
   broth

1 cup milk or half-and-half

Freshly ground pepper to taste

Oil for cooking polenta (optional)

2 tablespoons snipped fresh chives
   for garnish

1. Coat a 9-inch square baking pan with vegetable-oil cooking spray. In a medium, heavy saucepan, combine the milk or water, butter, sugar, and salt. Bring to a simmer over medium-low heat. Gradually whisk the polenta or cornmeal into the milk mixture. Reduce heat and stir constantly until the polenta or cornmeal thickens and pulls away from the side of the pan, about 10 minutes. Pour into the prepared pan. Let cool for 1 hour.

2. Preheat the broiler. Place a piece of aluminum foil on a broiler pan. Spread the corn kernels on the pan and cook as close as possible to the heat source until the kernels are lightly browned, about 3 to 5 minutes.

3. In a large skillet, melt the butter over medium-high heat and sauté the garlic and onion until soft 5 to 7 minutes. Add the roasted peppers and stock or broth. Cook for about 5 minutes.

4. In batches, puree the soup mixture in a blender or food processor until smooth. Return to saucepan. Place over low heat and add the milk or half-and-half. Stir in roasted corn and add pepper to taste. Simmer for 10 minutes; do not boil.

5. Meanwhile, cut the polenta into 3-inch squares. Under the broiler, cook the squares on each side until lightly browned, 2 to 3 minutes on each side. Cut each square in half diagonally.

6. Ladle the soup into bowls. Place 2 polenta triangles on top of each serving and garnish with the chives.

Roasted-Vegetable and Chicken Soup

SERVES 8

Roasted vegetables and chilies add a wonderful blend of hot and sweet tastes to this Southwestern-style soup. A delicious way to use up leftover roasted or grilled chicken.

1. Light a fire in a charcoal grill or preheat a gas grill or broilers. Grill the chicken 5 to 7 minutes on each side or until opaque throughout. Let cool, then cut into bite-sized pieces.

2. Preheat the oven to 450°F. Cover a baking sheet with aluminum foil. Place the tomatoes flat-side down on the baking sheet. Place the garlic cloves on the baking sheet with tomatoes. Roast for 30 minutes, or until the tomato skins are lightly browned and garlic has softened. Remove from oven and let cool slightly. Peel and chop the garlic. Peel and chop the tomatoes. Set aside.

3. Turn the oven to broil. Spread the corn kernels on a baking sheet roasting sheet and broil as close to the heat as possible, until lightly browned, 2 to 3 minutes. Set aside.

4. Flatten the pepper and chilies and place on a broiler pan lined with aluminum foil. Place under the broiler as close to the heat as possible and completely char, 10 to 15 minutes. Place in a closed paper bag and let cool for 15 minutes. Peel the charred skins from the pepper and chilies. Coarsely chop them and set aside.

5. In a soup pot, combine the stock or broth, tomatoes, garlic, chilies, pepper, corn, oregano, and cilantro. Bring to a boil, reduce heat, and simmer for 20 minutes.

6. Just before serving, add the chicken, lime juice, and avocado and cook just until heated through, about 5 minutes.

1 boneless, skinless whole chicken breast (about 12 ounces)

1 pound Roma or plum tomatoes (about 6), halved

Unpeeled cloves from 1 head garlic

1 cup of corn kernels (about 2 ears)

1 red bell pepper, halved lengthwise, seeded and deveined

2 serrano chilies, halved lengthwise and seeded

2 jalapeño chilies, halved lengthwise and seeded

8 cups Chicken Stock (page 61) or canned low-salt chicken broth

1 tablespoon dried oregano

2 fresh cilantro sprigs

3 tablespoons fresh lime juice

1 avocado, peeled, pitted, and chopped

Smoked Salmon and Rosemary Bisque

SERVES 6

This is a creative way to serve salmon inexpensively to a large group.
For a lower-fat soup, replace cream with half-and-half or milk.

WINE SUGGESTION BY KRIS HARRIMAN: FAR NIENTE CHARDONNAY

1 tablespoon butter

4 shallots, minced

2 celery stalks, finely chopped

4 cups water

1 cup Sauvignon Blanc or other
dry white wine

Juice of 1 lemon

2 salmon steaks, about 1 pound
total

1 pound Yukon Gold potatoes,
diced

1 cup heavy cream, half-and-half,
or milk

Freshly ground pepper to taste

7 ounces smoked salmon, chopped

4 teaspoons minced rosemary

1. In a large heavy saucepan, melt the butter over medium heat. Add the celery and shallots and continue cooking until vegetables are softened, about 10 minutes. Add water, wine, and lemon juice. Simmer for 10 minutes. Reduce heat to low and add the salmon steaks. Cover and cook for 10 minutes. Transfer the salmon steaks to a plate and let cool. Remove and discard the skin and bones. With a fork, coarsely flake the flesh. Set aside.

2. Meanwhile, stir the potatoes into the broth and simmer, partially covered, for 15 to 20 minutes, or until tender. Add the cream, half-and-half, or milk and the pepper and simmer for 5 minutes. Stir in the flaked salmon, smoked salmon pieces, and rosemary and cook for 5 minutes. Serve warm.

Burmese-Style Chicken Soup

SERVES 6

The ingredients for this bright yellow stew originate from Burma. Peanut oil is the oil of choice in Asian stir-frying because it has a very high burning temperature that allows the food to cook quickly. Serve this over cooked Asian noodles or steamed jasmine rice.

WINE SUGGESTION BY DEBBIE ZACHAREAS: IRON HORSE BRUT ROSÉ

1. In a large skillet over medium heat, heat 2 tablespoons of the peanut oil. Add the chicken and cook for about 5 to 7 minutes on each side, or until slightly firm. Remove the chicken from the pan and set aside. To the same skillet, add the garlic, ginger, tumeric, lemongrass, and cayenne and sauté for 2 to 3 minutes. Return the chicken to the pan and cook for 2 to 3 minutes. Reduce the heat, add chicken stock or broth, cook for additional 10 minutes. Add the coconut milk and simmer for 5 minutes; do not boil.

2. Meanwhile, over medium heat, in a small skillet, heat remaining 1 tablespoon peanut oil and sauté onion until soft, about 7 to 10 minutes. Set aside.

3. Steam carrots and broccoli over boiling water until tender, 5 to 7 minutes. Set aside.

4. To serve, divide noodles or rice, carrots, broccoli, cilantro, onion, and green onions into individual serving bowls. Ladle chicken mixture over each serving.

3 tablespoons peanut oil

3 boneless, skinless whole chicken breasts, cut into bite-size pieces

6 garlic cloves, minced

2 tablespoons minced fresh ginger

1 tablespoon ground turmeric

1 stalk lemongrass, white part only, cut into 1-inch pieces

½ teaspoon cayenne pepper

2 cups Chicken Stock (page 61) or canned low-salt chicken broth

One 14-ounce can unsweetened coconut milk

1 large yellow onion, chopped

1 cup sliced carrots

1 cup broccoli florets, chopped

Cooked Asian noodles, pasta, or steamed jasmine rice

1 cup chopped fresh cilantro

5 chopped green onions, white part only, chopped

Thai Spicy Prawn Soup

SERVES 6

This fragrant soup is easy to prepare. The spiciness comes from cayenne pepper, which is balanced by the lightly sweet coconut milk. Try to locate fresh kaffir lime leaves in an Asian market. They impart wonderfully perfumed flavor to the soup. (See photograph, page 69.)

WINE SUGGESTION BY KRIS HARRIMAN: ROEDERER ESTATE BRUT

2 tablespoons grated fresh ginger

1 teaspoon cayenne pepper

2 tablespoons peanut oil

6 cups Chicken Stock (page 61)
 or canned low-salt chicken
 broth

½ cup jasmine rice

1 cup unsweetened coconut milk

6 tablespoons Thai fish sauce
 (nam pla, found in the Asian
 section of most supermarkets)

8 ounces crimini or white
 mushrooms, sliced

1 small onion, chopped

1 small red bell pepper seeded,
 deveined, and cut into ¼-
 inch strips

2 tablespoons chopped fresh
 cilantro

1 stalk lemongrass, white part
 only, cut into 1-inch pieces

5 fresh or dried kaffir lime leaves
 (optional)

1 pound medium shrimp,
 shelled and deveined

2 to 3 tablespoons fresh lime juice

Chopped green onions, including
 green portion, and cilantro
 for garnish

1. In a large heavy saucepan, combine the ginger, cayenne, and peanut oil. Cook over medium-high heat for 1 to 2 minutes. Add stock or broth, and bring the mixture to a boil. Add the rice, reduce heat, and simmer for 15 to 20 minutes, or until the rice is tender.

2. Add the coconut milk, fish sauce, mushrooms, onion, pepper, cilantro, lemongrass, and lime leaves to the rice. Simmer for 5 minutes, stirring once or twice. Add the shrimp and cook for 3 to 5 minutes, or until they have turned pink. Stir in the lime juice. Serve hot, garnished with green onions and cilantro.

THOMAS KELLER, THE FRENCH LAUNDRY RESTAURANT: *Fresh ginger is a wonderful addition to many dishes. In order to keep fresh tasting ginger readily handy in your kitchen, store it in your freezer. This way you'll always have it available. Just grate it frozen into any recipe calling for ginger. It's also much easier to grate frozen than fresh ginger, and you don't have to peel it. It will last for up to 6 to 8 months in the freezer.*

Summer Squash Soup with Basil Crème Fraîche

SERVES 6

Basil adds a subtle summer flavor and a hint of color to this golden soup.
Garnish the soup plate with squash blossoms for a dramatic accent.

WINE SUGGESTION BY DEBBIE ZACHAREAS: FROG'S LEAP SAUVIGNON BLANC

1. In a large heavy saucepan over medium heat, melt the butter and sauté the leeks and the shallot for 4 to 5 minutes. Add the garlic and the squash and stir for 2 minutes. Add the stock or broth, and bring to a boil, reduce heat and simmer for 25 to 30 minutes, or until the squash is soft.

2. Meanwhile, finely chop the basil leaves in a food processor or with a sharp French chef's knife. In a small bowl, blend the crème fraîche and half cup of the chopped basil. Set aside.

3. In batches, puree the soup in a blender or food processor until smooth. Return to the saucepan over low heat. Stir in the crème fraîche mixture, the salt, and pepper. Simmer until heated through, about 5 minutes. Add the remaining basil and serve immediately.

4 tablespoons unsalted butter

3 leeks, white part only, washed and finely chopped

1 shallot, chopped

1 garlic clove, chopped

1¼ pounds yellow summer squash, cut into 1-inch pieces

5 cups Chicken Stock (page 61), or canned low-salt chicken broth, or Vegetable Stock (page 62)

1 cup loosely packed basil leaves

½ cup crème fraîche

½ teaspoon salt

Freshly ground pepper to taste

Strawberry Soup with Balsamic Vinegar

SERVES 6

Wood barrel aging gives balsamic vinegar a mellow character that complements both sweet and savory dishes. It enhances the summer's sweetest strawberries in this chilled soup.

2 cups ripe strawberries, hulled
  and halved

2 tablespoons sugar

2 tablespoons orange blossom or
  other mild honey˙

2 cups half-and-half

Pinch of salt

Pinch of ground white pepper

1 tablespoon balsamic vinegar

Fresh mint sprigs for garnish

1. In a blender or food processor, combine the strawberries, sugar, honey, half-and-half, salt, and pepper. Puree until smooth. Add the balsamic vinegar. Strain the soup through a meshed sieve. Pour into a medium bowl, cover, and refrigerate for at least 1 hour or overnight. Serve in chilled bowls, garnished with a mint sprig.

Tuscan Bean Soup

SERVES 6

This traditional Florentine bread soup, called *ribollita* in Italian, is made in two stages:
beginning on the stove top and finishing in the oven. (See photograph, page 70.)

WINE SUGGESTION BY DEBBIE ZACHAREAS: MCDOWELL SYRAH

1. In a large heavy stockpot, cover beans with 4 inches of water. Bring to a boil, then reduce heat. Cook until tender, about 2 hours. Allow to cool. In a blender or food processor, puree three-fourths of the beans with stock or broth.

2. In a soup pot over medium heat, heat the ¼ cup olive oil and sauté the chopped onion and pepper flakes for about 5 minutes, or until the onion is translucent. Add the tomatoes, tomato paste, and garlic and sauté for 3 minutes. Add the carrots, potatoes, fennel, spinach, cabbage or kale, and thyme. Pour in the bean puree, salt, and pepper. Bring to a boil, reduce heat to a simmer, and cook for 1½ hours, stirring occasionally. (To make ahead, let cool, cover, and refrigerate overnight. Reheat before baking.)

3. Preheat the oven to 350°F. Add the reserved whole beans to the soup. Add half of the soup mixture to a deep, 3-quart, casserole. Arrange the bread slices in a single layer over the soup. Ladle the remaining soup over the bread slices. Arrange the sliced onion in a single layer over the soup. Drizzle with a little olive oil and bake uncovered for 1 hour or until golden brown on top. Serve in large shallow bowls.

1 ½ cups dried cannellini beans

5 cups Chicken Stock (page 61) or canned low-fat chicken broth or vegetable stock

¼ cup olive oil, plus oil for drizzling

2 large yellow onions, 1 finely chopped and 1 thinly sliced

½ teaspoon red pepper flakes

3 tomatoes, peeled, seeded, and chopped (see page 40) or one 15-ounce can diced tomatoes, drained

1 tablespoon tomato paste

2 garlic cloves garlic, minced

2 carrots, peeled and cut into ½-inch pieces

2 medium Yukon Gold potatoes, cut into ½-inch pieces

1 small bulb fennel, trimmed and chopped

2 cups loosely packed fresh spinach

1 cup shredded cabbage or kale

2 tablespoons minced fresh thyme

Salt and freshly ground pepper to taste

6 or more slices hearty country bread, such as country sourdough, crusts removed

Spring Veal Ragout with Vegetables

This light and lemony stew can be made with or without the meat for a
one-bowl meal. Fava beans can be found fresh in many produce markets. If you can't
find them, use frozen lima beans. Try serving this over pasta or mashed potatoes.

¼ cup flour

Salt and freshly ground pepper

1 pound veal stew meat, cut into
  ½-inch cubes

3 tablespoons olive oil

1 pound fresh fava beans or
  lima beans, shelled

1 tablespoon minced fresh chervil

1 tablespoon minced fresh savory
  or sage

1 tablespoon minced fresh basil

1 tablespoon snipped fresh chives

1 tablespoon minced flat-leaf
  parsley

6 tablespoons unsalted butter

1. In a shallow dish, mix the flour, salt, and pepper together. Dredge the veal in the flour mixture, coating each piece evenly. In a large skillet, over medium heat, heat 2 tablespoons of the olive oil. Add the veal and cook, stirring, until pieces are golden brown on all sides, about 7 minutes. Transfer the veal to a plate and keep warm in a low oven.

2. Cook the beans in a pot of salted boiling water for 5 minutes. Transfer to a bowl of ice water. Skin the fava beans by inserting your thumbnail into the base of each bean and gently squeezing the bean out of the skin. Set aside.

3. In a small bowl, combine the herbs and set aside. In the same skillet, used to cook the veal, melt 2 tablespoons of the butter with the remaining 1 tablespoon oil over medium heat. Add the leeks and sauté for 1 minute. Add the mushrooms, carrots, garlic, half the herb mixture, and salt to taste. Sprinkle one tablespoon of the lemon juice over the mixture. Add the water and toss the ingredients together. Lower heat and cook for 2 minutes. Add the asparagus, peas, greens, and beans. Cover and cook for 2 more minutes.

4. Add the remaining 4 tablespoons butter and herbs. Cook until the vegetables are crisp-tender, about 2 minutes. Return the veal to the pan and heat through for 10 minutes. Taste for seasoning. Serve immediately in warm bowls.

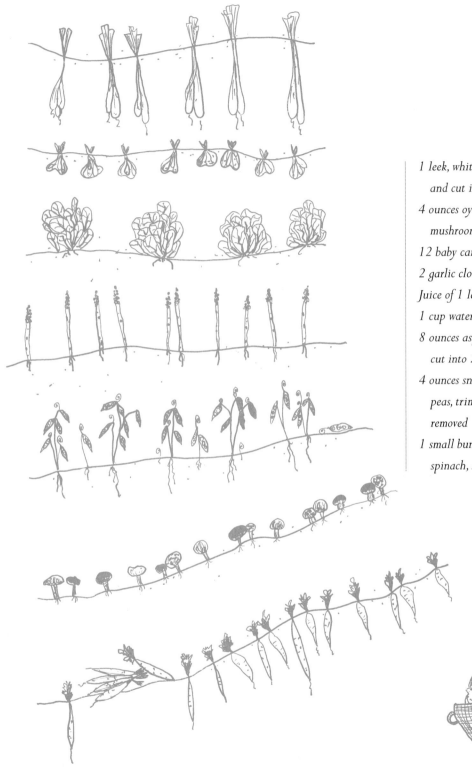

1 leek, white part only, washed
    and cut into ¼-inch rounds

4 ounces oyster or white
    mushrooms, chopped

12 baby carrots, cut into slices

2 garlic cloves, minced

Juice of 1 lemon

1 cup water

8 ounces asparagus, trimmed and
    cut into 2-inch pieces

4 ounces snow peas or sugar snap
    peas, trimmed and strings
    removed

1 small bunch tender chard or
    spinach, stemmed

Beef-Zinfandel Stew

SERVES 6

This updated winter classic is made in two stages to keep the vegetables
from turning red. Zinfandel grapes are the oldest wine grapes grown in California.
Use a good-quality Zinfandel, preferably the same one you serve with the stew.

WINE SUGGESTIONS BY DEBBIE ZACHAREAS: RAVENSWOOD OR FIFE ZINFANDEL "REDHEAD VINEYARD"

8 ounces thick-sliced bacon,
   cut into ½-inch pieces

2 pounds beef chuck or bottom
   round, cut into bite-sized pieces

1 large yellow onion, chopped

1 tablespoon minced garlic

3 tablespoons all-purpose flour

Salt and freshly ground pepper
   to taste

3 cups Zinfandel or other dry
   red wine

3½ cups Beef Stock (page 60) or
   canned low-salt beef broth

2 tablespoons tomato paste

1 tablespoon minced fresh thyme

4 carrots, peeled and cut into
   1-inch pieces

2 pounds Yukon Gold potatoes,
   peeled and cut into bite-sized
   pieces

12 ounces green beans, trimmed
   and cut into 1-inch pieces

1 cup pearl onions

1 tablespoon unsalted butter

6 ounces cremini or white
   mushrooms, thinly sliced

1. Preheat the oven to 350°F. In a large Dutch oven over medium heat, cook the bacon pieces until crisp. Using a slotted spoon, transfer to paper towels to drain. Drain all but 1 tablespoon of the bacon fat from the Dutch oven.

2. Heat the pan over medium-high heat, add the beef and cook until browned on all sides, 5 to 7 minutes. Add the onion, garlic, flour, salt, and pepper. Increase to high heat and cook, stirring constantly, for 5 minutes. Add the wine, stock or broth, tomato paste, bacon, and thyme. Bring to a boil, cover, and bake for 2 hours.

3. Meanwhile, steam the carrots in a covered pot over boiling water for 5 to 7 minutes or until tender. Using a steaming basket, rinse the carrots under cold running water. Transfer to a bowl. Steam the potatoes until tender, 10 to 15 minutes. Rinse under cold water and transfer to a bowl. Steam the beans for 7 to 9 minutes, or until crisp-tender. Rinse under cold water and transfer to a bowl. Peel the pearl onions and steam for 5 to 7 minutes, or until tender. Rinse under cold water and transfer to a bowl. In a small skillet, melt the butter over medium heat. Add the mushrooms and cook until soft, about 10 minutes. Set aside.

4. When the meat has finished cooking, place the Dutch oven over medium heat. Add the steamed vegetables and cook until heated through, about 7 minutes. Serve in warmed dishes.

White Bean and Chicken Stew

SERVES 8

The Mission District boasts the City's warmest weather. Long the center of
San Francisco's Latin community, the area markets sell traditional Mexican products.
Mexican crema and fresh oregano give this stew authentic flavor.

WINE SUGGESTION BY KRIS HARRIMAN: JOSEPH PHELPS LE MISTRAL

1. Pick over and rinse beans. Soak the beans overnight in water to cover by 4 inches. Drain.

2. Put the chicken in a large saucepan and add cold water to cover. Bring to a boil, reduce heat, and simmer, uncovered, for 15 minutes or until opaque throughout. Drain chicken and let cool, then cut in bite-sized pieces.

3. In a soup pot, over medium heat, heat the oil and sauté the onions until soft and translucent, about 10 minutes. Add the garlic, chilies, cumin, oregano, cloves, and cayenne and sauté for 2 minutes. Add the beans and stock or broth. Bring to a boil, reduce heat to a simmer, cover and cook for 2 hours, stirring occasionally.

4. Transfer 1 cup of the stock or broth to a small bowl and whisk in the cornstarch. Stir the cornstarch mixture into the stew and cook for 5 minutes, stirring once or twice. Add the chicken and 1 cup of the cheese to the pot. Stir until the cheese melts. Season with salt and pepper. Serve in warm bowls, garnished with the remaining cheese, the sour cream, and cilantro.

*2 cups dried Great Northern
beans*

*2 pounds boneless, skinless chicken
breasts*

1 tablespoon olive oil

2 yellow onions, finely chopped

4 garlic cloves, minced

*2 Anaheim chilies, roasted, seeded,
and chopped (see page 17)*

2 teaspoons ground cumin

1 teaspoon minced fresh oregano

¼ teaspoon ground cloves

½ teaspoon cayenne pepper

*6 cups Chicken Stock (page 61)
or canned low-salt chicken
broth*

2 tablespoons cornstarch

*3 cups (12 ounces) Monterey Jack
cheese, shredded*

*Salt and freshly ground pepper to
taste*

*Sour cream or Mexican crema and
chopped fresh cilantro for
garnish*

Roasted-Tomato Soup

SERVES 6

The soup is only as flavorful as the tomatoes. Look for meaty Beefsteak, Early Girl, Ace, or Viva tomatoes. If tomatoes are out of season, pass on this recipe.

16 large tomatoes, halved
(about 4 pounds)

1 tablespoon olive oil

6 tablespoons butter

2 large sweet white onions such as
Maui or Vidalia, chopped

1 teaspoon salt

1 teaspoon ground pepper

1 tablespoon minced fresh thyme
or 1 teaspoon dried

¼ cup shredded fresh basil

¼ cup crème fraîche

1. Preheat the oven to 350°F. Place the tomatoes cut side down on a baking sheet lined with aluminum foil. Drizzle with the olive oil and roast for 30 minutes. Remove from oven and let cool. Remove and discard the skins.

2. Meanwhile, in a large skillet, melt the butter over medium heat. Add the onions, salt, pepper, and thyme and cook, stirring constantly, for 15 minutes or until lightly browned.

3. In a blender or food processor process the tomatoes until smooth. Add the onions and puree until smooth. Pour the soup into a medium saucepan and cook over medium heat for 10 minutes. Taste for seasoning. Serve drizzled with crème fraîche and garnish with basil.

Fresh Pea and Arborio Soup

SERVES 8

A vibrant chicken-based soup with bright peas and Italian rice with a hint of mint. Because arborio rice continues to absorb the stock, serve immediately. If it becomes too thick add additional stock or water.

1. In a medium saucepan, bring Chicken Stock to a simmer. Add 1 cup of peas and 3 tablespoons of the mint and cook over low heat for 1 minute. Using a slotted spoon, transfer the peas to a food processor and add ¼ cup of the stock. Pulse the peas to a coarse puree. Keep the remaining stock warm.

2. In a large, heavy saucepan, add the butter and oil. Add onion and cook over medium heat until translucent and lightly browned, about 8 minutes. Add the garlic and cook 1 minute. Add the rice and stir until well coated and cook for 2 to 3 minutes. Add the remaining stock and cook over medium heat for 20 to 25 minutes until rice is cooked. Add the remaining 1 cup of uncooked peas and cook for 2 to 3 minutes or until the peas are cooked. Add the reserved puree, 1 tablespoon of mint, and all of the parsley. Season to taste with salt and pepper. To serve, ladle into bowls and sprinkle 1 tablespoon of Asiago cheese and a pinch of the remaining fresh mint over soup. Serve.

7 cups Chicken Stock (page 61) or low-salt chicken broth

2 pounds fresh green peas, shelled, or 2 cups frozen peas

5 tablespoons minced fresh mint

1 tablespoon unsalted butter

1 tablespoon olive oil

1 onion, chopped

2 cloves garlic, minced

1½ cups Arborio rice

Salt and freshly ground pepper to taste

¼ cup minced fresh flat-leaf parsley

1½ cups (6 ounces) aged Asiago or Parmesan cheese

SALADS

Mixed Baby Lettuce with Blood Orange Vinaigrette

Salad of Red Oakleaf Lettuce with Fuyu Persimmon and Candied Pecans

Salad of Tart Greens with Warm Balsamic Dressing

Asian Tri-Cabbage Coleslaw

Beet Salad with Orange and Tarragon Vinaigrette

Couscous with Olives, Lemon, and Mint

Grilled Shrimp and Cannellini Salad

Mediterranean Lentil Salad

Minted Lentil and Goat Cheese Salad

Miso Cabbage Salad

Panzanella with Grilled Chicken

Shrimp and Cherry Tomato Salad

Quinoa Salad

Roasted Portobello and Endive Salad

Spicy Vietnamese Beef Salad

Spinach Salad with Mint Leaves

Sweet White Corn and Rice Salad with Chicken-Apple Sausage

Mixed Baby Lettuce with Blood Orange Vinaigrette

SERVES 4 AS A FIRST COURSE

Blood oranges have striking red flesh and are deliciously sweet. The Napa Valley is the king of olive oil production outside of Spain, and many growers are bottling flavored varieties. This recipe features a local product, O Blood Orange olive oil (see Resources, page 311). Substitute Meyer Lemon olive oil, or Tahitian Lime olive oil (all from O Olive Oil Company) for an extravagant taste sensation in this simple vinaigrette.

1 tablespoon blood orange juice

2 teaspoons blood orange zest

2 teaspoons orange blossom honey

2 tablespoons white balsamic vinegar

1 garlic clove, minced

Salt and freshly ground pepper to taste

¼ cup blood orange olive oil, such as O Olive oil or extra-virgin olive oil

4 cups mixed baby lettuces or salad greens

2 blood oranges, peeled and segmented (see note)

1 small red onion, thinly sliced

1 ripe avocado, peeled, pitted, and sliced

1. In a small bowl, combine the juice, the zest, the honey, vinegar, garlic, salt, and pepper. Gradually whisk in the oil.

2. In a salad bowl, combine the greens, orange segments, onion, and avocado. Toss with the dressing and serve.

NOTE: To peel and segment oranges use a large French chef's knife, cut the top and bottom from each orange down to the flesh. Stand each orange on end and cut off the peel down to the flesh. Over a small bowl, cut in between each membrane to release the orange segments.

Salad of Red Oakleaf Lettuce with Fuyu Persimmon and Candied Pecans

SERVES 4 AS A FIRST COURSE

This is a fabulous salad to serve in fall, when crisp, squat Fuyu persimmons are in season. Make the candied pecans to use in other salads as well.

1. TO MAKE THE PECANS: Cook the nuts in boiling water for 30 seconds. Drain. In a large bowl, stir the powdered sugar and salt together. Add the nuts and toss until coated. In a large skillet over medium-high heat, heat the peanut oil and cook the pecans, stirring constantly, for 5 minutes, or until golden brown. Using a slotted spoon, transfer the nuts to a baking sheet lined with paper towels to cool.

2. TO MAKE THE DRESSING: In a small bowl, combine the mustard, vinegar, honey, salt, and pepper. Gradually whisk in the walnut oil until thoroughly combined. Taste for seasoning.

3. In a large salad bowl, gently toss the lettuce, persimmon, and red onion together. Toss with the vinaigrette. Add the pecans and serve.

CANDIED PECANS:

1 cup (4 ounces) pecan halves

½ cup powdered sugar, sifted

1 teaspoon salt

1 cup peanut oil or olive oil

DRESSING:

2 teaspoons tarragon mustard or Dijon mustard

2 tablespoons white balsamic vinegar or red wine vinegar

1 teaspoon wildflower honey or other mild honey

Salt and freshly ground pepper to taste

¼ cup walnut oil or olive oil

Leaves from 1 head red oakleaf lettuce, torn into bite-sized pieces

1 Fuyu persimmon, thinly sliced

1 small red onion, thinly sliced

Salad of Tart Greens with Warm Balsamic Dressing

SERVES 6

A simple dressing of balsamic vinegar and olive oil is favored for green salads by many chefs. Here, the wonderfully mellow flavor of balsamic tames the slight bitterness of radicchio and frisée. The various greens in this recipe may be replaced by 6 cups mixed salad greens.

1 red onion, thinly sliced and separated into rings

½ cup plus 3 tablespoons Cabernet or other red wine vinegar

Leaves from 1 small head romaine

Leaves from 1 small head radicchio

Leaves from 1 head red leaf lettuce

Leaves from 1 head curly frisée

1 cup pine nuts, toasted (see page 18)

3 to 4 whole scallions, cut into thin slices

3 ounces Parmesan cheese, shaved into thin curls with a vegetable peeler (¾ cup)

3 ounces thinly sliced prosciutto, torn into bite-sized pieces

1 cup fresh basil leaves

1 cup fresh flat-leaf parsley leaves

⅔ cup extra-virgin olive oil

8 large garlic cloves, thinly sliced

3 tablespoons balsamic vinegar

1 tablespoon packed dark brown sugar

Salt and freshly ground pepper to taste

1. In a small bowl, soak the onions in the ½ cup red wine vinegar for 30 minutes. Tear the lettuce leaves into bite-sized pieces. In a large bowl, toss the greens with all but 3 tablespoons of the pine nuts, most of the scallions, half of the cheese, half of the prosciutto, and the basil and parsley. Arrange the mixture on a large platter.

2. In medium, heavy saucepan over very low heat, heat the olive oil and cook the garlic cloves for 8 minutes, or until barely colored. Using a slotted spoon, transfer to a bowl. Increase heat to medium-high and add the 3 tablespoons red wine vinegar and the balsamic vinegar. Cook for 2 minutes, then stir in the brown sugar. Let bubble slowly for 1 minute. If the dressing is too sharp, simmer a bit longer to boil off some of the acid in the vinegar. Stir in the garlic cloves and season with salt and pepper.

3. Drain the red onions and discard the vinegar. Place the onions on top of the greens and scatter the remaining pine nuts, scallions, cheese, and prosciutto over the salad. Stir the dressing vigorously to blend and spoon over the salad. Serve immediately.

Asian Tri-Cabbage Coleslaw

SERVES 6 AS A SIDE DISH

This coleslaw is packed with bold Asian flavors and colorful crisp shreds of cabbage.
Napa and savoy cabbages both originated in Asia and have crinkly pale green leaves.
Choose a red cabbage with an intense color. (See photograph, page 71.)

1. Core the cabbages. In a food processor fitted with a shredding blade, shred the cabbages and carrots. Alternatively, shred the cabbages using a large French chef's knife, and shred the carrots using the large holes of a box grater. In a serving bowl, combine the cabbages, carrots, red onion, red pepper, lemongrass, ginger, and cilantro and mix thoroughly.

2. TO MAKE THE VINAIGRETTE: In a small bowl, combine the soy sauce, rice vinegar, sesame oil, sugar, pepper, and pepper flakes and stir well. Gradually whisk in the oil until combined. Pour over the salad and toss well. Refrigerate at least 2 hours before serving.

1 small napa cabbage

1 small red cabbage

1 small savoy cabbage

2 carrots, peeled

1 red onion, thinly sliced

1 red bell pepper, seeded,
   deveined, and thinly sliced

2 tablespoons grated lemongrass
   (white part only)

2 tablespoons grated fresh ginger

1 cup chopped fresh cilantro

VINAIGRETTE:

¼ cup soy sauce

3 tablespoons rice vinegar

2 tablespoons Asian sesame oil

1 tablespoon sugar

1 teaspoon ground pepper

Pinch of red pepper flakes

1 cup olive oil

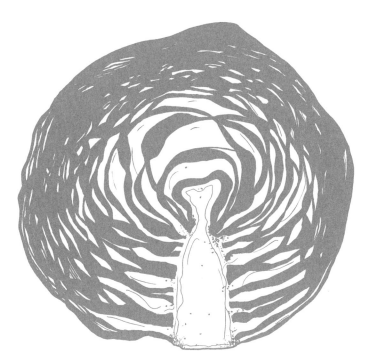

Beet Salad with Orange and Tarragon Vinaigrette

SERVES 4 AS A FIRST COURSE

Roasting beets brings out their natural sweetness. Using a combination of
red and golden beets makes this dish even more attractive. Look at
the leaves of beets as an indicator of freshness. (See photograph, page 72.)

4 red beets, greens trimmed to
 ½ inch
4 golden beets, greens trimmed
 to ½ inch

ORANGE AND TARRAGON
VINAIGRETTE:

2 tablespoons blood orange olive
 oil or extra-virgin olive oil
3 tablespoons fresh blood orange
 juice, or regular orange juice
2 teaspoons grated orange zest
2 tablespoons balsamic vinegar
2 tablespoons minced fresh
 tarragon, or 2 teaspoons dried
 tarragon
Salt and freshly ground pepper to
 taste

4 cups mixed salad greens
Tarragon sprigs and/or orange
 slices for garnish

1. Preheat the oven to 450°F. Wrap each color of beet in a separate aluminum foil packet. Put on a baking sheet and bake for 45 minutes, or until the beets can be easily pierced with the tip of a knife. Let cool completely. Trim the ends of the beets. Using paper towels, gently remove the skin. Cut the beets into ¼-inch slices and place in a bowl.

2. TO MAKE THE VINAIGRETTE: In a small bowl, combine all the ingredients. Whisk together and pour over the beets. Serve at room temperature, or cover and refrigerate overnight.

3. To serve, divide the greens among 4 plates. Place one quarter of the marinated beets on top of each serving. Spoon over additional vinaigrette, if desired. Garnish each serving with tarragon sprigs and/or orange slices.

Couscous with Olives, Lemon, and Mint

Couscous is a staple in the North African diet and has found its way into many California-style dishes. It is actually a pasta, not a grain, made from semolina flour. This recipe can be prepared ahead and finished in 15 minutes. Serve as a side dish for roasted chicken.

1. In a large, heavy saucepan, melt the butter over medium-low heat. Add the onions and sauté for 2 minutes. Cover and cook, stirring occasionally, until the onions are tender but not browned, 15 to 20 minutes. Stir in the ginger and turmeric.

2. In a medium saucepan, combine the stock or broth, olives, basil, mint, and lemon juice. Bring to a boil and add the couscous. Cover, turn off heat, and let stand until the couscous is tender and all the liquid is absorbed, about 12 minutes. Add the cooked onion mixture and gently mix. Fluff the couscous with a fork and season with salt and pepper. Mound the couscous in a serving bowl. Serve at room temperature.

4 tablespoons butter

6 onions, finely chopped (about 6 cups)

1 teaspoon grated fresh ginger

½ teaspoon ground turmeric

2¼ cups Chicken Stock (page 61) or canned low-salt chicken broth

1 cup kalamata olives, pitted

½ cup chopped fresh basil

⅓ cup chopped fresh mint, plus 2 or 3 fresh mint sprigs for garnish

¼ cup fresh lemon juice

2 cups couscous

Salt and freshly ground pepper to taste

Grilled Shrimp and Cannellini Salad

The sweet shrimp and delicate beans combine nicely with salty pancetta and peppery arugula. This is a delicious summer salad for a first course or a light dinner.

WINE SUGGESTION BY DEBBIE ZACHAREAS: ROSENBLUM SANTA BARBARA VIOGNIER

MARINADE:

¼ cup extra-virgin olive oil

1 tablespoon fresh lemon juice

Salt and freshly ground pepper to
taste

1 pound medium shrimp, shelled
and deveined

6 ounces orecchiette or other
small pasta

4 ounces pancetta or bacon, diced

2 cups cooked cannellini beans

1 tomato, chopped

3 tablespoons fresh lemon juice

1 tablespoon minced fresh thyme,
or 1 teaspoon dried thyme

Salt and freshly ground pepper to
taste

2 bunches arugula, stemmed and
chopped (about 4 cups)

1 small yellow onion, finely
chopped

1 tablespoon extra-virgin olive oil

1. TO MAKE THE MARINADE: In a medium bowl, combine all the ingredients. Add the shrimp, toss to coat, and let sit for 30 minutes.

2. Meanwhile, cook the pasta in a large pot of salted boiling water until al dente, about 10 minutes. Drain, rinse, drain again, and set aside.

3. Preheat the broiler. Place the shrimp on a broiling pan and broil for 2 to 3 minutes on each side, or until evenly pink. Set aside in a large bowl.

4. In a medium skillet over medium-high heat, cook the pancetta or bacon until golden brown, 7 to 10 minutes. Using a slotted spoon, transfer to paper towels to drain. Add the pasta, pancetta or bacon, beans, tomato, lemon juice, thyme, salt, and pepper. Toss to combine. Just before serving, toss the arugula, onion, and oil with the shrimp mixture. Serve at room temperature.

Mediterranean Lentil Salad

Fresh feta cheese, cured black olives, and ripe tomatoes are traditional ingredients in the classic Greek salad. Here, the tart flavors are mellowed with the addition of lentils. Serve as a picnic side salad, or double the recipe and serve over mixed salad greens as an entrée.

1. In a large saucepan, combine the lentils, garlic, and water and bring to a boil. Reduce heat and simmer, uncovered, until the lentils are tender but firm, about 15 to 20 minutes. Drain, transfer to a large bowl and let cool. Add the tomato, olives, feta, celery, and fennel. Stir to combine.

2. TO MAKE THE VINAIGRETTE: In a medium bowl, combine the lemon juice, garlic, and thyme. Gradually whisk in the oil. Add salt and pepper. Pour the vinaigrette over the salad and toss. Taste for seasoning. Garnish with parsley and serve.

1 cup dried French green lentils
    (lentilles de Puy)
1 garlic clove
5 cups water
1 Roma or plum tomato, cored
    and chopped, or 8 to 10 mixed
    cherry tomatoes, halved
½ cup oil-cured black olives,
    pitted and coarsely chopped
½ cup crumbled feta cheese
3 celery stalks, chopped
1 small fennel bulb, trimmed and
    chopped (optional)

VINAIGRETTE:
1 tablespoon fresh lemon juice
2 large garlic cloves, minced
2 tablespoons minced fresh thyme
¼ cup extra-virgin olive oil
Salt and freshly ground pepper to
    taste
1 tablespoon minced fresh
    flat-leaf parsley

Minted Lentil and Goat Cheese Salad

Goat cheese has become a regular addition to salads, and the Bay Area
produces some of the country's best goat cheese. Look for local labels such as
Laura Chenel, Redwood Farms, and Bodega Goat Cheese for a sample of the finest.

WINE SUGGESTION BY KRIS HARRIMAN: LATCHAM CABERNET FRANC

2 cups dried French green lentils
  (lentilles de Puy)

3 cups Chicken Stock (page 61) or
  canned low-salt chicken broth

½ teaspoon fennel seeds

2 teaspoons minced fresh thyme

3 tablespoons Cabernet or other
  red wine vinegar

3 tablespoons lemon olive oil or
  extra-virgin olive oil

Salt and freshly ground pepper to
  taste

1 small red onion, thinly sliced

4 ounces fresh white goat cheese,
  coarsely crumbled (¾ cup)

¼ cup minced fresh mint

1 teaspoon grated lemon zest

Mixed salad greens for serving

1. Pick over and rinse the lentils. In a large saucepan, combine the lentils
and stock or broth. Bring to a boil, reduce heat, and simmer uncovered
until the lentils are tender but firm, 15 to 20 minutes. Drain and let cool.
2. In a large bowl, combine the lentils, fennel seeds, thyme, vinegar, oil,
salt, pepper, and red onion and gently mix. Add the goat cheese, mint,
and zest and stir gently to incorporate. Taste for seasoning. Serve over
mixed salad greens.

Miso Cabbage Salad

Miso soup is familiar to all who have eaten in Japanese restaurants. A paste of fermented soybeans, miso, adds a delicate flavor to cabbage for an unusual twist on slaw. Toasted sesame seeds give a nice bite and nutty flavor. Miso paste can be found in many markets in the refrigerated section.

1. In a small bowl, combine the miso paste, vinegars, lemon juice, sugar, oils, and salt. Whisk until blended to a smooth consistency. Place equal amounts of cabbage on 4 salad plates. Layer equal amounts of onion, carrots, and cucumber on top of the cabbage. Spoon the dressing mixture evenly over each salad. Sprinkle with the toasted sesame seeds and serve.

3 tablespoons white miso paste

1 ½ teaspoons rice vinegar

1 teaspoon white wine vinegar

2 teaspoons fresh lemon juice

¼ teaspoon sugar

1 teaspoon canola or vegetable oil

1 teaspoon Asian sesame oil

Salt to taste

1 large napa or savoy cabbage,
   finely shredded (about 4 cups)

1 small onion, thinly sliced

2 carrots, peeled and shredded

¼ cup thinly sliced cucumbers

2 tablespoons sesame seeds, toasted
   (see page 18)

Panzanella with Grilled Chicken

Panzanella, a Tuscan bread salad, becomes more interesting with the addition of grilled chicken. Many markets carry authentic Italian breads. It is important that the day-old bread for this salad be firm and almost crumbly. Experiment with olive or rosemary bread, too.

½ cup fresh lemon juice

¼ cup extra-virgin olive oil

Salt and freshly ground pepper to taste

2 boneless, skinless whole chicken breasts

VINAIGRETTE:

3 tablespoons Cabernet or other red wine vinegar

1 tablespoon balsamic vinegar

4 garlic cloves, minced

Salt and freshly ground pepper to taste

⅔ cup extra-virgin olive oil

1 day-old loaf pugliese or other country bread, cubed

2 cups cherry tomatoes, halved

1 large red onion, thinly sliced

1 large English (hothouse) cucumber, thinly sliced

1 small fennel bulb, trimmed and thinly sliced

½ cup minced fresh basil

1 tablespoon minced fresh rosemary

½ cup (2 ounces) shaved Parmesan or aged Asiago cheese

1. In a medium bowl, whisk the lemon juice, ¼ cup olive oil and the salt and pepper together. Add the chicken and marinate at room temperature for 20 minutes.

2. Light a fire in a charcoal grill or preheat a gas grill or a broiler. Grill the chicken over a hot fire for about 8 minutes on each side, or until opaque throughout. Cut chicken into diagonal slices and set aside.

3. TO MAKE THE VINAIGRETTE: In a small bowl, whisk the vinegars, garlic, salt, and pepper together. Gradually whisk in the olive. Set aside.

4. In a large salad bowl, toss the bread cubes with 2 tablespoons of the vinaigrette. Add the tomatoes, onion, cucumber, fennel, basil, and rosemary; mix well. Add the remaining vinaigrette and cheese and let stand for ½ hour to 1 hour. Add the chicken and toss. Taste for seasoning and serve.

Shrimp and Cherry Tomato Salad

SERVES 4 AS A FIRST COURSE

Small, flavorful cherry tomatoes bring out the sweetness of the shrimp. Make this delicious and colorful salad in the summer after a trip to the farmers' market for Sweet 100 cherry tomatoes.

WINE SUGGESTION BY DAVID PAULEY: KUNDE VIOGNIER

1. In a large skillet, melt the butter with the 2 tablespoons olive oil over medium heat and sauté the shrimp for 3 to 4 minutes, or until pink. Set aside.

2. In a large bowl, whisk the jalapeño, vinegar, lime juice, ½ cup olive oil, salt, and garlic together. Stir in the tomatoes, onion, and pepper and mix until well coated. Arrange the lettuce leaves on plates. Spoon the tomato and onion mixture over the lettuce. Arrange 6 avocado slices in a flower pattern on top of the salad mixture and alternate shrimp between the avocado slices. Garnish with cilantro sprigs and serve.

1 tablespoon butter

2 tablespoons plus ½ cup extra-virgin olive oil

24 jumbo shrimp, shelled and deveined

1 small jalapeño chili, seeded and minced

1 tablespoon red wine vinegar

¼ cup fresh lime juice (about 2 large limes)

1 teaspoon salt

1 garlic clove, minced

2 cups mixed yellow and red cherry tomatoes, halved

1 small sweet white onion, cut into ¼-inch-thick slices and separated into rings

Freshly ground pepper to taste

Leaves from 2 heads butter lettuce, torn into bite-sized pieces

4 ripe avocados, peeled, pitted, and cut lengthwise into ⅛-inch-thick slices

Fresh cilantro sprigs for garnish

Quinoa Salad

Quinoa—pronounced "keen wa"— is a delicious mild-flavored grain of Latin American origin that cooks quickly and is higher in protein than rice. Ounce for ounce, quinoa has as much protein as meat, and has as much calcium as a glass of milk. Serve alongside grilled chicken or fish.

2 cups water

1 cup quinoa

½ cup extra-virgin olive oil

1 teaspoon minced fresh ginger

1 tablespoon fresh lime juice

1 teaspoon salt

1 teaspoon ground pepper

2 tablespoons finely chopped
scallions

1 tablespoon finely chopped red
bell pepper

1 tablespoon fresh cilantro,
minced

1. In a medium saucepan, bring the water to a boil. Rinse the quinoa and add to the boiling water. Reduce heat to a simmer and cook, uncovered, for 12 to 15 minutes, or until all the water is absorbed. Fluff with a fork and put in a serving bowl.

2. In a small bowl, whisk the olive oil, ginger, lime juice, salt, and pepper together. Pour over the cooked quinoa. Add the scallions, red pepper, and 2 teaspoons of the cilantro and stir to combine. Add the dressing as desired. Garnish with remaining cilantro and serve.

Roasted Portobello and Endive Salad

SERVES 4 AS A FIRST COURSE

Portobello mushrooms are recognized by their large size and firm texture
and appear on menus all over North Beach, the Italian enclave in San Francisco.
They are versatile in cooking and are often served unadorned.

1. In a shallow glass baking dish, combine the balsamic vinegar, soy sauce, ginger, and pepper and mix well. Place the mushrooms in the marinade and turn to coat. Place the mushrooms in the dish, gill-side down, and let sit for 1 hour.

2. Preheat the oven to 400°F. Roast the portobellos for about 6 minutes. Turn the mushrooms over and roast for an additional 6 minutes, or until lightly browned. Remove from the oven and let cool. Cut each mushroom into 5 to 6 pieces. Set aside.

3. In a blender or food processor, puree the bell pepper, olive oil, vinegar, shallots, garlic, salt, and pepper until smooth. Taste for seasoning.

4. Arrange the endive leaves on each of 4 individual plates. Place the portobello slices on the endive and drizzle the roasted-pepper puree on top. Serve.

¼ cup balsamic vinegar

¼ cup soy sauce

2 teaspoons grated fresh ginger

1 teaspoon ground pepper

4 large portobello mushrooms,
  stemmed

1 large red bell pepper, roasted,
  peeled, and chopped (see
  page 17)

½ cup extra-virgin olive oil

¼ cup champagne or other white
  wine vinegar

2 tablespoons minced shallots

2 garlic cloves, minced

Salt and freshly ground pepper to
  taste

8 endive leaves

Spicy Vietnamese Beef Salad

The complementing and contrasting flavors of this unique salad
explode on the palate. Once you start using fish sauce to season your
Asian dishes, you will have a new staple ingredient in your pantry.

2 tablespoons peanut or extra-
   virgin olive oil, plus oil for
   coating

2 tablespoons soy sauce

4 garlic cloves, crushed

2½ pounds sirloin steak

1 teaspoon ground pepper

4 shallots, thinly sliced

2 tablespoons grated fresh ginger

1 tablespoon sugar

1 small jalapeño chili, halved

¼ cup fresh lime juice

2 tablespoons fish sauce (nam pla
   or nuoc mam, available in
   Asian groceries)

1 small napa cabbage, cored and
   shredded

½ cup minced fresh mint

½ cup chopped fresh cilantro

2 cups (4 to 6 ounces) mung bean
   sprouts

¾ cup (4 ounces) unsalted
   peanuts, chopped

1. In a shallow dish, combine 1 tablespoon of the oil, the soy sauce, and 2 of the garlic cloves. Add the steak, cover, and marinate for 1 hour at room temperature or up to 24 hours in the refrigerator.

2. If refrigerated, remove the steak from the refrigerator 30 minutes before cooking. Sprinkle pepper on both sides of the steak. Heat a large skillet over medium-high heat. Add oil to coat the pan and cook the steak for about 5 minutes each side, or until well browned. Let rest for 10 minutes, then thinly slice across the grain into ¼-inch-wide strips.

3. In a small skillet over medium-high heat, heat the remaining 1 table-spoon oil. Add the shallots and sauté until lightly browned, about 3 minutes. Using a slotted spoon, transfer the shallots to paper towels to drain.

4. In a blender or food processor, puree the remaining garlic, the ginger, sugar, and jalapeño to a paste. Add the lime juice and fish sauce and blend well to make the dressing.

5. In a large bowl, combine the steak, cabbage, mint, and cilantro. Toss with the dressing and add the bean sprouts, peanuts, and fried shallots. Quickly toss until the salad is thoroughly coated. Serve.

Spinach Salad with Mint Leaves

SERVES 4 AS A FIRST COURSE

Tender baby spinach leaves are best for salads. Save the larger-leafed varieties for steaming or sautéing.

1. In a small bowl, soak the onion in the red wine vinegar for 30 minutes. In a medium saucepan over low heat, heat the olive oil and cook the garlic for 8 minutes, or until lightly colored. Using a slotted spoon, transfer to paper towels to drain. Increase heat to medium high and add 2 tablespoons of the red wine vinegar from the onions and the balsamic vinegar. Cook, stirring constantly, for 2 minutes and add the brown sugar. Let bubble slowly for 1 minute. If the dressing is too sharp, simmer a bit longer to boil off some of the acid in the vinegar. Remove from heat. Stir in the garlic and season with salt and pepper.

2. Drain the onions. In a large salad bowl, combine the spinach, cheese, mint, and onions and toss. Add the dressing and toss to coat the spinach leaves. Serve.

1 small red onion, thinly sliced

½ cup Cabernet or other red wine vinegar

⅓ cup extra-virgin olive oil

4 garlic cloves, thinly sliced

2 tablespoons balsamic vinegar

1 teaspoon packed brown sugar

Salt and freshly ground pepper to taste

6 cups baby spinach leaves

5 ounces feta cheese, crumbled (1 cup)

10 fresh mint leaves, thinly sliced

Sweet White Corn and Rice Salad with Chicken-Apple Sausage

SERVES 6 AS A SIDE DISH

Bruce Aidell's in San Francisco makes wonderful sausages, which are available by mail order (see Resources, page 311). The sweetness of the corn and apples makes a pleasant side dish to a spring buffet.

1 pound chicken-apple sausages;
  cut into bite-sized pieces

2 cups fresh white corn kernels
  (about 4 ears)

3 cups cooked jasmine rice

3 ounces Fontina or mozzarella
  cheese, cut into ¼-inch cubes
  (¾ cup)

¼ cup pine nuts, toasted (see
  page 18)

1 small red bell pepper, seeded,
  deveined, and chopped

1 tablespoon Dijon mustard

2 tablespoons Cabernet or other
  red wine vinegar

½ cup extra-virgin olive oil

Salt and freshly ground pepper to
  taste

Fresh basil or watercress sprigs for
  garnish

1. In a large skillet, cook the sausage over medium-high heat for about 5 minutes. Add the corn and cook until tender, about 5 minutes.

2. In a large bowl, combine the rice, sausage, and corn. Let cool slightly. Toss in the cheese. Add the pine nuts and bell pepper.

3. In a small bowl, whisk the mustard and vinegar together. Gradually whisk in the olive oil. Add salt and pepper. Add the dressing to the mixture and toss to coat. Taste for seasoning. Garnish with basil or watercress and serve.

ENTRÉES

Chilean Sea Bass with Tomatillo Salsa

Halibut and Bok Choy in Tomato-Lemongrass Broth

Seared Ahi Tuna Salad with Toasted Pumpkin Seeds

Pan-Seared Ahi with Olive-Wine Sauce

Seared Sea Scallops with Lime-Ginger Sauce and Caramelized Endives

Seared Sea Scallops with Fava Bean Puree and Shiitakes

Swordfish with Roasted Tomato, Red Pepper, and Onion Compote

Roasted Salmon Fillets with French Lentils

Thai Shrimp with Coconut Rice

Roasted Dungeness Crab with Fresh Herbs and Garlic

Roast Salmon with Fresh Corn, Tomatoes, and Zucchini

Salmon in Black Bean Sauce

Grilled Coriander Chicken with Cilantro-Walnut Pesto

Chicken Breasts with Wild Mushrooms and Balsamic Vinegar

Panfried Chicken Breasts with Asiago, Panko, and Fresh Tarragon

Chicken Pot Pie with Sage Biscuit Topping

Roast Chicken with Saffron and Lemons

Roasted Chicken with Carrots, Turnips, and Zucchini

Zinfandel-Braised Duck Legs

Orange Duck Breasts with Braised Bitter Greens

Lemon Pepper Duck with Red Wine Vinegar Sauce

Zucchini-Stuffed Pork Chops with Mustard Sauce

Moroccan-Style Pork Tenderloin

Butterflied Roasted Pork Loin with Fennel

Rosemary Pork Chops

Pork Tenderloin with Bourbon Sauce

Tamarind-Glazed Pork Tenderloin with Asian Pear Marmalade

Anchor Steam Beef Stew

Asian Flank Steak

Braised Veal Shanks with Porcini and Potatoes

Veal Chops with Spinach and Pancetta

Filet Mignons with Shallot Sauce and Onion Rings

Lamb with Potato-Tomato Gratin

Braised Lamb Shanks with Cabernet and California Prunes

Roasted Rack of Lamb with Artichokes and Sunchokes

Pappardelle with Caramelized Onions, Pancetta, and Arugula

Farfalle with Pancetta, Onions, and Cherry Tomatoes

Orecchiette with Roasted Asparagus, Lemon, and Basil

Rigatoni with Bread Crumbs and Arugula

Penne with Chicken and Spring Vegetables

Butternut Squash au Gratin

Curried Vegetable Stew

Vegetable Enchiladas with Tomatillo Sauce

Sweet Potato and Polenta Pie with Sautéed Bitter Greens and Vegetables

Morel, Asparagus, and Fresh Pea Risotto

Chilean Sea Bass with Tomatillo Salsa

SERVES 4

The sea bass is coated in polenta before it is fried, giving it a nice, slightly crunchy crust while keeping the fish moist. The tomatillo salsa gives the dish a tangy summertime taste. Highlight the south-of-the border flavors by serving this with black beans.

WINE SUGGESTIONS BY DEBBIE ZACHAREAS: DUCKHORN SAUVIGNON BLANC OR CALERA VIOGNIER

SALSA:

6 unhusked tomatillos

1 tablespoon olive oil

½ cup fresh or thawed frozen
   corn kernels

1 small red bell pepper, seeded,
   deveined, and diced

1 yellow bell pepper, seeded,
   deveined, and diced

2 serrano chilies, seeded and
   minced

⅓ cup coarsely chopped cucumber

2 tablespoons coarsely chopped
   fresh cilantro

1 tablespoon fresh lime juice

1 teaspoon kosher salt

1 teaspoon freshly ground pepper

½ cup polenta or cornmeal

Freshly cracked pepper to taste

Four 6-ounce Chilean sea bass or
   red snapper fillets

Kosher salt to taste

¼ cup olive oil

Lime wedges for garnish

1. TO MAKE THE SALSA: Heat a large cast-iron skillet over medium-high heat and add the tomatillos. Roast, turning occasionally, for 10 to 15 minutes, or until soft. Transfer to a plate and let cool. Remove and discard the husks and quarter the tomatillos. Heat the same pan over medium heat and add the oil. Add the corn kernels and cook for 5 minutes, or until lightly browned. Remove from heat. In a blender or food processor, puree the tomatillos until smooth. Transfer to medium bowl and add the corn and the remaining salsa ingredients. Stir to blend well. Refrigerate for 1 hour.

2. Spread the polenta on a plate and sprinkle it with pepper. Season the sea bass with salt. In a large cast-iron skillet over medium-high heat, heat the olive oil. Dredge the fish fillets in the polenta. Cook the fish until lightly browned on the outside and opaque throughout, 3 to 4 minutes per side. Transfer the fillets to plates and serve with the salsa and lime wedges.

Halibut and Bok Choy in Tomato-Lemongrass Broth

Lemongrass is an important ingredient in Vietnamese cooking and is more popular as
Asian cuisine continues to spread. Halibut in a delicious broth infused with lemongrass makes a nice
first course or light entrée. Pass steamed Jasmine Rice with Fresh Peas (page 206) or
Sugar Snap Peas with Mint Oil (page 191) to complete the meal. (See photograph, page 169.)

WINE SUGGESTION BY KRIS HARRIMAN: THOMAS FOGARTY GEWÜRZTRAMINER

TOMATO-LEMONGRASS BROTH:

- 4 pounds vine-ripened tomatoes, coarsely chopped
- 2 stalks lemongrass, white part only, coarsely chopped
- 1 Thai chili, seeded and minced, or 3 serrano chilies, minced

- 2 pounds halibut
- Kosher salt and freshly ground pepper to taste
- 4 cups fish stock, Chicken Stock (page 61), or canned low-salt chicken broth
- 4 baby bok choy, ends trimmed
- 10 red cherry tomatoes
- 10 yellow cherry tomatoes

1. TO MAKE THE BROTH: In a blender or food processor, puree the tomatoes. Strain through a sieve set over a bowl, stirring the pulp with a wooden spoon to extract the juice; discard the solids. You should have about 1½ cups tomato juice. Transfer to a small saucepan. Add the chopped lemongrass, cover, and simmer for 45 minutes. Add the chili and simmer 15 minutes longer. Strain the broth.

2. Sprinkle the halibut with salt and pepper. In a large skillet, bring the stock to a boil. Reduce heat to a simmer and add the halibut. Cover and cook for 6 to 8 minutes, or until opaque throughout. Transfer the fish to a plate and loosely cover with aluminum foil. Bring the stock or broth used to cook the fish to a boil. Add the bok choy, cover, and cook for 3 minutes, turning once. Add the cherry tomatoes and cook for 2 minutes. Remove from heat.

3. Divide the bok choy and cherry tomatoes among 4 soup bowls. Place a serving of fish in each bowl. Ladle the tomato broth over the fish until each bowl is half full; serve.

 ARNOLD WONG, EOS RESTAURANT: *Choose fresh-looking lemongrass stalks and use the flat side of a knife to bruise the stalks before using.*

Seared Ahi Tuna Salad with Toasted Pumpkin Seeds

SERVES 4

Ahi is a deep red tuna with loads of flavor. The spicy pumpkin crust complements the meaty texture of the fish without overpowering it. Served on a bed of greens and finished off with a lemony vinaigrette, this salad will star as an entrée. (See photograph, page 170.)

WINE SUGGESTION BY DAVID PAULEY: SILVER RIDGE SYRAH

1 cup hulled pumpkin seeds,
  coarsely chopped
Kosher salt and freshly ground
  pepper to taste
¼ cup dried bread crumbs
4 tablespoons olive oil
½ teaspoon red pepper flakes
½ teaspoon curry powder
2 egg whites
1 pound ahi tuna, sliced 1 inch
  thick

LEMON VINAIGRETTE:

¼ cup fresh lemon juice
Grated zest of 1 lemon
⅓ cup olive oil
2 shallots, minced
1 teaspoon honey mustard

4 cups mixed salad greens
2 blood oranges or navel oranges,
  peeled and sectioned (see page
  98)
Lemon wedges for garnish

1. In a blender or food processor, pulse the pumpkin seeds until coarsely chopped. In a dry heavy skillet over low heat, toast the seeds, stirring constantly, until fragrant. Transfer to a small bowl and add the salt, pepper, bread crumbs, 3 tablespoons of the olive oil, the pepper flakes, and curry. Mix well. In a medium bowl, whisk the egg whites until foamy. Place the pumpkin seed mixture on a plate large enough to hold the fish.

2. In a large nonstick skillet over medium-high heat, heat the remaining 1 tablespoon oil. Dip the fish into the egg whites, then coat on both sides in the pumpkin seed mixture. Cook for 3 to 5 minutes on one side, then turn and cook for 3 to 5 minutes on the second side, or until opaque on the outside and medium rare within.

3. TO MAKE THE VINAIGRETTE: In a small bowl, combine all the ingredients and whisk until combined. In a large bowl, combine the salad greens and orange segments. Toss gently with the vinaigrette. Place the salad on individual serving plates and top each with a tuna slice. Garnish with a lemon wedge and serve.

MARIA HELM, PLUMPJACK CAFÉ: *For cleaner tasting ahi, remove the dark red blood line before cooking or have your fishmonger do it for you.*

Pan-Seared Ahi with Olive-Wine Sauce

SERVES 4

The kalamata olives accent the fish with a delicate saltiness, which is balanced by the white wine. Flavorful and easy, this is a great dish to prepare after a busy day.

WINE SUGGESTION BY DEBBIE ZACHAREAS: IRON HORSE FUMÉ BLANC

1. In a medium skillet over low heat, heat 1 teaspoon of the olive oil. Add the fennel seeds and garlic and cook for 2 to 3 minutes. Add the olives, lemon juice, orange zest, pepper flakes, 1 teaspoon salt, and 1 teaspoon pepper and cook for 5 minutes. Remove from heat.

2. In a large, heavy skillet, heat the remaining 2 teaspoons oil over a medium heat. Salt and pepper the tuna steaks and add the tuna to the hot skillet. Cook for 3 minutes on each side for medium rare. Transfer the tuna to a serving plate and cover loosely with aluminum foil. Add the reserved olive mixture to the hot skillet and cook over medium-high heat for 2 minutes. Add the wine and cook for 3 minutes. Drizzle the olive mixture over the tuna steaks. Sprinkle with parsley and serve.

CHEF'S TIP

ARNOLD WONG, EOS RESTAURANT: *I recommend using No. 1 sushi grade ahi. It should be bright dark red, very moist and delicate, and have almost no odor. Trim away the dark flesh before cooking.*

3 teaspoons olive oil

1 teaspoon fennel seeds

2 garlic cloves, minced

¼ cup kalamata olives, pitted and chopped

2 tablespoons fresh lemon juice

2 teaspoons grated orange zest

¼ teaspoon red pepper flakes

1 teaspoon kosher salt, plus salt to taste

1 teaspoon ground pepper, plus pepper to taste

Four 6-ounce ahi tuna steaks

1 cup dry white wine

¼ cup minced fresh flat-leaf parsley

Seared Sea Scallops with Lime-Ginger Sauce and Caramelized Endives

SERVES 6 AS A FIRST COURSE, 4 AS AN ENTRÉE

These sea scallops are set atop sweetly braised endives and drizzled with a tangy sauce. Look for endives with perfectly white leaves with slightly yellow tips; any green is a sign of bitterness. Serve with steamed basmati rice. (See photograph, page 171.)

6 tablespoons butter

3 heads Belgian endive, halved
   lengthwise

Salt and freshly ground pepper to
   taste

1 tablespoon sugar

2 tablespoons fresh lime juice

1 pound sea scallops

1 tablespoon olive oil

2 shallots, sliced

2 garlic cloves, thinly sliced

2-inch piece fresh ginger, thinly
   sliced

¼ cup Chardonnay or other dry
   white wine

¼ cup heavy cream

2 tablespoons snipped fresh chives

1. In a large skillet, melt 2 tablespoons of the butter over medium-high heat and cook the endives for 8 minutes, or until lightly browned. Sprinkle the salt, pepper, sugar, and 1 tablespoon of the lime juice over the endives and cook, turning occasionally until caramelized and tender when pierced with a knife, about 15 minutes. Set aside and keep warm.

2. Rinse the scallops and pat dry with paper towels. Sprinkle with salt and pepper to taste. In a large skillet over medium-high heat, heat the oil and cook the scallops for 1 minute on each side. Add the remaining 1 tablespoon lime juice to the scallops. Transfer to a plate and cover loosely with aluminum foil to keep warm.

3. Cut the remaining 4 tablespoons butter into small dice. To the same skillet used to cook the scallops, add shallots, garlic, and ginger and sauté for 3 minutes. Add the wine and cook over high heat until almost all the liquid has evaporated. Add the cream and bring to a boil. Cook for 2 minutes. Strain the sauce into a small saucepan. Whisk in the diced butter a few pieces at a time. Season with salt and pepper to taste.

4. Place 1 endive half on each of 6 plates. Divide the scallops among the plates and spoon the sauce around them. Sprinkle with the chives and serve at once.

Seared Sea Scallops with Fava Bean Puree and Shiitakes

SERVES 6 AS AN APPETIZER, 4 AS AN ENTRÉE

Look for fresh fava beans in spring. They make a delicate
green puree that is a beautiful setting for scallops and mushrooms.

WINE SUGGESTION BY KRIS HARRIMAN: HENDRY BLOCK **9** CHARDONNAY

1. Cook the fava beans in a large saucepan of salted boiling water for 5 to 8 minutes, or until tender. Transfer to a bowl of ice water to cool. Drain. Slip the skins off the beans and place the beans in a blender or food processor. Add the stock or broth, cream, 1 teaspoon salt, and 1 teaspoon pepper. Process until smooth. Place in a small saucepan and heat gently over low heat. Set aside and keep warm.

2. In a medium nonstick skillet over medium-high heat, heat 2 teaspoons of the oil. Add the mushrooms and cook until soft and lightly browned, about 5 minutes. Season with salt and pepper to taste. Set aside and keep warm.

3. Brush a large cast-iron skillet with the remaining 1 teaspoon oil and heat over medium-high heat. Rinse the scallops and pat dry with paper towels. Sear the scallops until lightly browned on the outside and opaque throughout, about 1 minute per side. Sprinkle with the lemon juice and salt and pepper to taste.

4. Mound about ⅓ cup fava bean puree onto the center of each of 6 plates. Top with the scallops and mushrooms and sprinkle with parsley. Serve immediately.

5 pounds fava beans, shelled

½ cup Chicken Stock (page 61) or canned low-salt chicken broth

¾ cup heavy cream

1 teaspoon salt, plus salt to taste

1 teaspoon ground pepper, plus pepper to taste

3 teaspoons olive oil

1 pound shiitake mushrooms, stemmed and thinly sliced

1½ pounds sea scallops

1 tablespoon fresh lemon juice

4 teaspoons chopped fresh flat-leaf parsley

Swordfish with Roasted Tomato, Red Pepper, and Onion Compote

SERVES 6

Roasting fresh tomatoes is a simple process that adds a wonderful smokiness to this compote. French tarragon, the variety with long narrow leaves, has a subtle anise flavor that nicely accents the swordfish and compote. Make a double batch of the compote and freeze one for another time; delicious with any fish or chicken.

WINE SUGGESTION BY KRIS HARRIMAN: ALBAN ESTATE VIOGNIER

COMPOTE:

4 red vine-ripened tomatoes, preferably heirloom, cored

4 yellow vine-ripened tomatoes, preferably heirloom, cored

Olive oil for brushing, plus 2 tablespoons oil

3 teaspoons kosher salt

3 cups sliced sweet white onions, such as Vidalia, Walla Walla, or Maui onions

1 red bell pepper, roasted, peeled, and thinly sliced

2 teaspoons Cabernet or other red wine vinegar

1 tablespoon minced fresh tarragon

Freshly ground pepper to taste

3 large swordfish steaks (about 2½ pounds total)

Olive oil for brushing, plus 2 tablespoons

Salt and freshly ground pepper to taste

3 tablespoons minced fresh tarragon

1. TO MAKE THE COMPOTE: Preheat the oven to 350°F. Cut the tomatoes in half crosswise. Gently squeeze most of the seeds from each half and brush the tomatoes all over with olive oil. Arrange on a baking sheet, cut-side down, and roast in the oven for 30 minutes. Remove from the oven, cool slightly, and remove the skins. Coarsely chop the tomatoes and sprinkle with 1 teaspoon of the salt.

2. While the tomatoes are roasting, in a large skillet over medium heat, heat the 2 tablespoons oil. Add the onions and cook, stirring occasionally and adding water as necessary to prevent sticking, until soft, about 30 minutes. Add the bell pepper and continue cooking for 10 minutes. Add the tomatoes and stir in the vinegar. Cook until slightly thickened. Stir in the 1 tablespoon tarragon, the remaining 2 teaspoons salt, and the pepper. Remove from heat.

3. Twenty minutes before cooking, preheat the oven to 450°F. Brush the swordfish with olive oil, sprinkle with salt and pepper, and press the tarragon into the steaks. In a large cast-iron skillet over medium-high heat, heat the 2 tablespoons oil until very hot but not smoking. Add the steaks and sear on one side for about 3 minutes. Turn the steaks over, place the skillet in the oven, and roast, uncovered, for 10 to 12 minutes, or until the fish is opaque throughout. Serve the steaks topped with warm or room-temperature compote.

Roasted Salmon Fillets with French Lentils

SERVES 6

A rustic combination of roasted salmon, French lentils, and a rich butter sauce makes a cozy meal for a winter evening. Green lentils, originally from a small village in Puy, France, can be found in many gourmet stores and specialty markets.

WINE SUGGESTION BY DEBBIE ZACHAREAS: DEHLINGER CHARDONNAY

1. Rinse and pick over the lentils. In a large saucepan, combine the lentils and stock or broth. Slowly bring to a boil over medium heat. Tie the onion, carrot, thyme, parsley, and bay leaf in a square of cheesecloth and add to the pot. Reduce heat to low, partially cover, and simmer until tender, about 20 minutes. Drain, reserving 1 cup liquid for the sauce. Discard the bouquet garni. Season the lentils with salt and pepper and add 1 tablespoon of the butter. Set aside and keep warm.

2. Preheat the oven to 450°F. Brush the salmon on both sides with olive oil and sprinkle lightly with salt and pepper. Set aside.

3. In a small saucepan, heat the reserved stock or broth, and add the saffron. Cook over high heat to reduce the liquid to ½ cup. Reduce heat to low and whisk in the remaining 5 tablespoons butter a few pieces at a time. Add the lemon juice and salt and pepper to taste. Remove sauce to a small bowl, and set over a bowl of hot water to keep warm.

4. Coat a large cast-iron skillet with olive oil and heat over medium-high heat until very hot but not smoking. Sear the salmon fillets, skin-side up, for 2 minutes. Turn the fillets over and sear on the second side, for about 1 minute. Turn the fillets again, place the pan in the oven, and bake, uncovered, for 6 minutes, or until the salmon is barely translucent in the center.

5. To serve, place each fillet on a bed of warm lentils and pour some saffron sauce over the fillets.

1½ cups dried small green French lentils (lentilles de Puy)

4 cups fish stock, Chicken Stock (page 61), or canned low-salt chicken broth

1 small yellow onion, halved

1 small carrot, peeled and halved

1 fresh thyme sprig

1 fresh parsley sprig

1 bay leaf

Kosher salt and freshly ground pepper to taste

6 tablespoons cold unsalted butter, cut into pieces

6 salmon fillets, skin on

Extra-virgin olive oil for brushing, plus oil for cooking

½ teaspoon saffron threads

1 tablespoon fresh lemon juice

CHEF'S TIP

MARIA HELM, PLUMPJACK CAFÉ: *Save and freeze the shells when shelling shrimp. They make a great shellfish stock.*

Thai Shrimp with Coconut Rice

SERVES 4

Don't be scared off by the long list of ingredients for this dish. Once you measure them out, it's easy to assemble. The varied herbs and spices combine to produce the aromatic and somewhat spicy flavor of a great Thai dish. Try the pungent opal basil in this dish for a deep basil flavor.

WINE SUGGESTIONS BY DEBBIE ZACHAREAS: PRESTON VIOGNIER OR SINSKEY VIN GRIS OR PINOT NOIR

1½ pounds large shrimp, shelled
   and deveined

Juice of 1 lime

3 cups unsweetened coconut milk

½ cup water

1 cup jasmine rice

4 tablespoons sake, dry sherry, or
   Chardonnay wine

1½ teaspoons Chinese chili-garlic
   sauce

1 tablespoon sugar

1 teaspoon salt

1 teaspoon ground pepper

2 tablespoons butter

3 garlic cloves, minced

2 tablespoons minced fresh ginger

2 teaspoons grated lemongrass

2 shallots, minced

⅓ cup chopped fresh basil,
   preferably opal basil

⅓ cup chopped fresh mint

5 kaffir lime leaves

⅓ cup chopped scallions,
   including green portions

1½ tablespoons cornstarch mixed
   with 1½ tablespoons water

¼ cup peanuts, chopped

1. In a large bowl, combine the shrimp and lime juice and let stand for 30 minutes. In a small saucepan, bring 1½ cups of the coconut milk and the water to a boil. Reduce heat to medium low. Add the rice, cover, and simmer for 15 minutes, or until tender. Meanwhile, in a medium bowl, combine the remaining coconut milk, the sake, sherry, or wine, chili-garlic sauce, sugar, salt, and pepper. Set aside.

2. Drain the shrimp. In a large nonstick skillet, melt the butter over high heat. Add the shrimp, garlic, ginger, lemongrass, and shallots and cook for 2 minutes, or until the shrimp are pink. Add the seasoned coconut milk and bring to a boil. Add the basil, mint, kaffir lime leaves, and scallions and cook for 1 minute. Add the cornstarch mixture and cook for 2 minutes. Serve over rice, garnished with chopped peanuts.

Roasted Dungeness Crab with Fresh Herbs and Garlic

SERVES 4

If there were only one dish that was San Francisco, fresh Dungeness crab would surely be it. Fisherman's Wharf is bustling with locals and tourists alike during the crab season, which usually runs from October to May. For authentic presentation, cover your table with white butcher paper and serve the roasted crab with steamed artichokes. Forget about manners, and heap your discarded shells on the table.

WINE SUGGESTION BY DAVID PAULEY: CAYMUS SAUVIGNON BLANC

1. TO MAKE THE MARINADE: In a blender or food processor, combine all the ingredients and puree until smooth.

2. Place the crab pieces in a shallow baking dish. Pour the marinade over the crab. Cover and refrigerate for 1 hour, turning once or twice.

3. Preheat the oven to 400°F. Roast the crabs, uncovered, for 5 minutes. Remove from the oven, sprinkle the lemon zest over the crab, and mix thoroughly. Roast for 5 more minutes, or until golden brown and opaque throughout. Serve with lemon wedges.

NOTE: To clean and section Dungeness crabs, keep the crabs in a paper bag in the refrigerator until cooking. To stun the crabs, approach one from behind, grasp the legs and the claw on each side with each hand, and crack the center of the underside of the shell with a sharp blow against the hard edge of a table or counter. Pull the top shell off the crab and remove the gray gills and green tomalley (crab liver). To make serving easier, use a large cleaver to cut the crabs in half, then cut the body into portions, each with a leg. Crack the shells with a nutcracker or hammer.

MARINADE:

1 teaspoon fennel seeds

¼ cup chopped fresh flat-leaf parsley

2 teaspoons chopped fresh thyme

3 teaspoons chopped fresh oregano

4 garlic cloves, chopped

2 teaspoons red pepper flakes

1 teaspoon salt

1 teaspoon ground pepper

⅓ cup lemon olive oil or extra-virgin olive oil

2 live Dungeness crab (2 pounds each), cleaned and sectioned (see note)

1 tablespoon grated lemon zest

1 lemon, cut into wedges for garnish

Roast Salmon with Fresh Corn, Tomatoes, and Zucchini

SERVES 4

A festive summer entrée with a mélange of colorful vegetables. If the grill is fired up,
consider roasting the corn in the husk for a smoky, caramelized taste.
Let cool, then cut the kernels from the cobs and add to the cooked vegetables.

WINE SUGGESTION BY KRIS HARRIMAN: EL MOLINO CHARDONNAY

2 garlic cloves, minced

1 tablespoon grated lemon zest

2 tablespoons fresh lemon juice

Kosher salt and fresh ground
 pepper to taste

1 tablespoon minced fresh lemon
 thyme or regular thyme

1 teaspoon minced fresh rosemary

3 tablespoons lemon olive oil, or
 extra-virgin olive oil

4 salmon fillets, skinned and
 boned

2 tablespoons butter

2 cups fresh corn kernels (about
 4 ears)

1 small red bell pepper, seeded,
 deveined, and thinly sliced

2 zucchini, sliced

2 yellow crookneck squash, sliced

20 red or mixed red and yellow
 cherry tomatoes

2 tablespoons snipped fresh chives

Lemon wedges for garnish

1. In a small bowl, combine the garlic, lemon zest and juice, salt, pepper, 2 teaspoons of the thyme, and the rosemary. Whisk in the oil to emulsify. Place the salmon fillets in a glass baking dish, pour the marinade over, cover, and refrigerate for 2 hours, turning several times.

2. Preheat the oven to 400°F. In a large cast-iron skillet, melt the butter over medium-high heat until it foams. Add the corn, bell pepper, zucchini, squash, the remaining thyme, and salt and pepper to taste. Sauté until lightly browned, about 4 minutes.

3. Remove the salmon from the marinade and place on top of the vegetables in skillet. Add the tomatoes to the skillet. Place the skillet in the oven and roast for 10 minutes. Garnish with chives and lemon wedges and serve.

Salmon in Black Bean Sauce

SERVES 4

You'll find a version of this dish in many restaurants in San Francisco's Chinatown. All of the ingredients can be found in the supermarket. The oils and hoisin sauce are good to have on hand and can be stored in the refrigerator for up to a year. Serve this dish with steamed basmati rice.

WINE SUGGESTIONS BY DEBBIE ZACHAREAS: LOGAN CHARDONNAY OR ARROWOOD PINOT BLANC

1. In a large skillet over medium heat, heat the oils and stir-fry the black beans, ginger, and garlic for 2 minutes. Add the sake or wine, soy sauce, hoisin, brown sugar, stock or broth, and pepper, and stir-fry for 3 minutes. Add the salmon fillets to the pan and turn to coat with the sauce. Cover and cook for 4 minutes. Turn the fillets over, cover, and continue cooking for 4 minutes.

2. To serve, place a salmon fillet on each plate and garnish with scallions and cilantro.

MARIA HELM, PLUMPJACK CAFÉ: *For low-fat sautéing of salmon, place a dry nonstick pan over medium heat. Season the salmon and place in the pan. Do not turn until the fish exudes fat.*

2 tablespoons peanut oil

2 tablespoons Asian sesame oil

2 tablespoons fermented Chinese black beans, crushed, or black bean paste

1 tablespoon grated fresh ginger

2 garlic cloves, minced

2 tablespoons sake or dry white wine

3 tablespoons soy sauce

1 tablespoon hoisin sauce

1 tablespoon packed brown sugar

1 cup Chicken Stock (page 61) or canned low-salt chicken broth

1 teaspoon ground pepper

4 salmon fillets, skinned and boned

2 scallions, finely chopped, including green portions

¼ cup chopped fresh cilantro

Grilled Coriander Chicken with Cilantro-Walnut Pesto

SERVES 4

This marinated chicken dish combines the distinct flavors of toasted coriander and cumin seeds with garlic, peppercorns, cayenne, ginger, and saffron. Spread the cilantro pesto on warm torn pieces of pita bread. Top with some grilled chicken, roll up, and enjoy.

WINE SUGGESTION BY KRIS HARRIMAN: TRUCHARD SYRAH

MARINADE:

2 tablespoons coriander seeds

1 teaspoon cumin seeds

2 teaspoons peppercorns

8 garlic cloves

*2-inch piece fresh ginger, peeled
   and thinly sliced*

3 tablespoons olive oil

¼ cup water

1 tablespoon cayenne pepper

Pinch of saffron

2 tablespoons fresh lemon juice

2 teaspoons salt

½ cup fresh cilantro, chopped

*1 whole chicken, cut into 8 pieces
   and skinned*

*Cilantro-Walnut Pesto
   (recipe follows)*

Warm pita bread for serving

1. TO MAKE THE MARINADE: Heat a small dry skillet over medium heat. Add the coriander seeds, cumin seeds, and peppercorns, and stir constantly until fragrant, about 1 to 2 minutes. Transfer to a spice grinder and grind to a fine powder.

2. In a blender or food processor, combine the ground spices, garlic, ginger, olive oil, water, cayenne, saffron, lemon juice, and salt. Process to a paste. Transfer the paste to a large glass baking dish. Add the cilantro and stir to combine. Add the chicken pieces and thoroughly coat with the spice paste. Cover with plastic wrap and refrigerate for 4 hours or overnight.

3. Remove the chicken from the refrigerator 30 minutes before cooking. Light a fire in a charcoal grill or preheat a gas grill. Preheat the oven to 375°F. Bake the chicken for 15 minutes. Transfer the chicken pieces to the grill from the baking dish or to a broiler pan and place under the broiler and cook 8 to 10 minutes on each side or until the juices run clear when a thigh is pierced with a knife. Serve with the cilantro pesto and warm pita bread.

cilantro-walnut pesto

1. In a blender or food processor, combine the cilantro, garlic, jalapeño, walnuts, lemon juice, salt, pepper, and cumin. Process to a paste. Add the water and process to combine. Taste for seasoning. Pour into a serving container.

1 cup chopped fresh cilantro

4 garlic cloves

1 jalapeño chili, seeded, and cut into chunks

½ cup walnuts, toasted (see page 18)

½ cup fresh lemon juice

1 teaspoon salt

1 teaspoon freshly ground pepper

¼ teaspoon ground cumin

¼ cup water

Chicken Breasts with Wild Mushrooms and Balsamic Vinegar

SERVES 4

Mushrooms and balsamic vinegar make a rich, earthy sauce for chicken. Williams-Sonoma carries a good selection of balsamic vinegars, some aged twenty years (see Resources, page 311).

WINE SUGGESTION BY DEBBIE ZACHAREAS: DELOACH ZINFANDEL

4 boneless, skinless chicken breast halves

Salt and freshly ground pepper to taste

2 tablespoons flour

2 tablespoons olive oil

6 garlic cloves

8 ounces wild or mixed white and brown mushrooms, sliced

¼ cup balsamic vinegar

¾ cup Chicken Stock (page 61) or canned low-salt chicken broth

1 bay leaf

1 tablespoon minced fresh thyme, or 1 teaspoon dried thyme

1 tablespoon unsalted butter

1. Rinse the chicken and pat dry with paper towels. Sprinkle the chicken with salt and pepper. Spread the flour on a large plate, season with salt and pepper, and dredge the chicken breasts in the mixture. Shake off the excess and place on a clean plate.

2. In a large, heavy skillet over medium-high heat, heat the oil and cook the chicken breasts until nicely browned on one side, about 3 minutes. Add the garlic cloves and continue to cook for 2 to 3 minutes.

3. Turn the breasts and scatter the mushrooms over them. Continue cooking for 3 to 4 minutes, shaking the skillet to distribute the mushrooms. Add the vinegar, stock or broth, bay leaf, and thyme. Reduce heat to medium low. Cover and cook the breasts for 10 minutes, turning once or twice.

4. Using tongs, transfer the chicken breasts to a warm serving platter and cover loosely with aluminum foil. Cook the mushroom sauce, uncovered, over medium-high heat for about 5 minutes, or until the mushrooms are lightly browned. Whisk in the butter and continue to cook for 2 to 3 minutes. Remove and discard the bay leaf. Pour the mushroom sauce over the chicken breasts and serve.

Panfried Chicken Breasts with Asiago, Panko, and Fresh Tarragon

SERVES 6

Panko, Japanese-style bread crumbs, are the secret to this light version of fried chicken. They can be found in most supermarkets. Serve the breasts whole or slice crosswise into medallions. This is great picnic fare, served in sandwiches with Toasted Walnut and Ginger-Garlic Dip (page 16).

WINE SUGGESTION BY DAVID PAULEY: HONIG SAUVIGNON BLANC

1. In a wide, shallow bowl, beat the eggs until blended. On a large plate, combine the flour, salt, pepper, and herbs. Mix well. On another large plate, combine the bread crumbs and cheese. Mix well. Rinse and pat the chicken breasts dry with paper towels.

2. Coat each breast in the flour mixture, thoroughly shaking off excess. Coat in the beaten eggs, and then in the bread crumb mixture. Shake off the excess. In a large heavy skillet, melt the butter with the olive oil over medium heat. Add the chicken and cook for 7 to 8 minutes, or until golden brown on one side. Turn and cook on the second side for 7 to 8 minutes, or until the juices run clear when the chicken is pierced with a sharp knife. Transfer to a plate, garnish with parsley, and serve.

4 eggs

¾ cup all-purpose flour

1 teaspoon salt

1 teaspoon ground pepper

1 tablespoon minced fresh tarragon, or 1 teaspoon dried tarragon, thyme, or oregano

¾ cup panko or dried bread crumbs

¾ cup (3 ounces) grated aged Asiago or pecorino cheese

6 boneless, skinless chicken breast halves

3 tablespoons butter

1 tablespoon olive oil

Minced fresh flat-leaf parsley for garnish

Chicken Pot Pie with Sage Biscuit Topping

SERVES 6

Surprise your family and guests with this fabulous chicken pot pie.
A buttery crust with a hint of fresh sage tops off the flavorful filling which is baked
in the same pan in which it was cooked. (See photograph, page 172.)

WINE SUGGESTIONS BY DEBBIE ZACHAREAS: SWANSON CHARDONNAY
OR ROBERT SINSKY CABERNET FRANC

2 tablespoons olive oil

1 large onion, chopped

1 leek, white part only, chopped

4 boneless, skinless chicken breast
halves, cut into chunks

4 boneless chicken thighs, cut into
chunks

5 ounces mushrooms, chopped

3 garlic cloves, minced

¼ cup dry white wine

4 cups Chicken Stock (page 61) or
canned low-salt chicken broth

2 cups 1-inch-cubed potatoes

2 carrots, peeled and cut into
diagonal slices

2 tablespoons minced fresh thyme,
or 2 teaspoons dried thyme

1 teaspoon salt

1 teaspoon freshly ground pepper

1½ cups fresh or frozen peas

4 tablespoons unsalted butter

¼ cup all-purpose flour

1 cup half-and-half

salt and pepper to taste

Sage Biscuit Topping
(recipe follows)

1. TO MAKE THE FILLING: In a Dutch oven over medium-high heat, heat the oil and sauté the onion and leek for 5 minutes, or until lightly browned. Add the chicken pieces and cook for 5 minutes, or until lightly browned. Add the mushrooms and cook for 3 minutes. Add the garlic and cook for 1 minute. Add the wine and cook for 2 minutes. Add the stock or broth, potatoes, carrots, thyme, salt, and pepper and cook for 10 minutes, or until the potatoes can be easily pierced with a knife. Add the peas and remove from heat.

2. In a small saucepan, melt the butter over medium-high heat. Whisk in the flour and cook, whisking constantly, until the mixture begins to bubble, about 1 minute. Add the half-and-half, salt, and pepper and whisk until the mixture begins to bubble. Cook for 2 minutes, whisking constantly. Gently stir the white sauce into the chicken mixture until blended. Taste for seasoning.

3. Preheat the oven to 400°F. Prepare the Sage Biscuit Topping as directed. With your hands, gather dough and roughly shape the dough to fit the top of the Dutch oven. Place on top of chicken mixture using the same pan you cooked the chicken and vegetables. Don't worry about making the dough smooth. Bake for 20 to 30 minutes, or until the top is golden brown. Serve.

sage biscuit topping

1. In a food processor, combine the flours, salt, baking powder, baking soda, butter, and sage and pulse until the mixture resembles coarse meal. Add the buttermilk and pulse until the dough starts to come together. To make by hand, combine dry ingredients in a bowl and cut in the butter with a pastry cutter or 2 knives until the mixture resembles coarse meal. Stir in the buttermilk with a fork until all ingredients are moistened.

1 cup all-purpose flour

1 cup cake flour

1 teaspoon salt

2 teaspoons baking powder

¼ teaspoon baking soda

½ cup (1 stick) cold butter, cut into small cubes

2 tablespoons minced fresh sage, or 2 teaspoons dried sage

¾ cup buttermilk

Roast Chicken with Saffron and Lemons

Many fine meat markets and restaurants boast free-range chicken,
which has better flavor and texture than supermarket brands.
In this simply prepared dish, you will undoubtedly taste the difference.

WINE SUGGESTION BY DAVID PAULEY: SHENONDOAH VINEYARD SAUVIGNON BLANC

1 free-range chicken (about 3
  pounds) such as Rocky Junior

1 teaspoon saffron threads,
  slightly toasted in a dry small
  skillet

2 teaspoons kosher salt

1½ teaspoons peppercorns

2 tablespoons minced fresh
  rosemary, or ¾ tablespoon
  dried rosemary

2 tablespoons fresh flat-leaf
  parsley

2 lemons, 1 juiced and 1 thinly
  sliced

1. Preheat the oven to 425°F. Wash and pat the chicken dry with paper towels inside and out. In a blender or food processor, process all the other ingredients except the lemon slices for 15 seconds to form a paste. With your fingers, gently separate the skin from the meat of the chicken and spread the paste under and over the skin and inside the cavity. Place the slices of lemon under the skin and inside the cavity. Truss the chicken with the wings folded under.

2. Place the chicken, breast-side up, in a small roasting pan or baking dish. Roast for 15 minutes. Reduce the oven temperature to 375°F and roast, basting every 15 minutes, for 45 more minutes, or until a thermometer inserted in the thigh registers 160°F. Remove from the oven. Cover loosely with aluminum foil and let rest for 10 minutes before carving.

Roasted Chicken with Carrots, Turnips, and Zucchini

SERVES 4

An exotic blend of spices subtly infuses this roasted one-dish chicken meal.

WINE SUGGESTION BY DAVID PAULEY: PRESIDIO WINERY CHARDONNAY

1. Preheat the oven to 425°F. Pour the olive oil into a large roasting pan and spread over the bottom. Wash and pat the chicken dry inside and out with paper towels. Place the chicken in the pan, breast-side up. Set aside.

2. In a small bowl, mix the coriander, cumin, salt, garlic, and cilantro together. Reserve 3 tablespoons of the mixture in a cup and set aside. Stir 3 tablespoons of the butter into the mixture in the bowl. Using your fingers, gently separate the skin from the breast and thighs of the chicken. Spread the herbed butter mixture evenly under the skin on the breast, thighs, and legs. Put any remaining seasoned butter in the cavity. Truss the chicken with kitchen string and roast in the center of the oven for 15 minutes. Place the carrots and turnips around the chicken and add 1 tablespoon of the butter. Roast for an additional 30 minutes. Add the zucchini and sprinkle the reserved spice mixture in the pan over it. Toss all the vegetables. Roast 30 more minutes, or until a meat thermometer inserted in the thigh of the chicken registers 170°F. Transfer the chicken to a serving platter. Remove and discard the string. Using a slotted spoon, transfer the vegetables from the pan to the platter. Cover the platter loosely with aluminum foil.

3. Skim off any fat from the sauce in the roasting pan and place the pan over high heat. Add the wine and cook for 2 minutes. Add the stock or broth and reduce heat to medium-high. Stir to scrape up the browned bits from the bottom of the pan. Cook until reduced by half. In a small bowl, blend the remaining 1 tablespoon butter and the flour together. Stir the butter mixture into the pan and keep stirring until the sauce thickens, about 2 minutes. Taste for seasoning. Pour into a sauceboat. Serve the chicken and vegetables with the sauce alongside.

CHEF'S TIP

FLO BRAKER, COOKBOOK AUTHOR: *When handling chicken, meat, or dough, cover your faucet handle with a sandwich bag so that when you turn on the water to wash your hands, the handle stays clean.*

1 tablespoon olive oil

1 free-range chicken, such as Rocky Junior, about 4 pounds

½ teaspoon ground coriander seed

2 teaspoons ground cumin

1 teaspoon kosher salt

3 garlic cloves, minced

⅓ cup fresh cilantro leaves, minced

5 tablespoons unsalted butter at room temperature

5 carrots, peeled and cut into 1-inch diagonal slices

4 turnips, peeled and cut into 1-inch wedges

2 zucchini, halved lengthwise and cut into 1-inch pieces

¼ cup Chardonnay or other dry white wine

1 cup Chicken Stock (page 61) or canned low-salt chicken broth

1 tablespoon flour

Zinfandel-Braised Duck Legs

SERVES 6

Duck is readily available in many specialty markets today or you can ask your butcher to order it for you. The sweetness of the dried fruit holds up nicely to the assertive flavor of duck. Save the rendered fat to use as a richly flavored substitute for butter. It will keep several days in the refrigerator covered with plastic wrap.

6 duck legs, about 5 pounds total

Salt and freshly ground pepper to taste

½ cup Zinfandel or other dry red wine

2 heads garlic, separated into cloves and peeled

2 tablespoons minced fresh thyme, or 2 teaspoons dried thyme

1 cup mixed dried fruit such as cherries, apricots, prunes, and currants, chopped

5 cups Chicken Stock (page 61) or canned low-salt chicken broth

1. Preheat the oven to 350°F. Heat a large skillet over medium-high heat. Salt and pepper the duck legs and cook until the skin is evenly crisp and dark brown on one side, 10 to 15 minutes. With a bulb baster, remove the rendered fat and discard. Turn the legs and brown on the other side, 10 to 15 minutes. Transfer to a plate.

2. Pour off the remaining fat and heat pan over medium-high heat. Add the wine and stir to scrape up the brown bits in the bottom of the pan. Cook for 5 minutes. Add the garlic, thyme, and ½ cup of the fruit. Stir and arrange the duck legs on top of the fruit mixture. Add the stock or broth and bring to a simmer. Taste for seasoning. Bake, uncovered for 2 hours, or until very tender. Transfer the legs to serving platter and cover loosely with aluminum foil.

3. Use a fat separator to remove the fat from the pan liquid, or pour the liquid into a bowl and let stand until the fat rises to the top. Skim off the remaining fat and strain the liquid into a bowl. Pour the liquid into a medium saucepan and heat the pan over medium-high heat. Cook to reduce until slightly thickened. Add the remaining ½ cup fruit and cook until fruit is soft, about 5 minutes. Ladle the sauce around the duck and serve.

MARIA HELM, PLUMPJACK CAFÉ: *Soak garlic cloves in cold water for 15 minutes and the skins will slip off easily.*

Orange Duck Breasts with Braised Bitter Greens

SERVES 4

The duck marinates in orange juice, honey, and red pepper flakes,
then cooks to a deep mahogany color with a delicate, crisp skin.
Sliced and served on a bed of bitter greens, this entrée is a wonderful
mélange of flavors. Braised spinach may be substituted for the greens.

WINE SUGGESTION BY DEBBIE ZACHAREAS: BEAULIEU VINEYARDS CARNEROS RESERVE PINOT NOIR

1. With a sharp knife, halve the whole duck breasts and score the skin in a ¼-inch cross-hatch pattern. In a large bowl, whisk the zest, orange juice, soy sauce, oil, honey, vinegar, red pepper flakes, and the 1 teaspoon salt together. Mix well. Add the duck and cover all sides of it with marinade. Cover and refrigerate for at least 8 hours or overnight.

2. Remove the duck from the marinade, reserving the marinade. Pat the duck dry with paper towels and season with salt and pepper. In a large, heavy skillet over medium-high heat, cook the duck breasts, skin-side down, for 5 minutes. Pour off the fat, turn the duck over, and brown the other side. Reduce heat to medium and cook for 20 minutes, or until the duck is a dark mahogany color and a meat thermometer inserted in the center of a breast registers 145° to 150°F.

3. Meanwhile, in a large skillet, melt the butter over medium-high heat and sauté the garlic until it begins to turn golden, about 3 minutes. Add the bitter greens and water. Cover, stirring occasionally, for 8 to 10 minutes, or until just tender. Season the greens with salt and pepper to taste. Set aside and keep warm.

4. Transfer the cooked duck to a cutting board and let rest. Add the wine to the pan and stir to scrape up the browned bits from the bottom of the pan. Add the reserved marinade. Bring the mixture to a boil. Add any juices that have accumulated on the cutting board and cook the sauce for 2 minutes, or until slightly thickened. Strain the sauce through a fine-meshed sieve into a serving bowl.

5. Cut the duck across the grain into thick slices. Divide the greens among 4 plates and arrange the duck on top. Spoon the sauce over the duck and serve.

*2 whole boneless Muscovy duck
   breasts with skin*

1 teaspoon grated orange zest

½ cup fresh orange juice

¼ cup soy sauce

¼ cup olive oil

*2 tablespoons orange blossom or
   other mild honey*

1 tablespoon white wine vinegar

1 teaspoon red pepper flakes

1 teaspoon salt, plus salt to taste

Freshly ground pepper to taste

2 tablespoons butter

3 garlic cloves, sliced very thin

*6 cups mixed bitter greens such as
   frisée, escarole, radicchio,
   dandelion greens, mizuna, and
   arugula*

⅓ cup water

*¼ cup Cabernet Sauvignon or
   other dry red wine*

Lemon Pepper Duck with Red Wine Vinegar Sauce

SERVES 4

This delicious way of preparing duck is as easy as cooking chicken.
The Napa Valley produces the country's best Cabernet Sauvignon wine, and some
of the wineries use the wine for making vinegar. Williams-Sonoma carries
a good selection of red wine vinegars (see Resources, page 311).

WINE SUGGESTION BY DAVID PAULEY: DELOACH ZINFANDEL

1 tablespoon grated lemon zest

*1 tablespoon minced fresh thyme,
or 1 teaspoon dried thyme*

1 teaspoon salt, plus salt to taste

*1 teaspoon ground pepper, plus
pepper to taste*

*2 whole Muscovy duck breasts,
halved*

⅓ cup chopped pancetta or bacon

4 garlic cloves, minced

1 large onion, chopped

1 sprig fresh thyme

1 sprig fresh rosemary

1 sprig fresh sage

1 tablespoon flour

*½ cup Cabernet or other red wine
vinegar*

*2½ cups Beef Stock (page 60) or
canned low-salt beef broth*

1. Preheat the oven to 425°F. In a small bowl, combine the lemon zest, thyme, 1 teaspoon salt, and pepper. Spread the herb mixture under the skin of the duck breasts.

2. Heat a large cast-iron skillet or heavy roasting pan in the oven for 10 minutes. Place the duck breasts in the pan, skin-side down, and cook for 10 minutes. Turn and cook for 10 more minutes. Transfer the duck to a plate and cover loosely with aluminum foil. To prepare up to 1 day in advance, let cool to room temperature, cover tightly, and refrigerate.

3. In a large skillet over medium-high heat, cook the pancetta or bacon until brown. Add the garlic, onion, and herbs and sauté for 8 minutes. Sprinkle with the flour and cook, stirring constantly, until golden brown. Add the vinegar and stir for 1 minute. Reduce heat to low and add the stock or broth. Simmer for 15 minutes. Strain the sauce through a colander, pressing the solids with the back of a large spoon. Season with salt and pepper. Set aside and keep warm. To serve, slice the duck breasts on the diagonal and place on a serving plate. Pass the sauce separately.

Zucchini-Stuffed Pork Chops with Mustard Sauce

SERVES 4

A delicious mixture of zucchini and cheese enlivens thick, juicy loin chops.
A pool of tangy mustard sauce makes a beautiful presentation. The Napa Valley
Mustard Company has a wonderful variety of mustards including their own Dijon.
Experiment with other styles of mustard to alter the sauce slightly.

WINE SUGGESTION BY DEBBIE ZACHAREAS: FERRARI-CARANO CHARDONNAY

1. In a colander, combine the zucchini and 1 tablespoon salt. Let drain for 30 minutes, then squeeze dry. In a heavy skillet over medium-high heat, heat 3 tablespoons of the oil and sauté the zucchini for 8 minutes. Add the garlic and sauté for 2 minutes. Stir in the Parmesan and let cool for 5 minutes.

2. Cut a deep pocket in the side of each pork chop and fill the pocket with some stuffing. Salt and pepper the chops. In a large, heavy skillet over medium-high heat, heat the remaining 1 tablespoon oil and cook the chops for 7 to 8 minutes on each side, or until firm to the touch. Transfer the chops to an ovenproof platter and keep warm in a low oven.

3. In the oil remaining in the pan, sauté the onion over medium-high heat for 4 minutes. Add the wine and stir to scrape up the browned bits from the bottom of the pan. Whisk in the cream, mustard, and any juices that have accumulated on the platter. Add salt and pepper to taste. To serve, pool the sauce on heated plates and place a pork chop on top of each pool.

4 or 5 zucchini, grated

1 tablespoon salt, plus salt to taste

4 tablespoons olive oil

2 large garlic cloves, minced

¼ cup grated Parmesan cheese

Four ¾-inch-thick pork loin chops

Freshly ground pepper to taste

1 small onion, finely chopped

⅓ cup Chardonnay or other dry white wine

½ cup heavy cream

1 tablespoon Dijon mustard

Moroccan-Style Pork Tenderloin

SERVES 6

Cumin and garlic are familiar spices in Moroccan cooking. The red pepper flakes add a little heat. Serve with broccoli rabe or sautéed spinach and steamed basmati rice.

WINE SUGGESTION BY KRIS HARRIMAN: J. FRITZ OLD VINE ZINFANDEL

1 or 2 small pork tenderloins
   (about 2¼ pounds total)
Salt and freshly ground pepper to
   taste
3 garlic cloves, chopped
4 teaspoons grated orange zest
1 tablespoon cumin seed
1 teaspoon red pepper flakes

1. Preheat the oven to 475°F. Salt and pepper the pork. In a mortar or spice grinder, grind the garlic, zest, cumin, and pepper flakes to a paste. Spread the paste over the pork.

2. Put the pork in a roasting pan and roast in the center of the oven for 30 minutes. Reduce the oven temperature to 325°F and continue to roast for 12 to 15 minutes, or until a meat thermometer inserted into the pork registers 145°F. Transfer to a carving board, cover loosely with aluminum foil, and let rest for 10 minutes before carving and serving.

Butterflied Roasted Pork Loin with Fennel

SERVES 6

Fennel has a subtle licorice character and a crisp texture. The fennel seeds are mixed with pancetta, sage, and rosemary to make a flavorful paste. The sliced bulb fennel is cooked until soft and served with the pork for additional flavor and provides some crunch.

WINE SUGGESTIONS BY DEBBIE ZACHAREAS: ARROWOOD CHARDONNAY OR MACROSTIE PINOT NOIR

1. TO MAKE THE PASTE: In a blender or food processor, combine all the ingredients and process to a paste.

2. Trim the excess fat from pork, leaving a ⅛-inch layer on the outside. Set the pork, fat-side down, in a roasting pan and, with the tip of a sharp knife, make several small incisions all over the pork loin. Rub the pancetta mixture over the pork, pushing some of the mixture into the incisions. Cover with plastic wrap and refrigerate for at least 2 hours or overnight.

3. Remove the pork from the refrigerator 30 minutes before roasting. Preheat oven to 375°F. Put the pork in a large roasting pan and roast for 1 hour, basting occasionally, or until a thermometer inserted into the center of the roast registers 140°F. Remove the pork from the oven and turn on the broiler. Broil the pork for about 5 minutes, or until lightly browned. Transfer to a cutting board, cover loosely with aluminum foil, and let rest for 10 minutes.

4. Place the roasting pan over medium-high heat, add the wine, and cook for 2 minutes. Add any accumulated juices from pork and cook for 2 minutes, stirring to scrape up the browned bits from the bottom of the pan. Add the stock or broth and cook for 3 minutes. Add the fennel and cook stirring constantly, until the fennel is tender, about 5 minutes. Cut the meat into diagonal slices and serve with the fennel.

GERALD HIRIGOYEN, FRINGALE RESTAURANT AND PASTIS RESTAURANT: *After being cooked, most meat should be allowed to rest for 10 to 15 minutes before you slice into it. This allows the blood and juices to more evenly permeate the meat, resulting in improved taste and tenderness.*

PANCETTA AND FENNEL PASTE:

Six ¼-inch-thick slices pancetta, chopped

10 garlic cloves

2 teaspoons fennel seeds

2 tablespoons olive oil

1 tablespoon balsamic vinegar

2 tablespoons Cabernet or other red wine vinegar

1 tablespoon minced fresh sage

1 tablespoon minced fresh rosemary

1 teaspoon kosher salt

1 teaspoon ground pepper

1 boneless pork loin, about 3 pounds, untied

¼ cup Chardonnay or other dry white wine

2 cups Beef Stock (page 60) or canned low-salt beef broth

2 fennel bulbs, trimmed and thinly sliced

Rosemary Pork Chops

SERVES 4

This is a delicious and simple recipe for your family. Serve it with
Mashed Potatoes with Leeks and Fresh Thyme (page 201). Center loin chops
offer more flavor, and the thickness of the chops keeps the pork moist.

WINE SUGGESTIONS BY DEBBIE ZACHAREAS: BYRON CHARDONNAY OR SINSKEY PINOT NOIR

Four 1-inch-thick center-loin
    pork chops
Kosher salt and freshly ground
    pepper to taste
2 tablespoons minced fresh
    rosemary, or 2 teaspoons dried
    rosemary
2 tablespoons grapeseed or olive
    oil
1 tablespoon butter
2 shallots, minced
2 garlic cloves, chopped
½ cup Chardonnay or other dry
    white wine
1 cup Chicken Stock (page 61) or
    canned low-salt chicken broth
4 fresh rosemary sprigs for
    garnish (optional)

1. Rinse and pat the pork chops dry with paper towels. Salt and pepper the chops. Sprinkle the rosemary on each side and lightly press the rosemary into the chops. In a large cast iron skillet over medium-high heat, heat the oil and cook the chops for 3 to 4 minutes on one side. Turn the chops over and cook for 3 more minutes. Reduce heat to medium, cover, and cook, turning once, until the juices run clear when a chop is pierced with a knife, about 4 minutes. Remove the chops to a serving plate and cover loosely with aluminum foil.

2. In the same skillet, melt the butter over medium-low heat, and sauté the shallots for 3 to 4 minutes, or until softened. Add the garlic and cook for 1 minute. Add the wine and cook for 2 minutes, stirring to scrape up the browned bits from the bottom of the pan. Add the stock or broth and any juices that have accumulated from the reserved chops. Simmer the sauce for 5 to 6 minutes, or until slightly syrupy. Pour the sauce over the chops. Garnish with rosemary sprigs, if you like, and serve.

Pork Tenderloin with Bourbon Sauce

SERVES 6

This quick and simple tenderloin dish is delicately spiked with bourbon and roasts up with a nice sugary crust. Try this sliced cold, with Brie cheese and roasted red peppers, for sandwiches.

WINE SUGGESTION BY DEBBIE ZACHAREAS: FROG'S LEAP ZINFANDEL

1. In a glass baking pan, whisk together all the ingredients except the pork. Remove and reserve ¼ cup of the marinade. Add the tenderloins to the remaining marinade, cover with plastic wrap, and refrigerate overnight, turning once or twice.

2. Remove the pork from the refrigerator 30 minutes before cooking. Light a fire in a charcoal grill or preheat a gas grill or a broiler. Drain the tenderloins. Grill or broil the pork 6 inches from the heat source, basting often with the reserved marinade and turning occasionally with tongs for 15 to 25 minutes, or until the pork has reached an internal temperature of 140°F. Cut into ½-inch slices to serve as a main course, or ¼-inch slices to serve cold for sandwiches.

¼ cup Jack Daniel's or other bourbon

¼ cup soy sauce

¼ cup packed brown sugar

3 garlic cloves, minced

¼ cup Dijon mustard

1 teaspoon minced fresh ginger, or ¼ teaspoon ground ginger

1 teaspoon Worcestershire sauce

¼ cup peanut oil

2 pork tenderloins, about 1 pound each

Tamarind-Glazed Pork Tenderloin with Asian Pear Marmalade

SERVES 4

An Asian twist on the American pork chops with applesauce, this recipe calls for pears and Chinese five-spice powder, a mixture of star anise, fennel, ginger, cinnamon, and Szechwan peppercorns. Tamarind paste, used in the glaze, may be found in Asian markets. The pear marmalade may be made the day ahead and makes a great sandwich accompaniment.

WINE SUGGESTIONS BY DEBBIE ZACHAREAS: SAINTSBURY PINOT NOIR OR HANDLEY BRIGHTLIGHTER CHARDONNAY

TAMARIND GLAZE:

2 tablespoons tamarind paste

1 tablespoon water

1 tablespoon orange marmalade

½ teaspoon ground cinnamon

¼ cup Chardonnay or other dry
    white wine

Salt and freshly ground pepper
    to taste

2 pork tenderloins

1 tablespoon olive oil

Asian Pear Marmalade
    (recipe follows)

1. TO MAKE THE GLAZE: In a small bowl, combine the tamarind paste, water, orange marmalade, cinnamon, wine, salt, and pepper. Pour over the tenderloins, thoroughly coating all sides. Marinate at room temperature for 1 hour.

2. Preheat the oven to 375°F. Heat a large cast-iron skillet over medium-high heat for 10 minutes. Add the oil and quickly cook the tenderloins until browned on all sides. Transfer the skillet to the oven and roast for 30 minutes, or until faintly pink in the center. Cut the pork into medallions and serve with the Asian pear marmalade.

asian pear marmalade

1. In a medium saucepan, combine all the marmalade ingredients. Bring to a boil, reduce heat, cover, and simmer for 3 minutes. Uncover and continue cooking, stirring occasionally, for 15 minutes, or until soft but not mushy. Remove and discard the cinnamon stick. Let cool and use now, or cover and refrigerate for up to 3 days. Bring to room temperature before using.

One 2-inch piece ginger, peeled and grated

½ cup water

Grated zest of 1 orange

2 tablespoons fresh orange juice

½ cup packed brown sugar

1 teaspoon Chinese five-spice powder

½ teaspoon vanilla extract

1 cinnamon stick, or ½ teaspoon ground cinnamon

1 tablespoon unsalted butter

4 Asian pears, or a combination of Bartlett and Asian pears, peeled, cored, and chopped into ½-inch pieces

Anchor Steam Beef Stew

SERVES 6

Anchor Steam, San Francisco's premier micro-brewery beer, adds a distinctive flavor
to this stew. Be sure to serve ice-cold Anchor Steam beer with the stew.

1 boneless chuck roast, 4 to 5
    pounds

5 tablespoons butter

1 tablespoon olive oil

2 onions, chopped

2 garlic cloves, minced

2½ cups Anchor Steam beer or
    other dark beer

2 teaspoons minced fresh thyme,
    or ¾ teaspoon dried thyme

3 bay leaves

1 teaspoon salt

1 teaspoon freshly ground pepper

1 tablespoon blackberry jam

1 tablespoon cornstarch

1. Cut the beef into 1-inch cubes. In a Dutch oven, melt 2 tablespoons of the butter with the oil over medium-high heat and brown the beef in batches on all sides, transferring it to a plate when done. Reduce heat to medium, add the remaining 3 tablespoons butter, and sauté the onions and garlic for 3 to 5 minutes. Add 1 cup of the beer and cook the onion mixture another 3 to 5 minutes. Return the beef to the pan and add the thyme, bay leaves, 1 cup of the beer, and the salt and pepper. Bring to a boil, then reduce heat, cover, and simmer gently for 1½ hours, or until tender.

2. Let the beef cool for 5 minutes, then stir in the jam. Mix the cornstarch with the remaining ½ cup beer. Add the beer mixture to the Dutch oven and stir over medium heat until thick, 3 to 5 minutes. Serve.

THOMAS KELLER, THE FRENCH LAUNDRY RESTAURANT: *In Northern California, the bay laurel is a common backyard tree. Instead of purchasing bottled bay leaves, pick some right from your tree. Clean, then dry the leaves in a cool, dark spot, for 1 to 2 weeks. Store in an airtight jar. Because bay laurel leaves are stronger that the ones you buy at the market, use half as much as suggested in your recipes. I like to use bay leaves in soups, winter stews, and hearty fall dishes.*

Asian Flank Steak

In this recipe, ginger acts as a natural meat tenderizer while infusing the flank steak with a wonderful flavor. Do not marinate the meat for longer than 2 hours, or it will begin to break down. Serve this with Sautéed Red and Yellow Cherry Tomatoes (page 184).

WINE SUGGESTION BY KRIS HARRIMAN: FLORA SPRINGS MERLOT

1. In a 9-by-13-inch glass baking dish, combine the lemon juice, hoisin, soy sauce, Worcestershire, pepper, cilantro, and ginger. Mix until well blended. Add the steak, cover with plastic wrap, and marinate for 2 hours at room temperature, turning once or twice.

2. Light a fire in a charcoal grill or preheat a gas grill or a broiler. Transfer the steak from the marinade and grill or broil for 5 to 6 minutes on each side for medium rare. Transfer to a carving board, cover loosely with aluminum foil, and let rest for 10 minutes. Slice the meat crosswise on the diagonal. Garnish with chives and serve.

2 tablespoons fresh lemon juice

1 tablespoon hoisin sauce

3 tablespoons soy sauce

¼ cup Worcestershire sauce

1 teaspoon freshly ground pepper

2 tablespoons chopped fresh
  cilantro

1 tablespoon minced fresh ginger

One 2-pound flank steak

2 tablespoons snipped fresh chives
  for garnish

Braised Veal Shanks with Porcini and Potatoes

SERVES 4

Fresh porcini mushrooms are difficult to find, but they are sold dried. Rehydrate the mushrooms in hot water and add the soaking liquid to the stew for a heightened mushroom flavor.

WINE SUGGESTION BY DEBBIE ZACHAREAS: ROBERT KEENAN MERLOT

1 ounce dried porcini mushrooms

2 cups boiling water

4 tablespoons olive oil

2 large onions, chopped

2 garlic cloves, minced

1 tablespoon minced fresh rosemary, or 1 teaspoon dried rosemary

2 bay leaves

1 pound fresh cremini or white mushrooms, sliced

3 large red potatoes, cut into ½-inch-thick slices

Four 1-inch-thick veal shanks

Salt and freshly ground pepper to taste

Flour for coating

1 cup dry red wine

1½ cups Beef Stock (page 60), or canned low-salt beef broth

2 tablespoons fresh lemon juice

3 tablespoons minced fresh flat-leaf parsley

1 tablespoon minced lemon zest

1. Place the dried mushrooms in a bowl. Pour the boiling water over and let stand until soft, about 30 minutes. Drain the mushrooms and squeeze dry over a bowl. Reserve the liquid. Chop the mushrooms and set aside.

2. Preheat the oven to 350°F. In a large Dutch oven over medium-high heat, heat 2 tablespoons of the oil. Add the onions, garlic, rosemary, and bay leaves and cook until the onions are tender, about 10 minutes. Add the porcini, fresh mushrooms, and potatoes; cook for 4 minutes, stirring frequently.

3. Season the veal with salt and pepper and lightly dredge in the flour. In large, heavy skillet over high heat, heat the remaining 2 tablespoons oil. Brown the shanks for about 4 minutes on each side. Place atop the vegetables in the Dutch oven. Add the wine, stock or broth, lemon juice, and the reserved mushroom liquid. Stir to scrape up the browned bits from the bottom of the pan. Pour the mixture over the veal. Cover and bake for about 1 hour and 15 minutes, or until tender.

4. Remove the stew from the oven. Place over medium-high heat and cook, uncovered, stirring occasionally, until the liquid is thickened, about 15 minutes. Season with salt and pepper to taste. Remove and discard the bay leaves.

5. Mix the parsley and lemon zest in a bowl. Garnish the stew with the parsley mixture or sprinkle it on top of each serving.

Veal Chops with Spinach and Pancetta

SERVES 4

These simple pan-seared veal chops are set on a bed of sautéed spinach,
pancetta, and chopped vine-ripened tomatoes for a colorful presentation.
This dish can be prepared in less than 45 minutes. Serve with buttered egg noodles.

WINE SUGGESTION BY DEBBIE ZACHAREAS: ROBERT SINSKEY CLARET

1. Heat a large cast-iron skillet over medium-high heat for 10 minutes.
Add the oil. Salt and pepper the veal and sear on each side for about
5 minutes. Reduce heat to low, cover, and cook, occasionally turning
with tongs for 15 to 20 minutes, for medium. Remove the chops from
the pan and set aside.

2. In the same skillet, cook the pancetta or bacon over medium-high
heat, for 3 minutes. Add the garlic and cook for 2 minutes. Stir in the
chopped tomatoes and cook for 3 minutes. Add the spinach to the pan
in batches, stirring as it wilts and adding more until all has been cooked.
Add the 1 teaspoon salt and pepper to taste. Cook for 2 minutes more.
Serve the chops on a bed of spinach.

2 teaspoons olive oil

Four 1-inch-thick veal loin chops

*Kosher salt and freshly ground
 pepper to taste*

*4 ounces pancetta or bacon, cut
 into ¼-inch dice*

4 large garlic cloves, minced

2 vine-ripened tomatoes, chopped

*1 pound spinach, stemmed,
 washed, and torn*

1 teaspoon salt

GERALD HIRIGOYEN, FRINGALE RESTAURANT AND PASTIS
RESTAURANT: *When I cook at home, I make sure to line up
everything I need in the way of ingredients and utensils, then I carefully select music
to accompany the mood I am in. Have fun while you're cooking—that's what life's
all about!*

Filet Mignons with Shallot Sauce and Onion Rings

Go to a good butcher for this cut—or, better yet, order the steak from Niman Ranch (see Resources, page 311). If you don't feel like splurging, use rib-eye steak instead. Serve with garlic mashed potatoes and braised Swiss chard.

WINE SUGGESTION BY DEBBIE ZACHAREAS: T-VINE CABERNET SAUVIGNON

SHALLOT SAUCE:

2 tablespoons olive oil

4 shallots, halved

¼ cup sugar

½ cup balsamic vinegar

1 cup Chicken Stock (page 61) or
   canned low-salt chicken broth

1 cup Beef Stock (page 60) or
   canned low-salt beef broth

3 tablespoons minced fresh thyme,
   or 1½ teaspoons dried thyme

Kosher salt and freshly ground
   pepper to taste

Four 1-inch-thick filet mignon
   steaks, preferably Niman Ranch

Salt and freshly ground pepper to
   taste

Oil for brushing

Onion Rings (recipe follows)

1. TO MAKE THE SAUCE: In a large, heavy skillet over medium heat, heat the olive oil and cook the shallots for 10 minutes, or until soft. Add the sugar and stir for 5 minutes, or until the shallots are golden brown. Add the vinegar and cook for 3 to 5 minutes, or until reduced to a syrup. Add the stocks or broths and boil until the liquid is reduced by half, about 10 minutes. Add the thyme, salt, and pepper.

2. Season the steaks with salt and pepper. Brush a cast-iron grill pan with oil and heat over medium heat. Grill the steaks about 8 minutes on each side for medium rare. Transfer the steaks to a plate. Spoon the shallot sauce around the steaks and garnish the top with onion rings.

onion rings

1. Preheat the oven to 250°F. In a large bowl, combine the buttermilk and onions and soak for 1 hour. Drain. In a large bowl, combine the flour, the 2 teaspoons salt, and the pepper and mix well. Add the onion slices in batches and toss to coat. In a Dutch oven or deep fryer, heat the oil to 375°F. Shake the excess flour from the onion rings and add a couple of handfuls to the hot oil. Fry until golden brown, about 2 minutes. Using a slotted spoon, transfer to paper towels to drain. Transfer to a large baking sheet, season lightly with salt, and keep warm in a low oven while cooking the remaining onion slices.

2 cups buttermilk

2 Vidalia, Maui, or red onions, thinly sliced and separated into rings

1 cup all-purpose flour

2 teaspoons salt, plus salt to taste

Freshly ground pepper to taste

8 cups peanut oil or vegetable oil

Lamb with Potato-Tomato Gratin

SERVES 6

The juices from the lamb drip onto the vegetables as it roasts creating a rich-tasting gratin to serve alongside. If you can't find top round of lamb, ask your butcher to prepare it for you from the meaty portion of the leg of lamb.

WINE SUGGESTION BY KRIS HARRIMAN: HARRISON MERLOT

4 garlic cloves, 1 halved, 3 minced

Extra-virgin olive oil for coating, plus ⅓ cup

2 pounds Yellow Finn or Yukon Gold potatoes, thinly sliced

Kosher salt and freshly ground pepper to taste

1 tablespoon minced fresh thyme

2 onions, thinly sliced

5 vine-ripened tomatoes, thinly sliced

⅔ cup Chardonnay or other dry white wine

2 top rounds of lamb, about 1½ pounds each

1. Preheat the oven to 400°F. Rub the bottom and side of a 10-by-16-inch gratin dish with the halved garlic and coat the bottom with olive oil. Arrange the potatoes in a single layer in the dish and season with salt, pepper, and ⅓ of the minced garlic and thyme. Place the sliced onions in a single layer over the potatoes and season with salt, pepper, and ⅓ of the minced garlic and thyme. Repeat with the layer of tomatoes. Pour the wine and ⅓ cup olive oil over the entire layered mixture.

2. Sprinkle the meat with salt and pepper. Set a sturdy cake rack directly on top of the gratin dish and set the meat on the rack so the juices will drip through. Put the gratin dish in the oven and roast, uncovered, for 45 minutes to 1 hour, until a meat thermometer inserted in the center of the roast reaches 130° to 135°F for medium rare. Transfer the meat to a serving platter and cover loosely with aluminum foil. Let rest for 10 to 20 minutes. Allow the gratin to finish cooking in the oven while the lamb rests. Carve and serve with the gratin.

Braised Lamb Shanks with Cabernet and California Prunes

SERVES 6

The hot, dry climate of California is ideal for sun-drying fruit. California prunes add a rich dimension to this dish, as they practically melt into the braised shanks and offset the tart tomatoes with a hint of sweetness. This hearty entrée is even better if made the day before and gently reheated. Serve on top of mashed potatoes or creamy polenta.

WINE SUGGESTIONS BY KRIS HARRIMAN: PLUMPJACK ESTATE OR RESERVE SAUVIGNON

1. Preheat the oven to 325°F. Salt and pepper the lamb shanks. Put the flour on a large plate and dredge each piece of meat evenly. In a Dutch oven over medium-high heat, heat the olive oil. Add half of the lamb shanks in one layer and brown on each side. Transfer to a plate. Repeat with the remaining lamb shanks. Set aside.

2. In the same Dutch oven over medium heat, sauté the onion, scraping the bottom of the pan thoroughly, until the onion is lightly browned, about 12 minutes. Add the carrots and fennel and sauté for 5 minutes. Add the garlic and sauté for 1 minute. Add all the remaining ingredients and cook for 5 minutes.

3. Add the lamb shanks to the pan and mix thoroughly. Cover and bake, turning the lamb occasionally with tongs, for 2 hours, or until the meat is falling off the bones. Taste for seasoning and serve.

THOMAS KELLER, THE FRENCH LAUNDRY RESTAURANT: *When setting your table with linens that have been folded, use a spray bottle of water to spritz the creases in the linen. Use only the finest mist or spray setting. Once the cloth is on your table, very lightly spray any creases that persist and smooth them with your hands. The creases will fall right out.*

Salt and freshly ground pepper to taste

6 lamb shanks, cut in half

Flour for dusting

¼ cup olive oil

1 large onion, chopped

4 carrots, peeled and cut into diagonal slices

1 fennel bulb, trimmed and chopped

6 garlic cloves, minced

3 tablespoons minced fresh thyme

3 tablespoons chopped fresh basil

3 cups Cabernet Sauvignon or other dry red wine

2 cups Beef Stock (page 60) or canned low-salt beef broth

2 cups diced fresh or canned tomatoes

3 tablespoons tomato paste

1½ cups pitted California prunes

Roasted Rack of Lamb with Artichokes and Sunchokes

SERVES 4

The town of Watsonville, south of San Francisco, is the artichoke capital of the world,
so San Franciscans enjoy bumper crops of artichokes almost year-round. In this recipe,
the inner leaves of the artichoke are kept attached to the heart, and only the spiny purple choke
and tough outer leaves are removed. The artichokes are then roasted with the lamb and
beautifully presented as a bed for the lamb chops. Sunchokes, or Jerusalem artichokes,
as they are also called, are no relation to the artichoke, but they are delicious!

WINE SUGGESTION BY KRIS HARRIMAN: NIEBAUM COPPOLA CLARET

1 lemon, quartered

4 large artichokes

2 teaspoons salt, plus salt to taste

4 tablespoons olive oil

1 pound sunchokes or Jerusalem artichokes, peeled and cut into quarters

4 red onions, each cut into 6 wedges, with root ends attached

22 garlic cloves, 16 whole and 6 minced

1 teaspoon freshly ground pepper, plus freshly ground pepper to taste

2 racks of lamb, frenched (have your butcher do this for you)

3 tablespoons minced fresh oregano

¼ cup Chardonnay or other dry white wine

½ cup Chicken Stock (page 61) or canned low-salt chicken broth

1. Squeeze one of the lemon quarters into a large bowl of water. Cut off the stems of artichokes and remove the tough outer leaves. Cut ¼-inch off the tops and cut each artichoke into quarters. Using a teaspoon, scoop out the fuzzy purple choke and discard. Rub one lemon quarter on the artichokes and place them in the lemon water. Soak for several minutes.

2. Bring a large saucepan of water to a boil. Squeeze the remaining two lemon quarters into the water and add 1 teaspoon of the salt. Add the artichokes, and cook for 5 minutes. Transfer the partially cooked artichokes to a bowl of ice water to stop the cooking. Drain.

3. Preheat the oven to 450°F. In a large roasting pan, heat 1 tablespoon of the oil over medium-high heat and sauté the artichokes, sunchokes, onions, and whole garlic cloves. Transfer the pan to the oven and roast, uncovered, for 20 minutes.

4. In a large, heavy skillet, heat 1 tablespoon of the oil over medium-high heat. Salt and pepper the racks of lamb, add the lamb and cook on one side for 2 minutes, or until browned. Turn and brown the other side. Transfer the lamb to a plate, leaving the oven on.

5. In a small bowl, combine the minced garlic, the oregano, the remaining 1 teaspoon salt, the 1 teaspoon pepper, and the remaining 2 tablespoons olive oil. Mix well. Rub this mixture over the lamb. Place the lamb, rib-side down, on top of vegetables in the roasting pan and roast for 15 minutes, or until a thermometer inserted in the center of a rack registers 130°F for medium rare.

6. Place the cooked vegetables on a serving platter. Place the rack of lamb on a cutting board and cover loosely with aluminum foil. Place the roasting pan over medium-high heat. Add the wine and cook for 3 minutes, stirring to scrape up the browned bits from the bottom of the pan. Add the stock or broth and continue to cook for 5 minutes, or until the sauce is slightly thickened. Add salt and pepper to taste. Pour the sauce into a sauceboat. Cut the lamb racks into individual chops, place the chops on top of the vegetables, and serve with the sauce alongside.

 THOMAS KELLER, THE FRENCH LAUNDRY RESTAURANT:
To keep herbs fresh in your refrigerator, wrap them in moistened newspaper or paper towels. This works much better than plastic bags because it allows the herbs to breathe. This should prolong the life of your herbs by up to 1 week.

Pappardelle with Caramelized Onions, Pancetta, and Arugula

SERVES 4

Try to find the sweet Vidalia, Walla Walla, and Maui onions for this casual dinner dish of pasta ribbons tossed in a broth of sweet onions, smoky pancetta, and tart arugula.

WINE SUGGESTION BY KRIS HARRIMAN: FERRARI-CARANO "SIENA" CABERNET

2 tablespoons extra-virgin olive
   oil

6 ounces pancetta or bacon,
   chopped

2 tablespoons butter

2 sweet white or onions, sliced

1 teaspoon sugar

4 cups Chicken Stock (page 61) or
   canned low-salt chicken broth

Salt and freshly ground pepper to
   taste

1 pound dried pappardelle pasta

2 cups arugula

⅓ cup grated romano cheese

1. In a large cast-iron skillet over medium high, heat 1 tablespoon of the oil. Add the pancetta or bacon and cook until crisp, stirring occasionally. Transfer to paper towels to drain. Pour off all but 1 tablespoon of fat from the skillet.

2. In the same skillet, melt 1 tablespoon of the butter with the remaining 1 tablespoon oil over medium-high heat. Add the onions and sugar and cook, stirring frequently, until well browned, about 10 minutes. Reduce heat to low and continue cooking, stirring occasionally, for 20 minutes, or until very soft and caramel-colored. Remove half the onions and reserve them.

3. Turn heat to high, and gradually add the stock or broth to the onions in the pan, stirring to scrape up the browned bits from bottom of the pan. Cook for 10 minutes. Add salt and pepper.

4. In a large pot of salted boiling water, cook the pasta until not quite al dente, about 9 minutes. Drain and add to the mixture in the skillet. Add the arugula, cover, and cook for 1 minute, or until the pasta is al dente. Stir in the remaining 1 tablespoon butter and the pancetta or bacon. Serve immediately in shallow bowls, garnished with the reserved onion and the cheese.

 REED HEARON, ROSE PISTOLA RESTAURANT: *Make sure to salt the water for boiling pasta very generously. When under-salted, pasta can be a flavor sponge and suck the flavor out of a sauce.*

Farfalle with Pancetta, Onions, and Cherry Tomatoes

SERVES 4

A lighter rendition of the Italian favorite *spaghetti all'amatriciana,* this is made with cherry tomatoes instead of Roma tomatoes. Look for Sweet 100s or the yellow Sungold variety. Add additional red pepper flakes for a very spicy sauce.

WINE SUGGESTION BY KRIS HARRIMAN: ROBERT MONDAVI LA FAMIGLIA BARBERA

1. In a large cast-iron skillet over medium heat, heat 1 tablespoon of the oil and cook the pancetta or bacon until crisp. Using a slotted spoon, transfer to paper towels to drain. Pour off all but 1 tablespoon fat. Add the remaining 1 tablespoon oil and sauté the onion until golden, about 5 minutes. Add the wine and simmer for 3 minutes, until reduced by half. Increase heat to high, add the cherry tomatoes, and sauté for 3 minutes. Reduce heat to medium. Stir in the reserved pancetta or bacon, pepper flakes, thyme, and basil. Add the butter and salt and simmer for 15 minutes.

2. Cook the farfalle in a large pot of salted boiling water until al dente, about 10 minutes. Add ¼ cup of the pasta water to the sauce. Drain the pasta and toss. Pour into a warm pasta serving bowl, sprinkle with the cheese, and toss. Serve immediately.

REED HEARON, ROSE PISTOLA RESTAURANT: *Remember, the sauce or flavoring is an enhancement for pasta. Pasta is a grain dish, not a stew with noodles. Don't overwhelm the pasta with sauce.*

2 tablespoons olive oil

8 ounces pancetta or thick bacon slices, cut into strips

1 large onion, chopped

¼ cup Chardonnay or other dry white wine

2 cups red or mixed red and yellow cherry tomatoes, halved

¼ teaspoon red pepper flakes

2 tablespoons minced fresh thyme, or 1 tablespoon dried thyme

½ cup fresh basil leaves, shredded

2 tablespoons unsalted butter

1 teaspoon kosher salt

1 pound dried farfalle pasta

⅓ cup grated aged Asiago cheese

Orecchiette with Roasted Asparagus, Lemon, and Basil

SERVES 4 AS AN ENTRÉE, 6 AS A SIDE DISH

Orecchiette, a round, cup-shaped pasta, means "little ears" in Italian. If asparagus
is not available, tender peas make a wonderful substitute in this simple sauce.

WINE SUGGESTION BY KRIS HARRIDAN: SWANSON ROSATO SANGIOVESE

1 pound dried orecchiette or other
   short shaped pasta

1 pound thin asparagus, trimmed
   to 3-inch pieces

6 tablespoons olive oil

Juice of 1 lemon

1 teaspoon minced lemon zest

1 shallot, minced

½ cup fresh basil leaves, shredded

Kosher salt and freshly ground
   pepper to taste

¼ cup shaved Parmesan cheese

1. Preheat the oven to 400°F. In a large pot of salted boiling water, cook the pasta until al dente, about 10 minutes.

2. While the pasta is cooking, spread the asparagus pieces in one layer on a baking sheet. In a small bowl, combine 3 tablespoons of the oil with half of the lemon juice and mix. Pour over the asparagus to coat well and roast for 10 minutes, turning twice.

3. In large skillet over medium-high heat, heat the remaining 3 tablespoons oil and sauté the lemon zest and shallot for 1 minute. Add the asparagus pieces and the remaining lemon juice into pan. Stir briefly and turn off heat.

4. Drain the pasta and place in a large serving bowl. Add the asparagus mixture, basil, salt, and pepper. Serve immediately in warm pasta bowls, topped with the Parmesan.

THOMAS KELLER, THE FRENCH LAUNDRY RESTAURANT:
When I lived in Italy, a charming Italian woman taught me to make fresh pasta dough. One of the best tips she gave me was a test for knowing when the dough has been kneaded enough (if you over knead it, it will be tough): when the pasta feels like your earlobe, it's ready!

Rigatoni with Bread Crumbs and Arugula

SERVES 4

Bread crumbs add a nice balance to the peppery bite of arugula.
For young eaters in your house, put aside some tomato sauce just before adding
the arugula, toss with the rigatoni, and sprinkle with extra bread crumbs.

WINE SUGGESTION BY KRIS HARRIMAN: KENT RASMUSSEN DOLCETTO

1. In a large skillet over medium heat, heat 1 tablespoon oil and sauté the bread crumbs and the oregano until the crumbs are golden, about 8 minutes. Transfer the mixture to a bowl. In a large pot of salted boiling water, cook the pasta until al dente. Meanwhile, add the remaining 4 tablespoons oil to the skillet and sauté the garlic for 2 minutes. Add the pepper flakes and sauté another 2 minutes. Add the tomatoes and salt, and sauté for 2 minutes. Add the arugula and sauté until wilted. Season with pepper. Set aside and keep warm.

2. Drain the pasta and transfer to a serving bowl. Toss with the sauce and serve immediately, with the seasoned bread crumbs sprinkled on top of each serving.

REED HEARON, ROSE PISTOLA RESTAURANT: *When cooking dried pasta, be sure to cook it al dente. Almost everyone overcooks dried pasta.*

5 tablespoons olive oil

½ cup fresh bread crumbs

2 tablespoons minced fresh
   oregano, or 2 teaspoons dried
   oregano

1 pound rigatoni

4 garlic cloves, minced

¼ teaspoon red pepper flakes

4 ripe tomatoes, peeled, seeded,
   and chopped (see page 40)

1 teaspoon kosher salt

1 bunch arugula, stemmed

Freshly ground pepper to taste

Penne with Chicken and Spring Vegetables

SERVES 4 TO 6

This will take the place of the old standby "spaghetti and meatballs" in your house. Lots of fresh vegetables make this a healthy choice for the whole family. You can use boneless, skinless chicken breasts to quicken the process. If doing so, sear for 2 minutes per side and shorten the cooking time by 10 minutes.

WINE SUGGESTIONS BY DEBBIE ZACHAREAS: ROSENBLUM ZINFANDEL
OR DELORIMIER SPECTRUM WHITE MERITAGE

1 tablespoon olive oil

Kosher salt and freshly ground
pepper to taste

2 whole chicken breasts, halved

¼ cup Chardonnay or other dry
white wine

2 cups Chicken Stock (page 61) or
canned low-salt chicken broth

4 vine-ripened tomatoes, chopped,
or one 14-ounce can whole
tomatoes, drained and chopped

2 tablespoons minced fresh thyme,
or 2 teaspoons dried thyme

1 pound dried penne pasta

3 leeks, white part only, washed
and cut into diagonal slices

4 carrots, peeled and cut into
diagonal slices

1 pound asparagus, trimmed and
cut into 2-inch diagonal slices

1 cup fresh or frozen peas

1. In a large skillet over medium-high heat, heat the oil. Salt and pepper the chicken breasts. Sear the chicken for 5 minutes on each side, or until golden brown. Pour in the wine and cook for 1 minute, stirring to scrape up the browned bits from the bottom of the pan. Add the stock or broth and simmer for 1 minute. Stir in the tomatoes and half of the thyme. Cover and simmer for 15 minutes. Remove the chicken from the sauce and let cool to the touch. Pull the meat from the bones and shred into bite-sized pieces. Set aside.

2. In a large pot of salted boiling water, cook the pasta until al dente, about 10 minutes.

3. Meanwhile, add the leeks to the sauce and cook for 5 minutes. Stir in the carrots and remaining thyme and cook another 5 minutes. Add the asparagus and peas and continue cooking until the asparagus is crisp-tender, about 3 minutes. Stir in the chicken and heat through. Season with salt and pepper to taste. Drain the pasta and toss with the sauce. Serve immediately.

Butternut Squash au Gratin

SERVES 6

This satisfying vegetarian dish is a great way to enjoy squash.
The sweetness of the winter squash is enhanced by the tangy Gruyère cheese.

WINE SUGGESTION BY DAVID PAULEY: CHALONE CENTRAL COAST CHARDONNAY

1. In a large skillet over medium-high heat, heat the olive oil and sauté the chopped onion and garlic until lightly browned, about 8 minutes. Add the thyme, bay leaf, and salt. Add the wine and simmer until reduced by half, about 5 minutes. Add the cayenne, pepper, and tomatoes. Reduce heat to low and simmer for 15 minutes.

2. Meanwhile, preheat the oven to 450°F. Brush a large baking sheet with oil, add the squash, and roast until lightly browned on both sides and soft to the touch, about 8 minutes on each side. Reduce heat to 375°F. Spread one-third of the tomato sauce over the bottom of a 9-by-13-inch baking pan. Layer one-third of the squash slices over tomato sauce and sprinkle one-third of the cheese. Repeat, ending with a layer of cheese. Bake for 20 minutes, or until the tomato sauce is bubbling and the cheese is melted.

2 tablespoons olive oil, plus oil for brushing

1 onion, finely chopped

3 garlic cloves, minced

2 teaspoons minced fresh thyme, or ¾ teaspoon dried thyme

1 bay leaf

1 teaspoon salt

¾ cup Chardonnay or other dry white wine

¼ teaspoon cayenne pepper

Freshly ground pepper to taste

6 vine-ripened tomatoes (about 2 pounds), seeded and finely chopped

1 butternut squash, about 4 pounds, peeled, seeded, and cut into ¼-inch slices

2 cups (8 ounces) shredded Gruyère cheese

Curried Vegetable Stew

SERVES 4 TO 6

The long list of ingredients should not in any way deter you from making
this hearty vegetarian stew. Pungent spices give the stew a fragrant finish.
Many stores, including Whole Foods in the Bay Area, sell spices in bulk so you can
buy just the amount needed for the recipe. Serve over steamed jasmine rice.

WINE SUGGESTION BY DEBBIE ZACHAREAS: CHALONE CHENIN BLANC

6 tablespoons butter

1 large onion, cut into ¼-inch-
thick slices

3 large garlic cloves, minced

1 tablespoon grated fresh ginger

2 teaspoons ground coriander

2 teaspoons ground cumin

1 teaspoon mustard seeds

1 teaspoon ground cardamom

¼ teaspoon cayenne pepper

1 teaspoon ground turmeric

3 cups unsweetened coconut milk

10 baby carrots, halved
length-wise, or 4 carrots,
peeled and sliced

Juice of ½ lemon

1 large parsnip, peeled, quartered,
and halved

1. In a large Dutch oven, melt the butter over medium-high heat and sauté the onion, garlic, and ginger until the onion is lightly browned, about 8 minutes. Lower the heat and add all the spices. Cook for several minutes, then add the coconut milk, carrots, and lemon juice. Cover and simmer for 10 minutes. Add the parsnip, mushrooms, and potatoes and cook for 10 minutes. Add the cauliflower, broccoli, and snap peas and cook for 5 to 6 minutes or until the cauliflower is almost tender. Add the spinach and cook until wilted, about 2 minutes. Add the salt and pepper. Serve over jasmine rice, garnished with the cilantro and nuts.

GERALD HIRIGOYEN, FRINGALE RESTAURANT AND PASTIS RESTAURANT: *A simple but useful tip for cooking in general is to prepare a mise-en-place, that is, to assemble all the ingredients that you'll need to prepare a particular dish. Place them all right at hand beside your sink or a bowl of warm water. This enables you to rinse each utensil as you go. Always keep a dish towel handy as well. It is a good habit to constantly clean up after yourself, as it is much easier and more pleasant to cook in a clean and neat environment.*

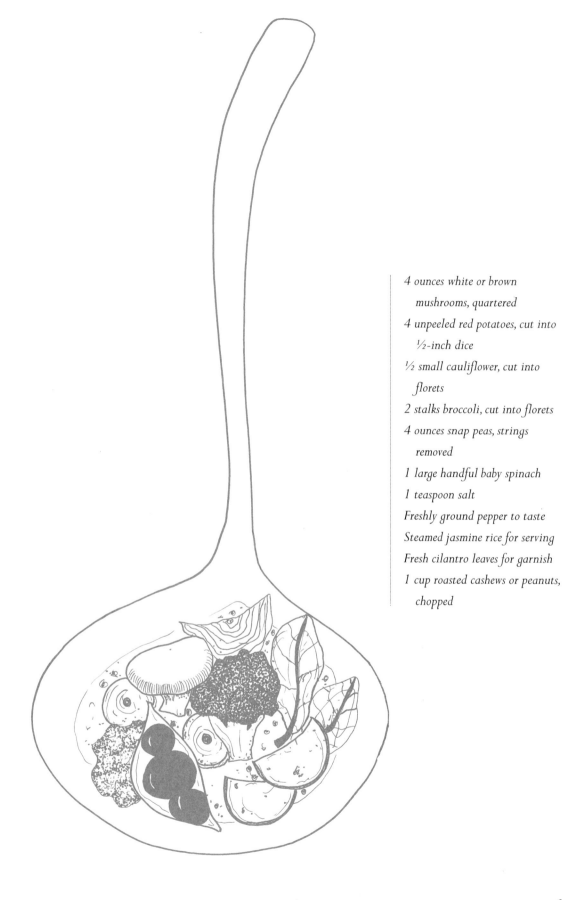

4 ounces white or brown
    mushrooms, quartered
4 unpeeled red potatoes, cut into
    ½-inch dice
½ small cauliflower, cut into
    florets
2 stalks broccoli, cut into florets
4 ounces snap peas, strings
    removed
1 large handful baby spinach
1 teaspoon salt
Freshly ground pepper to taste
Steamed jasmine rice for serving
Fresh cilantro leaves for garnish
1 cup roasted cashews or peanuts,
    chopped

Vegetable Enchiladas with Tomatillo Sauce

SERVES 6

Cooked black beans are available at local markets in San Francisco's Mission District and in many other cities, or use drained and rinsed canned beans.

WINE SUGGESTION BY DEBBIE ZACHAREAS: HUSCH CHENIN BLANC

FILLING:

2 tablespoons olive oil

1 red onion, diced

¼ teaspoon salt

¼ teaspoon cayenne pepper or
   to taste

4 large garlic cloves, minced

½ yellow, red, or green bell
   pepper, seeded, deveined, and
   chopped

1 zucchini, diced

1 teaspoon ground cumin

6 cremini or white mushrooms,
   sliced

2 cups fresh corn kernels (about
   4 ears)

2 cups cooked black beans

2 tablespoons chopped fresh
   cilantro

2 tablespoons corn or vegetable oil

12 corn tortillas

Tomatillo Sauce (recipe follows)

½ cup sour cream

¾ cup (3 ounces) shredded
   Monterey jack cheese

2 tablespoons chopped fresh
   cilantro

1. TO MAKE THE FILLING: In a large skillet over medium-high heat, heat the oil and sauté the red onion, salt, and cayenne for 8 minutes, or until the onion is wilted. Add the garlic, bell pepper, zucchini, and cumin. Cook for 5 to 7 minutes. Add the mushrooms, corn, and beans. Cook for another 5 minutes, or until the mushrooms are soft and corn is crisp-tender. Remove from heat. Stir in the cilantro and set aside.

2. In a medium, heavy skillet over medium-high heat, heat the oil to just below the smoking point. Using tongs, fry a tortilla in the hot oil for about 3 seconds on each side. Transfer to paper towels to drain. Repeat to cook the remaining tortillas, layering a paper towel between each tortilla.

3. Preheat the oven to 400°F. Ladle 2 cups Tomatillo Sauce into a 9-by-13-inch baking dish. Lay 1 tortilla out on a clean surface. Spread 1 tablespoon sour cream down the center of the tortilla. Spoon 3 to 4 tablespoons of the filling over the sour cream and sprinkle 2 tablespoons cheese on top. Roll the tortilla and place seam-side down in the baking dish. Repeat with all the remaining tortillas. Ladle the remaining sauce on top and sprinkle with the remaining cheese. Cover with aluminum foil and bake for 20 to 25 minutes, or until the sauce is bubbling. Remove the foil and bake another 5 to 7 minutes, or until the cheese is browned. Sprinkle with the cilantro and serve.

tomatillo sauce

1. In a large saucepan, combine the water, onion, salt, and cayenne. Bring to a boil, reduce heat to a simmer, cover, and cook for 5 minutes, or until the onion is soft. Add the bell pepper, tomatillos, and chilies. Cover and simmer until the tomatillos are soft and have released their juices, about 10 to 15 minutes. In a blender or food processor, puree the mixture, in batches if necessary. Taste and adjust the seasoning. Add a little sugar if the sauce is too acidic.

1 cup water

1 large red onion, thinly sliced

1 teaspoon salt

½ teaspoon cayenne pepper or to taste

1 large green bell pepper, seeded, deveined and coarsely chopped

2 pounds tomatillos, husked, or canned tomatillos

2 serrano chilies, seeded and chopped

Pinch of sugar (optional)

Sweet Potato and Polenta Pie
with Sautéed Bitter Greens and Vegetables

SERVES 4

Creamy polenta combined with mashed sweet potato is accented by sage and
pecorino cheese and cut into wedges. Robust bitter greens tempered with
sautéed vegetables are then spooned over the polenta wedges. (See photograph, page 173.)

WINE SUGGESTION BY DAVID PAULEY: CHALONE CENTRAL COAST CHARDONNAY

1 small sweet potato, peeled and
chopped

2 cups cooked Polenta (page 209)

2 tablespoons butter at room
temperature

1 tablespoon minced fresh sage

2 tablespoons grated pecorino
cheese

1 tablespoon olive oil

3 carrots, peeled and diced

1 small red onion, thinly sliced

1 small red bell pepper, seeded,
deveined, and chopped

2 leeks, white parts only, washed
and chopped

6 cups mixed bitter greens such as
escarole, radicchio, mizuna, and
arugula

2 teaspoons balsamic vinegar

2 tablespoons Chardonnay or
other white wine

2 teaspoons fresh lemon juice

Pinch of red pepper flakes

Kosher salt and freshly ground
pepper to taste

Grated pecorino or Parmesan
cheese for garnish (optional)

1. Preheat the oven to 425°F. Line the center rack with a piece of aluminum foil, add the sweet potato, and bake for about 45 minutes, or until tender. Remove from the oven, let cool slightly, and peel. Place the flesh in a medium saucepan and mash. Stir in the hot polenta, butter, sage, and pecorino. Lightly oil a 9-inch glass pie plate. Add the polenta and spread it evenly in the plate. Refrigerate until completely cooled, at least 1 hour or up to 1 day.

2. Preheat the oven to 425°F. Cut the polenta into 8 wedges. Transfer to an oiled baking sheet and bake for 12 minutes, or until golden brown.

3. Cook the carrots in salted boiling water for 3 minutes, or until crisp-tender, drain and set aside. In a large skillet over medium-high heat, heat the olive oil and sauté the onion, red pepper, and leeks until the onions are golden, about 8 minutes. Stir in the carrots, then the bitter greens, vinegar, wine, lemon juice, and pepper flakes. Cook, stirring, until the greens are wilted, adding a little water if necessary to help steam the greens. Remove from heat and add the salt and pepper. To serve, place 2 polenta wedges each on the plate and spoon the greens over. Sprinkle with Parmesan cheese, if you like.

HALIBUT AND BOK CHOY IN TOMATO-LEMONGRASS BROTH, *page 119*

SEARED AHI TUNA SALAD WITH TOASTED PUMPKIN SEEDS, *page 120*

SEARED SEA SCALLOPS WITH LIME-GINGER SAUCE
AND CARAMELIZED ENDIVES, *page 122*

CHICKEN POT PIE WITH SAGE BISCUIT TOPPING, *page 134*

SWEET POTATO AND POLENTA PIE WITH SAUTÉED BITTER GREENS
AND VEGETABLES, *page 168*

ASPARAGUS IN LEMON-GINGER VINAIGRETTE, *page 180*

GRILLED LEEKS WITH HAZELNUT VINAIGRETTE, *page 190*

MOREL, ASPARAGUS, AND FRESH PEA RISOTTO, *opposite*

Morel, Asparagus, and Fresh Pea Risotto

Stopping by the farmers' market on the Embarcadero to pick up fresh produce for dinner is a pleasure on weekends in the city. Fresh peas are one of the great rewards. You will often see shoppers strolling with freshly split pea pods, eating the raw peas like peanuts. This lovely spring risotto can be served as either a first course or a vegetarian meal. (See photograph opposite.)

WINE SUGGESTION BY DEBBIE ZACHAREAS: HESS SELECT PINOT NOIR

1. Blanch the peas in salted boiling water for 2 minutes. Using a strainer, transfer to ice water for 5 minutes. Blanch the asparagus in salted boiling water for 3 minutes and transfer to ice water for 5 minutes. Drain the vegetables and set aside.

2. In a large skillet, melt the butter over medium-high heat. Add the mushrooms, salt, and pepper and sauté until lightly browned, about 10 minutes. Set aside. In a saucepan, bring the stock or broth to a boil, then reduce to a simmer.

3. In a large, heavy saucepan over medium-high heat, heat the olive oil and sauté the onion for 5 minutes, stirring constantly. Add the garlic and stir for 1 minute. Add the rice and stir to coat well. Pour in the wine and stir for 2 minutes. Stir in the reserved mushrooms. Add ½ cup hot broth and stir constantly until almost all the liquid is absorbed into the rice. Repeat, adding the remaining broth in ½-cup increments until the rice is al dente, 20 to 25 minutes. Stir in the peas, asparagus, parsley, and cheese. Taste and adjust the seasoning. Serve immediately.

1 pound fresh green peas, shelled, or 1 cup frozen peas

1 pound asparagus, trimmed and cut into 2-inch diagonal pieces

4 tablespoons butter

8 ounces morels or other wild mushrooms, sliced

2 teaspoons kosher salt

¼ teaspoon ground pepper

8 cups Chicken Stock (page 61) or canned low-salt chicken broth

2 tablespoons olive oil

1 onion, chopped

3 garlic cloves, minced

1 pound Arborio rice

½ cup Chardonnay or other dry white wine

¼ cup minced fresh flat-leaf parsley

½ cup (2 ounces) grated Parmesan cheese

SIDE DISHES

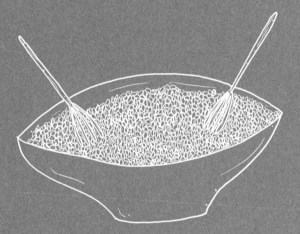

Asparagus in Lemon-Ginger Vinaigrette

Braised Brussels Sprouts

Brussels Sprouts with Walnut Oil and Meyer Lemon Zest

Broccoli Rabe Sautéed with Currants

Sautéed Red and Yellow Cherry Tomatoes

Zucchini and Tomato Gratin

Zucchini and Squash Sauté

Caramelized Carrots

Cauliflower with Capers and Olives

Curried Vegetable Ratatouille

Grilled Leeks with Hazelnut Vinaigrette

Sugar Snap Peas with Mint Oil

Sauté of Spring Vegetables

Fennel with Mushrooms and Prosciutto

Farmers' Market Sauté

Green Beans with Pesto and Balsamic Vinegar

Chinese Long Beans with Mushrooms and Garlic-Soy Sauce

Italian Spinach with Garbanzo Beans and Raisins

Orzo with Tomato and Fennel

Orzo with Sautéed Mushrooms and Pinot Grigio

Firecracker Noodles

Mashed Potatoes with Leeks and Fresh Thyme

Creamy Potatoes with Pinot Noir

Wild Mushroom Potato Lasagna

Potatoes au Gratin with Leeks and Oregano

Wild Mushroom Barley Risotto

Jasmine Rice with Fresh Peas

Rice Pilaf with Scallions and Mustard Seeds

Wild Rice Sauté

Polenta

Wild Mushroom and Rosemary Polenta

Asparagus in Lemon-Ginger Vinaigrette

SERVES 4

Serve this as a side dish with roast chicken or with an Asian meal.
To prepare ahead of time, refrigerate the vinaigrette and asparagus separately
and combine them just before serving. (See photograph, page 174.)

LEMON-GINGER
VINAIGRETTE:

½ cup fresh lemon juice (about
   3 lemons)

2 teaspoons grated fresh ginger

1 teaspoon soy sauce

1 tablespoon Asian sesame oil

½ teaspoon salt

¼ teaspoon ground white pepper

⅓ cup canola or safflower oil

2 pounds asparagus, trimmed

Lemon slices for garnish

1. TO MAKE THE VINAIGRETTE: In a small bowl, combine all the ingredients except the canola or safflower oil. Gradually whisk in the oil. Set aside.

2. Steam the asparagus over boiling water in a covered pot for 5 to 6 minutes, or until crisp-tender. Transfer the asparagus to a bowl of ice water to stop cooking. Remove after 5 minutes and drain.

3. Place the asparagus on a serving dish and drizzle with the vinaigrette. Garnish with lemon slices and serve.

Braised Brussels Sprouts

Braising softens the bitterness of Brussels sprouts and the wine and chicken stock adds a savory richness.

1. In a medium skillet over medium-high heat, heat olive oil and sauté the onion, garlic, and sprouts until the sprouts are lightly browned, about 4 minutes. Add the salt and pepper. Add the wine and stir. Add the stock or broth and cook until it has evaporated, about 3 minutes. Serve.

1 tablespoon extra-virgin olive oil

1 small onion, chopped

1 garlic clove, minced

1 pound Brussels sprouts, halved

Salt and freshly ground pepper
  to taste

¼ cup dry white wine

½ cup Chicken Stock (page 61)
  or canned low-salt broth

Brussels Sprouts with Walnut Oil and Meyer Lemon Zest

SERVES 6

Walnut oil and Meyer lemon zest add a depth of flavor to these crunchy little cabbages.

1 ½ pounds Brussels sprouts, trimmed

1 teaspoon salt

1 tablespoon butter

1 ½ tablespoons walnut oil

2 teaspoons grated lemon zest, preferably Meyer lemon

1 tablespoon snipped fresh chives

1. Cook the Brussels sprouts in salted boiling water for 8 to 10 minutes, or until easily pierced with a knife. Drain and put in a serving dish. Immediately add the remaining ingredients. Mix thoroughly and serve.

Broccoli Rabe Sautéed with Currants

SERVES 6

Broccoli rabe is a long-stemmed green vegetable with a mustardlike flavor, often served in Italian restaurants as a side dish. Red pepper flakes and sweet currants nicely balance the strong rabe flavor. Serve this with chicken or fish.

1. Cook the broccoli rabe in salted boiling water for 5 minutes, or until you can easily pierce stem with a knife. Transfer to a bowl of ice water and let cool. Drain and set aside.

2. In a large skillet over medium heat, heat 2 tablespoons of the oil and sauté the garlic for 2 minutes, or until golden. Do not let the garlic burn. Add the broccoli rabe, currants, salt, and pepper flakes and sauté for about 8 minutes. Drizzle the remaining 2 tablespoons oil over the mixture and toss again. Serve hot or at room temperature.

2 pounds broccoli rabe, chopped

4 tablespoons extra-virgin
   olive oil

3 garlic cloves, minced

⅓ cup currants

1 teaspoon kosher salt

½ teaspoon red pepper flakes

Sautéed Red and Yellow Cherry Tomatoes

SERVES 4

A fresh, quick, and colorful side dish to serve with grilled meat or chicken.

2 tablespoons butter

2 cups red cherry tomatoes

2 cups yellow cherry tomatoes

Salt and freshly ground pepper to
taste

2 tablespoons snipped fresh chives

1. In a large skillet over medium-high heat, melt the butter. Add the tomatoes, salt, and pepper and sauté for 4 to 5 minutes, or until the tomatoes almost burst. Add the chives and mix well. Serve at once.

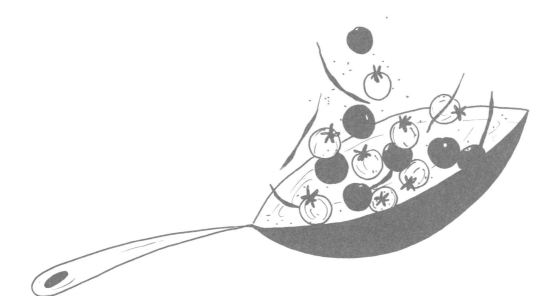

Zucchini and Tomato Gratin

SERVES 6

Vary this summery gratin by using green, gold, or striped tomatoes.
Serve as a delicious side dish with a grill dinner.

1. Preheat the oven to 400°F. In a 5- to 6-cup gratin dish, alternately layer the zucchini, squash, and tomatoes, spreading each layer with a little garlic, salt, and pepper. Sprinkle the cheese over the top and bake for 30 minutes, or until golden brown. Serve.

4 zucchini, cut into ¼-inch-thick slices

4 yellow crookneck squash, cut into ¼-inch thick slices

6 tomatoes, sliced

4 garlic cloves, sliced

Salt and freshly ground pepper to taste

⅓ cup grated pecorino or Parmesan cheese

Zucchini and Squash Sauté

Toasted pine nuts give a nice crunch to this simple side dish. Serve with any roasted meats or fish.

2 tablespoons extra-virgin olive
  oil

2 zucchini, sliced

1 summer squash, sliced

1 yellow crookneck squash, sliced

2 shallots, minced

3 tablespoons balsamic vinegar

2 garlic cloves, minced

2 tablespoons minced fresh
  flat-leaf parsley

Salt and freshly ground pepper to
  taste

¼ cup pine nuts, toasted
  (see page 18)

1. In a large skillet over medium high heat, heat the oil and sauté the zucchini and squashes for 3 minutes. Add all the remaining ingredients except the nuts, reduce heat to medium, and cook until crisp-tender, 5 to 8 minutes. Add the nuts and serve.

Caramelized Carrots

SERVES 6

Red grapes pair their sweetness with these carrots, and walnuts add their crunch and nutty taste to the savory-sweet sauce. If time is short, try using packaged baby carrots for this dish.

1. In a medium skillet, melt the butter over medium-high heat. Add the carrots, stock, and brown sugar and bring to a boil. Reduce heat to medium-low and simmer until the carrots are soft, about 8 minutes. Add the grapes and walnuts and cook until just heated through, about 2 minutes. Serve.

4 tablespoons butter

1½ pounds carrots, peeled and sliced

1 cup Chicken Stock (page 61) or canned low-salt chicken broth

3 tablespoons packed brown sugar

1 cup red or green seedless grapes, halved

½ cup chopped walnuts, toasted (see page 18)

Cauliflower with Capers and Olives

SERVES 4

Capers and olives add a sweet-and-sour Mediterranean flair
to an otherwise bland vegetable. This dish is even better the next day
and can be taken on a picnic and served at room temperature.

4 teaspoons extra-virgin olive oil

1 head cauliflower, cut into florets

4 garlic cloves, crushed

1 teaspoon anchovy paste

1 cup kalamata olives, pitted

¼ teaspoon red pepper flakes

¼ cup capers, drained

¼ cup chopped fresh flat-leaf
   parsley

Freshly ground pepper to taste

½ cup Chicken Stock (page 61)
   or canned low-salt chicken
   broth

2 tomatoes, chopped

1 tablespoon sugar

1 tablespoon balsamic vinegar

1. In a large skillet over medium-high heat, heat 2 teaspoons of the olive oil and sauté the cauliflower for 3 minutes, or until lightly browned. Transfer the cauliflower to a dish and set aside.

2. In the same skillet over medium-high heat, heat the remaining 2 teaspoons of olive oil and sauté the garlic, anchovy paste, olives, pepper flakes, capers, parsley, and pepper, stirring frequently for 3 to 5 minutes, or until the garlic is soft. Add the cauliflower and mix. Add the stock or broth and tomatoes and cook, stirring frequently until the cauliflower is crisp-tender, 3 to 4 minutes. Remove from heat.

3. In a small saucepan, combine the sugar and balsamic vinegar and bring to a boil. Cook for 30 seconds and add to the cauliflower. Mix well and serve.

Curried Vegetable Ratatouille

SERVES 6

This version of ratatouille brings the Provençal classic to life with the addition
of curry, chilies, and potatoes. Do not allow the vegetables to become too soft
and mushy. Make this dish the day before to allow the flavors to mingle.
Store, covered, in the refrigerator and serve reheated or at room temperature.

1. In a large skillet over medium-high heat, heat the olive oil, add the curry and cumin seeds, and stir for 3 to 4 minutes. Add the eggplant, chilies, potatoes, onions, tomatoes, salt, chili powder, and turmeric and mix thoroughly. Cover and reduce heat to medium low. Cook for 45 minutes, or until the vegetables are soft. Add the cilantro, cover, and cook for another 2 minutes. Serve warm or at room temperature.

3 tablespoons extra-virgin olive oil

1 tablespoon curry powder

½ teaspoon cumin seeds

1 eggplant, cut into ½-inch crosswise rounds, then cut into 8 wedges

3 jalapeño chilies, minced

4 Yukon Gold potatoes, cut into ½-inch dice

1 yellow onion, coarsely chopped

3 yellow or red tomatoes, cut into ½-inch dice

1 teaspoon salt

½ teaspoon chili powder

½ teaspoon ground turmeric

¼ cup coarsely chopped fresh cilantro

Grilled Leeks with Hazelnut Vinaigrette

SERVES 4

A wonderful springtime dish to prepare when leeks are small and tender.
Serve this alongside chicken or fish or as a first course. (See photograph, page 175.)

½ cup hazelnuts or walnuts,
   toasted, skinned, and coarsely
   chopped

16 baby leeks, including light
   green parts

¼ cup hazelnut oil or walnut oil

2 tablespoons extra-virgin olive
   oil

2½ tablespoons heavy cream

2 tablespoons balsamic or red
   wine vinegar

1 teaspoon salt

1 teaspoon ground pepper

2 tablespoons minced flat-leaf
   parsley

1. TO TOAST AND SKIN NUTS: Preheat the oven to 350°F. Toast the nuts on a baking sheet for 8 to 10 minutes, tossing several times, until they are lightly browned. Remove the nuts to a rough kitchen towel or several layers of paper towels and rub to remove the skins, if necessary.

2. Cut about halfway through down the center of each leek. Wash the leeks under running water. In a large pot of salted boiling water, cook the leeks for 2 to 3 minutes, or until the white part is tender when gently pierced with a knife. Transfer to a bowl of ice water. Drain well and gently dry with paper towels.

3. In a small bowl, combine the oils, cream, vinegar, salt, and pepper. Whisk until fully incorporated. Add the nuts and taste for seasoning.

4. Light a fire in a charcoal grill or preheat a gas grill or a broiler. Grill or broil the leeks for about 5 minutes on each side, or until golden brown. Transfer to a serving platter. Pour the vinaigrette over the leeks and sprinkle with the parsley. Serve warm or at room temperature.

Sugar Snap Peas with Mint Oil

SERVES 6

Bright green sugar snap peas coated with mint oil are a sweet and refreshing accompaniment to a spring or summer meal. Store the leftover mint oil in an airtight container in the refrigerator for up to 1 week and use in vinaigrette.

1. In a medium saucepan, bring the water to a boil. Add the mint leaves and cook for 30 seconds, or until limp and bright green. Using a slotted spoon, transfer to a bowl of cold water for 3 minutes; reserve the saucepan of hot water. Drain and transfer the mint to paper towels; pat them dry.

2. In a blender or food processor, puree the mint. With the machine running, gradually add the oil and puree until smooth. Add the salt and pepper.

3. Bring the reserved pan of water to a boil and cook the sugar snap peas until crisp-tender and bright green, about 3 minutes. Drain well, transfer to a bowl, and toss with 1 tablespoon of the mint oil. Serve.

3 cups water

¼ cup packed fresh mint leaves

¼ cup extra-virgin olive oil

Salt and freshly ground pepper to taste

12 ounces sugar snap peas, trimmed and strings removed

Sauté of Spring Vegetables

SERVES 4

This uncomplicated dish is full of color and flavor, and takes minutes to prepare.
Experiment with various types of herbs, like lemon thyme and opal basil.
If baby vegetables are not in season, use diagonally sliced mature vegetables.

2 tablespoons butter or olive oil

1 shallot, minced

12 baby carrots

8 ounces baby zucchini, or 2
zucchini, sliced

8 ounces baby yellow crookneck,
or 2 yellow crookneck squash,
sliced

8 ounces sugar snap peas

1 tablespoon minced fresh thyme,
basil, or oregano

Salt and freshly ground pepper to
taste

1. In a saucepan or skillet over medium-high heat, melt the butter or heat the oil. Add the shallot and carrots and sauté for 3 minutes. Add the zucchini, squash, peas, and herb and sauté for about 5 minutes, or until crisp-tender. Season with salt and pepper and serve.

Fennel with Mushrooms and Prosciutto

SERVES 6

The slight licorice flavor of fennel complements earthy mushrooms and salty prosciutto. Parma prosciutto, imported from Italy, is considered the best; however, there are excellent domestic brands available as well. Ask for a sample of each and compare.

1. Trim the fennel stalks and reserve the feathery greens. Mince the greens to make ¼ cup. Arrange the fennel bulbs in a single layer in a large saucepan. Pour the stock or broth and wine over the bulbs, cover, and bring to a boil. Reduce heat to medium-low and simmer until the fennel is very tender, about 35 minutes. Set aside to cool.

2. While the fennel is simmering, combine the mushrooms, prosciutto, 2 tablespoons of the minced fennel greens, the thyme, salt, and pepper in a medium skillet. Cover and cook over medium-high heat for 7 minutes. Uncover and cook, stirring frequently, until the liquid evaporates and the mushrooms are browned, about 10 minutes. Set aside.

3. Preheat the oven to 400°F. With a small knife and spoon, scoop out the inner part of each fennel bulb to leave a ¼-inch-thick shell. Spoon the mushroom mixture equally into the fennel bulbs and place them in a baking dish. Sprinkle the cheese on top of the fennel. (The recipe can be made several hours ahead to this point.) Bake for 15 minutes, or until cheese is lightly browned. Serve warm garnished with the remaining fennel greens.

6 fennel bulbs, each 3 inches wide at base

1½ cups Chicken Stock (page 61) or canned low-salt chicken broth

¾ cup dry white wine

1 pound cremini or other white mushrooms, sliced

2 ounces thinly sliced prosciutto, minced

1 tablespoon minced fresh thyme, or 1 teaspoon dried thyme

1 teaspoon salt

1 teaspoon ground pepper

½ cup (2 ounces) grated Parmesan cheese

Farmers' Market Sauté

SERVES 4

The height of summer is the best time to make this dish. As the title suggests,
let the freshest vegetables at the farmers' market govern your choice of ingredients.

2 tablespoons olive oil

1 shallot, minced

1 cup fresh corn kernels (about 2
ears)

2 pounds green peas, shelled, or 2
cups thawed frozen peas

6 asparagus stalks, trimmed and
cut into 1-inch diagonal pieces

12 baby carrots, green ends
trimmed and scrubbed, or
2 carrots, peeled and sliced on
the diagonal

2 tablespoons minced fresh
oregano

2 garlic cloves, minced

Salt and freshly ground pepper to
taste

1 tablespoon fresh lemon juice

1. In a large skillet over medium-high heat, heat the oil and sauté the shallot for 2 minutes. Add the corn, peas, asparagus, and carrots and sauté for 4 minutes, or until the carrots can easily be pierced with a knife. Add the oregano, garlic, salt, and pepper, and sauté for 1 minute. Add the lemon juice and serve.

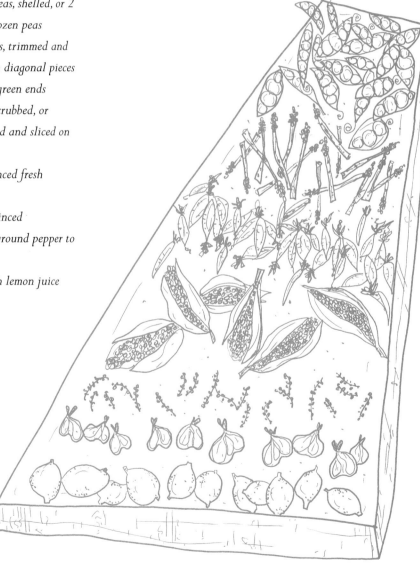

Green Beans with Pesto and Balsamic Vinegar

SERVES 6

Make this delicious summer side dish when green beans and basil come to market.
Unlike classic basil pesto, this recipe calls for balsamic vinegar and brown
sugar for a sweeter taste. Take this along on a picnic and serve at room temperature.

1. TO MAKE THE PESTO: In a blender or food processor, puree all ingredients until smooth.

2. Steam the beans over boiling water in a covered pot for 3 minutes, or until crisp-tender. Transfer the beans to a serving dish. Add the pesto and toss until the beans are well coated. Add the salt and pepper, garnish with basil leaves, and serve.

PESTO:

¼ cup extra-virgin olive oil

1 large garlic clove

1 large bunch fresh basil, stemmed

¾ cup (3 ounces) grated
   Parmesan cheese

1 tablespoon balsamic vinegar

½ teaspoon packed dark brown
   sugar

1½ pounds green beans, trimmed
   and cut into 1-inch pieces

Salt and freshly ground pepper to
   taste

Fresh basil leaves for garnish

Chinese Long Beans with Mushrooms and Garlic-Soy Sauce

SERVES 6

This dish is found in many restaurants in San Francisco's Chinatown. Chinese long beans, which grow up to 18 inches long, make a flavorful side dish for Asian chicken or seafood dishes. You can also use regular green beans.

GARLIC-SOY SAUCE:

¼ cup soy sauce

2 garlic cloves, minced

1 teaspoon orange honey

3 teaspoons grated fresh ginger

Freshly ground pepper to taste

2 tablespoons extra-virgin olive oil

1½ pounds Chinese long beans or regular green beans, trimmed

6 ounces cremini or white mushrooms

1. TO MAKE THE SAUCE: In a small bowl, whisk all the ingredients together.

2. In a wok or a large skillet over medium-high, heat the oil and stir-fry the beans and mushrooms until the beans are crisp-tender, about 5 minutes. Pour the sauce over the beans, increase heat to high, and cook until the sauce slightly thickens and coats the vegetables, 2 to 3 minutes. Transfer to a bowl and serve.

Italian Spinach with Garbanzo Beans and Raisins

SERVES 4

Sautéed spinach with garbanzo beans, a typical side dish in Italy,
is easy to prepare and full of flavor and nutrition. This rendition
adds golden raisins and toasted pine nuts for a bit of sweetness and crunch.

1. In a large, heavy saucepan or skillet, heat the oil and sauté the garlic until golden, about 3 minutes. Add the pepper flakes and cook for 30 seconds. Stir in the garbanzo beans and cook until heated through, about 3 minutes. Increase heat to high and add the spinach, raisins, and salt. Cook, stirring constantly, for 2 to 3 minutes, or just until the spinach wilts. Add the pine nuts and serve.

1 tablespoon extra-virgin olive oil

2 garlic cloves, crushed

Pinch of red pepper flakes

2 cups canned garbanzo beans,
*   drained*

8 cups baby spinach leaves

¼ cup golden raisins

½ teaspoon salt

¼ cup pine nuts, toasted
*   (see page 18)*

Orzo with Tomato and Fennel

SERVES 4

This side dish is a great alternative to steamed rice and goes well with
roasted chicken or grilled fish. Both fennel and fresh tarragon have a mild licorice
characteristic that mixes with the tomatoes for a flavorful orzo dish.

1 cup orzo pasta

1 tablespoon butter

1 tablespoon olive oil

1 small fennel bulb, trimmed and
　finely chopped

1 small onion, finely chopped

6 Roma or plum tomatoes,
　chopped

2 teaspoons minced fresh tarragon

Salt and freshly ground pepper to
　taste

1. In a large saucepan of salted boiling water, cook the orzo until al dente, 5 to 8 minutes. Drain. Meanwhile, in a heavy skillet, melt the butter with the oil over medium-high heat and sauté the fennel and onion for 4 to 5 minutes, or until the onion is translucent. Add the tomatoes, tarragon, salt, and pepper and cook until the fennel is tender, 7 to 10 minutes.

2. Add the orzo to the skillet and quickly mix to thoroughly incorporate. Taste for seasoning and serve.

Orzo with Sautéed Mushrooms and Pinot Grigio

SERVES 6

Orzo, a rice-shaped pasta, is the base for a good vegetarian entrée.
Pinot Grigio's dry, crisp taste complements the mushrooms.

1. In a medium skillet, melt the butter over medium-high heat until it foams. Add the mushrooms, salt, and pepper and sauté for 4 minutes. Add the wine and cook until most of the liquid has evaporated. Set aside.
2. In a large saucepan of boiling water, cook the orzo until al dente, 5 to 8 minutes. Drain. Put the orzo in a large bowl and add the mushroom mixture, parsley, and oil. Add the cheese, toss, and serve.

3 tablespoons butter

1 pound cremini or white mushrooms, cut into ⅛-inch slices

Salt and freshly ground pepper to taste

¾ cup Pinot Grigio or other dry white wine

1 pound orzo pasta

¼ cup minced fresh flat-leaf parsley

2 tablespoons extra-virgin olive oil

½ cup (2 ounces) grated Parmesan cheese

Firecracker Noodles

A spicy Asian-style pasta to serve alongside roasted meat, such as
Asian Flank Steak (page 149). A touch of chili oil sets the fiery
tempo for this dish. Use less or more according to your tolerance level.

1 pound thin dried Chinese egg
   noodles

4 tablespoons peanut oil

1 tablespoon red wine vinegar

⅓ cup soy sauce

3 tablespoons honey

1 tablespoon chili oil

1 teaspoon red pepper flakes

Freshly ground pepper to taste

1 shallot, minced

5 to 6 shiitake mushrooms,
   stemmed and sliced

6 scallions, cut in ¼-inch
   diagonal slices including green
   portions

1. In a large pot of salted boiling water, cook the noodles until tender, about 7 minutes. Drain. In a medium bowl, whisk the peanut oil, vinegar, soy sauce, honey, chili oil, pepper flakes, and pepper together. Pour a third of mixture into a wok or medium skillet. Heat over medium heat and stir-fry the shallots for 2 to 3 minutes, or until softened. Add the mushrooms and stir-fry for 1 to 2 minutes. Add one third of the scallions to the pan and stir-fry for an additional 1 to 2 minutes. Add the noodles and remaining sauce mixture. Stir-fry for 1 to 2 more minutes. Serve topped with the remaining scallions.

Mashed Potatoes with Leeks and Fresh Thyme

SERVES 6

Add extra flavor to everybody's favorite, mashed potatoes, with sautéed leeks
and fresh thyme. You can change the nuance of these potatoes by
substituting other fresh herbs such as rosemary, oregano, sage, or dill.

1. In a large pot of salted boiling water, cook the potatoes until tender, about 20 minutes. Meanwhile, in a heavy skillet, melt 6 tablespoons of the butter over medium-low heat. Add the leeks and cook, stirring occasionally, until softened and slightly browned, 15 to 20 minutes. Stir in the thyme.

2. Drain the potatoes in a colander. Force the potatoes through a ricer back into the pot and add the remaining 6 tablespoons butter, milk, and cream. Or, return them to the pot and mash with an electric mixer or potato masher. Stir to blend. Add the leek mixture and stir until blended. Add salt and pepper and serve warm.

*3 pounds russet potatoes (about
6), peeled and cut into chunks*

12 tablespoons butter

*6 leeks, including pale green
portions, washed and chopped*

1 tablespoon minced fresh thyme

1 cup milk

½ cup heavy cream

*Salt and freshly ground pepper to
taste*

Creamy Potatoes with Pinot Noir

SERVES 6

Pinot Noir is a fragrant, supple red wine that is increasingly available from
Northern California and Oregon wineries. Its fruity taste combines with garlic, potatoes,
and cream for a satisfying creamy side dish that goes wonderfully with a juicy cut of beef.

*2 pounds red potatoes, scrubbed
and coarsely chopped*

*1 head garlic, cloves separated
and peeled*

*2 cups Pinot Noir or other dry red
wine*

*Salt and freshly ground pepper to
taste*

¾ cup half-and-half

*Minced fresh flat-leaf parsley for
garnish*

1. Preheat the oven to 375°F. In a large gratin dish or glass baking dish, combine the potatoes and garlic cloves. Add the wine, salt, and pepper. Cover with aluminum foil and bake for 90 minutes. Add the half-and-half and stir. Uncover and continue to bake for another 20 to 30 minutes. Garnish with chopped parsley and serve.

Wild Mushroom Potato Lasagna

SERVES 6

A wildly flavorful lasagna made with potato layers filled with a variety of mushrooms.
Look for golden and black chanterelles when they come to the market in the fall;
both will lend wonderful flavor and color to this dish. Use your food processor
to slice the potatoes—the thinner the better. This also makes a great first course.

WINE SUGGESTION BY KRIS HARRIMAN: ROBERT PEPI SANGIOVESE

1. Preheat the oven to 375°F. Slice or break the mushrooms into ⅛-inch-thick pieces. In a large saucepan, melt the butter over medium-high heat. Add the mushrooms and cook until lightly browned, about 5 minutes. Stir in the thyme and garlic and cook for 2 minutes. Season with salt and pepper.

2. Lightly butter a gratin dish or square Pyrex dish. Add a layer of half the potatoes and season with salt and pepper to taste. Spread the mushrooms over the potatoes. Layer the remaining potatoes on top. Season with salt and pepper to taste.

3. In a small bowl, mix the stock or chicken broth and cream together. Pour over the potatoes and bake for 40 to 45 minutes, or until the liquid is absorbed and the potatoes have a golden crust. Cut into wedges or squares and serve warm.

1 pound wild mushrooms, such as chanterelles, oysters, stemmed shiitakes, or cremini

3 tablespoons butter

1 tablespoon minced fresh thyme

2 garlic cloves, minced

Salt and freshly ground pepper to taste

4 russet potatoes, peeled and cut into ⅛-inch slices

½ cup Chicken Stock (page 61) or canned low-salt chicken broth

1 cup heavy cream

Potatoes au Gratin with Leeks and Oregano

A classic dish updated with the addition of sautéed leeks and fresh oregano.
Use the best Gruyère cheese you can find. For quick and uniform slicing,
use a food processor or mandoline for the potatoes. Partially cooking the potatoes
before baking them assures that the final dish will be perfectly seasoned.

1 tablespoon butter

3 leeks, white part only, washed
  and sliced

Salt and freshly ground pepper

2½ cups half-and-half

1 tablespoon minced fresh
  oregano or thyme

1½ cups (6 ounces) shredded
  Gruyère cheese

4 garlic cloves, minced

2 pounds russet potatoes, peeled
  and thinly sliced crosswise

1. Preheat the oven to 350°F. Butter a 5- to 6-cup gratin dish.

2. In a large skillet, melt the butter over medium-high heat. Add the leeks, salt, and pepper and cook, stirring frequently, for 10 minutes, or until golden brown. Set aside.

3. In a large saucepan, combine the half-and-half, oregano, 1 cup of the Gruyère, the garlic, and salt and pepper to taste. Heat over medium heat until bubbles begin to form around the sides. Do not boil. Add the potato slices to the pan and gently mix. Cook for 3 minutes. Taste for seasoning.

4. Add half the potatoes to the prepared gratin dish. Add the cooked leeks and cover with the remaining potatoes. Sprinkle the remaining cheese over the potatoes. Bake until golden brown, about 30 minutes. Serve warm.

Wild Mushroom Barley Risotto

SERVES 6 AS A SIDE DISH, 4 AS AN ENTRÉE

Barley is a wonderful and nutritious alternative to the Arborio rice usually used to make risotto. A rich side dish for meat and fish, this also makes an excellent vegetarian entrée.

1. In a large saucepan over medium-high heat, heat the oil and sauté the onion until translucent, about 5 minutes. Add half the garlic and sauté for 2 minutes. Add the barley, stirring to coat the grains. Pour in the wine and cook, stirring, for 2 minutes. Add the thyme, stock or broth, salt, and pepper. Reduce heat to medium and cook, stirring occasionally, for 50 minutes, or until most of the liquid is absorbed.

2. Meanwhile, in a large skillet, melt the butter over medium-high heat and sauté the mushrooms for 5 minutes, or until lightly browned. Stir in the remaining garlic and cook for 2 minutes. Add the mushrooms, cheese, and parsley to the cooked barley and stir. Taste for seasoning and serve at once.

2 teaspoons olive oil

1 medium onion, finely chopped

4 garlic cloves, minced

1 cup pearl barley

¼ cup Chardonnay or other dry white wine

2 teaspoons minced fresh thyme leaves, or 1 teaspoon dried thyme

4½ cups Chicken Stock (page 61) or canned low-salt chicken broth, heated

Salt and freshly ground pepper to taste

1 tablespoon butter

1 pound assorted wild mushrooms, sliced

2 tablespoons minced fresh parsley

¼ cup grated Parmesan cheese

Jasmine Rice with Fresh Peas

SERVES 4

Jasmine is a long-grain rice with a delicate perfume typically used in Thai cooking.
Try serving this at room temperature as a salad, sprinkled with chopped peanuts.

1 cup jasmine rice

2 cups water

½ teaspoon ground turmeric

1 pound green peas, shelled, or
   1 cup thawed frozen peas

¼ cup minced fresh cilantro

5 tablespoons rice vinegar

2 teaspoons Asian sesame oil

¼ cup chopped peanuts (optional)

1. In a medium saucepan, combine the rice, water, and turmeric and bring to a boil over high heat. Reduce heat to low, cover, and cook for 15 minutes. Fluff the rice with fork and add the remaining ingredients. Stir, cover, and let sit for 5 minutes. Add the peanuts if desired and serve.

Rice Pilaf with Scallions and Mustard Seeds

SERVES 6

Although Rice-A-Roni is still advertised on cable cars as the
"San Francisco Treat," fortunately there are alternatives to the boxed
rice dish. Instead, try this fragrant pilaf for your next dinner party.

1. In a heavy, medium saucepan over medium-low heat, heat olive oil
and sauté the shallots until softened, about 5 minutes. Add the mustard
seeds and stir for 1 minute. Add the rice and cook for 1 minute. Add the
water and salt, bring to a boil, and reduce heat to low. Cover and cook
for 20 minutes, or until tender. Remove from heat and let stand for
5 minutes. Fluff the rice with a fork and mix in the scallion tops.
Serve immediately.

3 tablespoons extra-virgin olive oil

3 shallots, thinly sliced

4 teaspoons mustard seeds

1 ½ cups jasmine rice

3 cups water

3 teaspoons salt

½ cup thinly sliced scallion tops

Wild Rice Sauté

Wild rice is more closely related to wheat than rice. It has a nutty flavor that is complemented by sweet corn and balsamic vinegar. Serve alongside Roast Chicken with Saffron and Lemons (page 136) or Zinfandel Braised Duck Legs (page 138).

1½ cups water

¾ cup wild rice, rinsed

1 teaspoon extra-virgin olive oil

2 garlic cloves, minced

2 shallots, minced

1 tablespoon Chardonnay or other
    dry white wine

¼ cup Chicken Stock (page 61)
    or canned low-salt chicken
    broth

1 cup fresh corn kernels (about
    2 ears)

4 Roma or plum tomatoes,
    chopped

1 tablespoon balsamic vinegar

Salt and freshly ground pepper to
    taste

¼ cup chopped fresh basil

1. In a large saucepan, bring the water to a boil. Add the rice, reduce heat to a simmer, cover, and cook for 20 minutes, or until cooked. Drain and let cool.

2. In medium skillet over medium-high heat, heat the oil and sauté the garlic and shallots until softened, about 2 minutes. Add the wine and cook for 2 minutes. Add the stock or broth, corn and tomatoes, and cook for 2 minutes. Add the rice and cook for 4 minutes. Stir in the vinegar, salt, pepper, and basil. Serve.

Polenta

A foolproof method for cooking polenta, a great accompaniment for lamb, chicken, or sausages. For another side dish, spread the cooked polenta in a 9-by-13 baking dish, cover, and refrigerate overnight. Cut the chilled polenta into triangles and deep-fry, grill, or bake until lightly browned.

1. Add the water and salt to a large saucepan, and gradually whisk in the polenta. Cook over medium-low heat stirring frequently, until the polenta is thick and not granular, about 30 minutes. Taste for seasoning and serve.

VARIATION: Stir 1 cup (4 ounces) grated Parmesan cheese or 4 ounces crumbled Gorgonzola and 3 tablespoons of butter into the hot polenta.

8 cups cold water

1 teaspoon salt

2 cups polenta

Wild Mushroom and Rosemary Polenta

SERVES 6 AS FIRST COURSE, 4 AS AN ENTRÉE

Make this polenta in the fall when appetites are healthy and wild mushrooms are plentiful.
Serve as a first course, or with some crusty bread and a salad for a hearty dinner.

WINE SUGGESTION BY DAVID PAULEY: RAVENSWOOD ZINFANDEL

2 tablespoons butter

3 tablespoons olive oil

3 shallots, minced

1 pound assorted wild
   mushrooms, sliced

Salt and freshly ground pepper to
   taste

2 teaspoons minced fresh rosemary

¼ cup Chardonnay or other dry
   white wine

¼ cup Chicken Stock (page 61)
   or canned low-salt chicken
   broth

Polenta (page 209)

1. In a large skillet over medium high-heat, melt the butter with the olive oil and sauté the shallots for 2 minutes. Add the mushrooms, salt, pepper, and rosemary and cook until the mushrooms are lightly browned and most of the liquid has evaporated, about 10 minutes. Add the wine and cook for 2 minutes. Add stock or broth and cook for 2 minutes, or until all the liquid has evaporated. Add the mushroom mixture to the cooked polenta and stir well to combine. Serve at once.

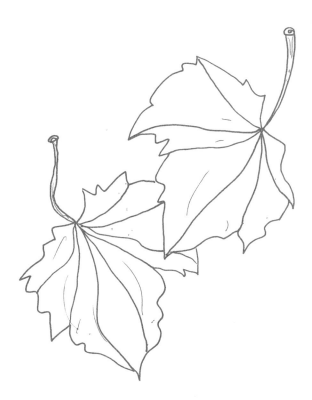

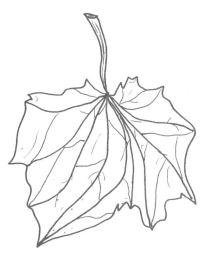

BRUNCHES

Orange-Raspberry Muffins

Raisin-Pecan Coffee Cake

Smoked Salmon and Dill Biscuits

Rosemary-Shallot Popovers

Corn Popovers

Asparagus and Gorgonzola Frittata

Scrambled Eggs with Goat Cheese and Cherry Tomatoes

Scrambled Eggs with Asparagus, Goat Cheese, and Prosciutto

Potato Omelette with Lemon-Garlic Mayonnaise

Soufflé Omelette with Canadian Bacon and Sharp Cheddar Cheese

Fuji Apple and Ricotta Pancakes

Pumpkin Pancakes with Crystallized Ginger Syrup

QUICK OVEN PANCAKES WITH SPICED HONEY SYRUP

Cornmeal Pancakes with Chèvre and Red Pepper Sauce

POTATO PANCAKES WITH BACON AND CHIVES

Chicken and Pancetta Crêpes with Apples, Leeks, and Shiitakes

ASIAN PORK WITH CHIVE-GINGER CRÊPES

Banana-Stuffed French Toast with Streusel Topping

BAKED FRENCH TOAST WITH BLUEBERRY SAUCE

Grand Marnier Stuffed French Toast

VEGETABLE, CHEESE, AND SAUSAGE BREAD PUDDING

San Francisco–Style Eggs Benedict

ESCAROLE TORTA WITH A SWEET POTATO CRUST

Wine Country B.L.T.

GREEK SALAD SANDWICH WITH OREGANO VINAIGRETTE

Crab Salad Niçoise

SALMON HASH WITH HORSERADISH-DILL SAUCE

Panfried Trout with Bacon and Sage

PECAN-CRUSTED TROUT WITH ORANGE-ROSEMARY SAUCE

Orange-Raspberry Muffins

MAKES 12 STANDARD MUFFINS

This basic recipe makes delicious and moist muffins. Substitute other fresh
or frozen berries. Use miniature muffin pans to make bite-sized treats
for tea or your children's lunch box. Adjust the baking time to 12 to 14 minutes.

3 cups all-purpose flour

1 tablespoon baking powder

½ teaspoon baking soda

1 teaspoon salt

½ cup (1 stick) plus 2 tablespoons
    unsalted butter at room
    temperature

1 cup sugar

2 teaspoons grated orange zest

2 eggs at room temperature

2 teaspoons pure vanilla extract

1½ cups plain low-fat yogurt

1½ cups fresh or frozen
    unsweetened raspberries

1. Preheat the oven to 375°F. Spray 12 standard muffin cups with vegetable-oil cooking spray, or butter them.

2. In a medium bowl, combine the flour, baking powder, baking soda, and salt and stir to blend. In a medium bowl, cream the butter, sugar, and orange zest together until light and fluffy. Beat in the eggs one at a time. Blend in the vanilla and mix. Add half of the dry mixture and stir until barely blended. Gently blend in one-third of the yogurt. Alternately add the remaining dry mixture and yogurt in two batches, stirring until just blended; the batter should be slightly lumpy. Gently fold in the raspberries (do not defrost frozen raspberries). Fill each muffin cup three-fourths full.

3. Bake for 25 minutes, or until the muffins are golden brown and a toothpick inserted in the center of one comes out clean. Let cool in the pan on a wire rack for 3 minutes, and then unmold and serve.

Raisin-Pecan Coffee Cake

SERVES 8 TO 10

A just-baked coffee cake makes a sweet morning wake-up call for the family.
Make two of these and keep one in the freezer for later use.

1. Preheat the oven to 350°F. Butter and flour an 8- or 9-inch round springform pan.

2. In a large bowl, cream the butter and the 1 cup sugar together until light and fluffy. Beat in the eggs one at a time. Add the vanilla and mix. Sift the flours, baking powder, baking soda, and salt together. Blend the flour mixture into the butter mixture just until smooth. Blend the sour cream or crème fraîche into the batter. Pour half of the mixture into the prepared pan.

3. In a small bowl, mix the cinnamon, raisins, and the ¼ cup sugar together. Sprinkle half this mixture over the batter in the pan. Top with the remaining batter, then the remaining cinnamon mixture and the pecans. Bake for 40 to 45 minutes, or until a toothpick inserted in the center comes out clean. Let cool in the pan on a wire rack for 30 minutes. Serve warm.

½ cup (1 stick) unsalted butter at
    room temperature

1 cup plus ¼ cup sugar

2 eggs at room temperature

1 teaspoon pure vanilla extract

1 cup cake flour

½ cup all-purpose flour

1½ teaspoons baking powder

1 teaspoon baking soda

1 teaspoon salt

1 cup sour cream or crème fraîche

1½ teaspoons ground cinnamon

⅓ cup raisins

⅓ cup chopped pecans

Smoked Salmon and Dill Biscuits

MAKES ABOUT 6 BISCUITS

These biscuits are buttery and richly flavored. Serve them warm with scrambled eggs
or an omelette. To serve as an appetizer, fill them with cream cheese and smoked salmon.

1 cup all-purpose flour

2 teaspoons baking powder

¼ teaspoon sugar

¼ teaspoon salt

4 tablespoons cold unsalted
    butter, cut into small pieces

6 tablespoons half-and-half

2 ounces sliced smoked salmon,
    chopped

2 tablespoons snipped fresh dill

1. Preheat the oven to 425°F. In a food processor, combine the flour, baking powder, sugar, and salt. Quickly pulse. Add the butter and pulse until it resembles small peas. Add the half-and-half, salmon, and dill and pulse just until the dough forms a ball. Or to make by hand, stir the dry ingredients together in a medium bowl. Cut in the butter with a pastry cutter or 2 knives until mixture resembles coarse meal. Stir in the half-and-half, salmon, and dill until the dry ingredients are moistened. Form into a ball.

2. On a floured board, roll the dough out to a 1-inch thickness. Using a 2-inch biscuit cutter, cut into rounds. Place the rounds 1-inch apart on an ungreased baking sheet. Bake until puffed and golden, about 15 minutes. Let cool slightly before serving.

Rosemary-Shallot Popovers

MAKES 6 POPOVERS

Serve with any brunch entrée or for dinner with chicken, lamb,
or beef. These popovers are good for soaking up sauce.

1. Preheat the oven to 450°F. In a small skillet, melt the 1 teaspoon butter over low heat. Add the shallots and cook until translucent, about 3 minutes. Add the rosemary and set aside.

2. In a blender, combine the milk, flour, salt, and eggs and blend for 3 to 4 minutes. Stir in the shallots and rosemary.

3. Divide the melted butter among 6 popover cups. Place the pan in the oven to heat for 5 minutes. Remove from the oven and divide the batter evenly among the cups. Bake for 20 minutes, or until the popovers are golden brown and their sides are crisp and firm. Poke the side of each popover with a sharp knife to release the steam. Serve immediately.

1 teaspoon unsalted butter, plus
    3 tablespoons melted butter

4 shallots, minced

1 tablespoon minced fresh
    rosemary, or 1 teaspoon dried
    rosemary

1½ cups milk

1½ cups all-purpose flour

1 teaspoon salt

4 large eggs at room temperature

Corn Popovers

Delicious with pork or a hearty stew. Omit the chives, and you can serve these with fruity preserves.

1 cup all-purpose flour

1½ tablespoons yellow cornmeal

1 teaspoon sugar

½ teaspoon salt

Freshly ground pepper to taste

1 cup milk

3 eggs, lightly beaten

½ cup fresh corn kernels (about 1 ear), lightly mashed with a fork

1 tablespoon minced fresh chives or scallion tops

1 tablespoon butter, melted and cooled

1. Preheat the oven to 425°F. Butter a 12-cup popover or muffin pan. In a medium bowl, stir the flour, cornmeal, sugar, salt, and pepper together. Stir in the remaining ingredients until just blended. Do not overmix. Pour ¼ cup batter into each cup and bake until puffy and golden brown, about 25 minutes. Serve immediately.

Asparagus and Gorgonzola Frittata

SERVES 6

Fresh, sweet asparagus and rich tangy cheese are put together
in this elegant egg dish. Serve this frittata hot for brunch.
Any leftover frittata makes a wonderful sandwich filling the next day.

1. Preheat the oven to 350°F. Cook the asparagus pieces in salted boiling water until crisp-tender, about 2 minutes. Transfer to a bowl of ice water, then drain.

2. In a large bowl, whisk the eggs, salt, and pepper together just until blended. Stir in the asparagus and Gorgonzola. In a 9- or 10-inch ovenproof nonstick skillet over medium heat, heat the olive oil. Add the scallions and sauté until soft, about 4 minutes. Add the egg mixture and stir to incorporate the scallions. Place the skillet in the oven and bake for 20 to 25 minutes, or until the frittata is puffed and lightly browned. Let rest for 5 minutes before slicing into wedges. Serve warm or at room temperature.

18 asparagus stalks, trimmed and cut into 1-inch pieces

6 large eggs at room temperature

¼ teaspoon salt

Freshly ground pepper to taste

⅓ cup crumbled Gorgonzola cheese

1½ tablespoons extra-virgin olive oil

¼ cup chopped scallions

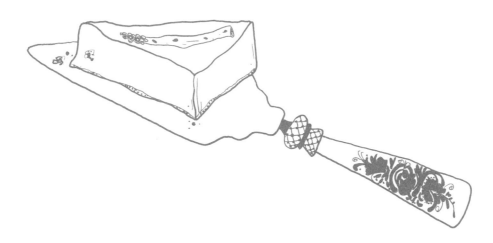

Scrambled Eggs with Goat Cheese and Cherry Tomatoes

SERVES 4

Cherry tomatoes liven up these basic scrambled eggs. Look for
a mixture of yellow and red tomatoes, both round and pear shaped.

8 eggs at room temperature

2 tablespoons milk

Salt and freshly ground pepper to
taste

2 teaspoons butter

1 cup cherry tomatoes, stemmed
and halved

4 ounces fresh white goat cheese,
crumbled (¾ cup)

3 tablespoons snipped fresh chives

1. In a medium bowl, beat the eggs, milk, salt, and pepper until just blended. In a heavy medium saucepan, melt 1 teaspoon of the butter. Add the tomatoes and cook until just warmed through. Using a slotted spoon, transfer to a dish and pour off any liquid.

2. In the same pan, melt the remaining 1 teaspoon butter over low heat. Add the egg mixture and stir to scramble. When eggs are almost set, fold in the goat cheese, tomatoes, and chives. Cook for 1 to 2 minutes, or until the goat cheese begins to soften. Transfer to a serving dish and serve immediately.

Scrambled Eggs with Asparagus, Goat Cheese, and Prosciutto

San Franciscans are lucky to be near some of the best goat cheese makers in the country. This creamy cheese adds richness to the eggs and nicely coats the asparagus.

1. Cook the asparagus in salted boiling water until just crisp-tender, about 2 minutes. Transfer to a bowl of ice water, then drain well and set aside.

2. In a small bowl, whisk the eggs, milk, salt, and pepper just until blended. In a medium skillet, melt 1 tablespoon of the butter over medium heat. Add the egg mixture and stir to scramble until barely set. Remove the eggs from heat and mix in goat cheese and chives. Spoon the eggs into a shallow bowl and set the bowl in a pan of warm water to keep the eggs hot until ready to serve.

3. In the same skillet, melt the remaining 2 tablespoons butter over medium heat. Add the asparagus and cook for 1 minute. Remove 8 asparagus tips and reserve for garnish. Add the prosciutto to the asparagus in skillet and sauté until heated through, about 15 seconds. Gently stir the asparagus mixture into the eggs. Garnish with the reserved asparagus tips. Serve immediately.

12 asparagus stalks, trimmed, peeled, and cut into ½-inch pieces

8 eggs at room temperature

2 tablespoons milk

3 tablespoons unsalted butter

½ cup (3 ounces) crumbled fresh white goat cheese such as Cypress Grove

1 tablespoon snipped fresh chives

2 thin slices prosciutto, cut into 2-inch strips

Salt and freshly ground pepper to taste

Potato Omelette with Lemon-Garlic Mayonnaise

SERVES 6 TO 8

Also known as a *tortilla español,* this flat potato omelette is popular at
San Francisco's tapas bars and is traditionally served at room temperature.
The dense potato cake has a moist creamy texture. Be sure to slice the potatoes thinly,
using a mandoline or a very sharp knife. Wrap this up and take it on a picnic.

½ cup extra-virgin olive oil

2 Yukon Gold potatoes, peeled,
thinly sliced and submerged in
a bowl of cold water

1 onion, thinly sliced, and rings
separated

4 ounces mild Italian sausage,
removed from casing and
crumbled

3 extra large eggs at room
temperature

1 teaspoon salt

1 teaspoon ground pepper

1 small red or yellow bell pepper,
seeded, deveined, and chopped

½ cup cooked fresh or thawed
frozen peas

6 asparagus stalks, cooked and cut
into ½-inch pieces

Lemon-Garlic Mayonnaise (recipe
follows)

1. In a 9-inch nonstick ovenproof skillet, heat the oil over medium heat. Drain the potatoes and pat dry with paper towels. Add the onions and potatoes in alternating layers and cook over medium heat until tender but not browned, about 12 minutes. Using a slotted spoon, transfer to paper towels to drain, and cool. Reserve the leftover oil in a separate heatproof container. Wipe the skillet clean.

2. While the potatoes are cooling, brown the sausage in a skillet over medium heat. Using a slotted spoon, transfer the sausage to paper towels to drain. In a medium bowl, whisk the eggs, salt, and pepper until slightly foamy. Add the potatoes and onion to the eggs and set aside for 15 minutes.

3. Wipe the skillet clean again. Add 1 tablespoon of the reserved oil to the skillet and place over medium heat. Add the bell pepper and cook for 3 minutes. Add the peas and asparagus and cook for 2 minutes. Remove from heat and let cool in the skillet.

4. Add the cooled vegetables and sausage to the egg and potato mixture and let sit for 5 minutes.

5. Wipe the skillet clean once again. Add enough of the reserved oil to coat the skillet and place over medium heat. Add the egg mixture and cook for several minutes. Occasionally, and very gently, peek at the bottom of the omelette by slipping a narrow knife or spatula under it.

6. Turn on the broiler. When the bottom of the omelette is lightly browned, place the skillet under broiler for 2 minutes, or until the eggs begin to set. Remove from the broiler. Cover the skillet with a large plate and gently invert the skillet, flipping the omelet onto the plate.

7. Add enough oil to coat the skillet and slide the omelette back into the skillet to brown on the second side. Cook until the omelette is completely set and the bottom is browned, about 10 minutes. Transfer to a serving plate and let cool to room temperature. To make several hours in advance, cover and refrigerate. Bring to room temperature, or cover the omelette with a damp paper towel and heat on high in a microwave for 30 seconds. Cut into wedges and serve with the mayonnaise.

lemon-garlic mayonnaise

MAKES ABOUT ⅔ CUP

Use any leftover mayonnaise for sandwiches. For an authentic Spanish taste, try adding a finely chopped anchovy fillet to this mayonnaise. To give the mayonnaise a rich orange color, boil a small dried red pepper until tender. Drain, stem, seed, and mince, and add to the sauce.

1. In small bowl combine all the ingredients and whisk until smooth. Cover and refrigerate for 1 hour, or up to 1 week.

4 tablespoons butter, melted and cooled slightly

⅓ cup good-quality mayonnaise

Juice from ½ lemon

2 garlic cloves, minced

1 tablespoon minced fresh chopped flat-leaf parsley or dill

2 to 3 drops hot pepper sauce

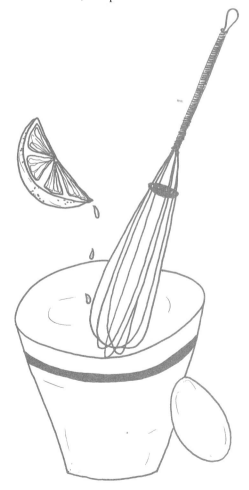

Soufflé Omelette with Canadian Bacon and Sharp Cheddar Cheese

SERVES 4

Bring this golden soufflé directly from the oven to the table for a spectacular, yet easy brunch entrée. Serve with green salad or fresh fruit.

6 ounces Canadian bacon,
　chopped

1 red pepper or green bell pepper,
　seeded, deveined, and diced

1 cup heavy cream

3 tablespoons flour

8 eggs at room temperature

2 teaspoons minced fresh thyme

2 teaspoons minced fresh parsley

1 teaspoon salt

1 teaspoon ground pepper

2 tablespoons butter, melted

¾ cup (3 ounces) shredded sharp
　Cheddar cheese

1. Preheat the oven to 450°F. In a small skillet, cook the bacon and bell pepper over medium heat until the bacon is lightly browned but not crisp. Using a slotted spoon, transfer to paper towels to drain.

2. In a medium bowl, combine the cream, flour, eggs, thyme, parsley, salt, and pepper and beat just until blended. Add the bacon and bell pepper.

3. In a flameproof 6-cup baking dish, melt the butter over medium-high heat. Tilt the dish to coat the sides. Add the egg mixture, sprinkle the cheese over the top, and bake in the center of the oven for 15 to 20 minutes, or until puffed and golden. Serve immediately.

Fuji Apple and Ricotta Pancakes

SERVES 4

These sophisticated pancakes are loved by children and adults alike.
Experiment with some of the heirloom apples available in many markets today.

1. In a medium bowl, combine all the ingredients except the egg whites, butter, and suggested toppings. Beat until blended.

2. In a large bowl, beat the egg whites until stiff, glossy peaks form. Fold the whites into the batter. In a large nonstick skillet, melt 1 tablespoon of the butter over medium-high heat. Pour ¼-cup portions of batter into the pan. Cook until bubbles appear all over the surface and the pancakes becomes dry near the edges. Flip over and cook for 1 minute on the second side, or until lightly browned on the bottom. Transfer to a low oven to keep warm. Repeat to cook the remaining batter. Serve at once. Serve with maple syrup, preserves, fresh fruit, or cinnamon sugar.

1 cup ricotta cheese

2 Fuji apples, peeled, cored, and
   grated

¾ cup all-purpose flour

1 tablespoon lavender honey or
   other mild-flavored honey

1 teaspoon fresh lemon juice

1 tablespoon almonds, toasted and
   chopped

1 teaspoon ground cinnamon

½ teaspoon ground nutmeg

4 eggs, separated, at room
   temperature

½ teaspoon salt

¼ cup frozen orange juice
   concentrate

2 tablespoons butter

Maple syrup, preserves, fresh fruit,
   or cinnamon sugar for serving

Pumpkin Pancakes with Crystallized Ginger Syrup

SERVES 4

Pumpkin puree and crystallized ginger syrup add an exotic flair to these pancakes.
Serve with smoky ham or sweet sausage. The Spiced Honey Syrup (page 229),
also makes a great syrup for these pancakes. For a cocktail party, make
bite-sized pancakes and top with smoked turkey and a dollop of pear chutney.

2 cups all-purpose flour

2 tablespoons sugar

2 teaspoons baking powder

1 teaspoon salt

½ teaspoon ground coriander

1 teaspoon ground cinnamon

¼ teaspoon freshly grated nutmeg

1 ⅓ cups milk

1 cup canned pumpkin puree

4 eggs, separated, at room
   temperature

½ cup (1 stick) butter, melted

1 tablespoon pure vanilla extract

1 tablespoon vegetable oil

Crystallized Ginger Syrup (recipe
   follows)

1. Preheat the oven to 200°F. Sift the dry ingredients together into a large bowl. In a medium bowl, combine the milk, pumpkin puree, egg yolks, butter, and vanilla and beat until smooth. Pour the mixture into the dry ingredients and stir until blended. In a large bowl, beat the egg whites until stiff, glossy peaks form. Fold into the pumpkin batter until blended.

2. In a large nonstick skillet over medium-high heat, heat the oil. Pour ¼-cup portions of batter into the pan and cook for 2 to 3 minutes. Flip each pancake and cook for 1 minute on the second side. Keep warm in a low oven while cooking the remaining batter. Serve pancakes with Crystallized Ginger Syrup.

crystallized ginger syrup

MAKES 3 CUPS

1. In a medium saucepan, bring all the ingredients to a boil. Reduce heat and simmer for 15 minutes, or until the consistency of maple syrup. Strain the syrup and transfer to a small pitcher for serving.

1½ cups filtered apple cider

1 cup packed brown sugar

1 cup corn syrup

4 tablespoons butter

1 tablespoon grated lemon zest

2 tablespoons fresh lemon juice

1 teaspoon ground cinnamon

2 teaspoons grated crystallized
  ginger

Quick Oven Pancakes with Spiced Honey Syrup

A cross between a soufflé and a pancake, this makes a light morning meal.
Serve with Spiced Honey Syrup, fruit compote, warm sautéed pears,
or just powdered sugar and syrup. For a more sophisticated version,
add cooked and crumbled bacon or pancetta to the batter before baking.

3 eggs at room temperature

½ cup all-purpose flour

½ cup milk

1 teaspoon grated lemon zest

½ teaspoon pure vanilla extract

1 teaspoon salt

2 tablespoons unsalted butter

Spiced Honey Syrup (recipe
  follows)

1. Preheat the oven to 450°F. In a blender or medium bowl, combine all the ingredients except the butter and blend or whisk until smooth.

2. Put the butter in a 12-inch heavy ovenproof skillet, and set the skillet in the oven for 3 minutes, or until the butter melts. Using a hot pad, remove the skillet from the oven and swirl the butter around the sides of the pan. Add the batter and bake for 20 minutes, or until golden brown and puffed all over. Serve immediately, with Spiced Honey Syrup.

spiced honey syrup

MAKES 2 CUPS

An alternative to maple syrup for pancakes and waffles,
this is also delicious over ice cream.

1. In a small saucepan, combine all the ingredients and cook over medium-low heat for 30 minutes. Strain and pour into a serving bowl, or store in an airtight container at room temperature.

2 cups lavender honey or other
  mild honey

3 star anise pods

4 cinnamon sticks

Grated zest of 1 orange

Grated zest of 1 lemon

5 whole cloves

Cornmeal Pancakes with Chèvre and Red Pepper Sauce

SERVES 4

Savory pancakes are topped with goat cheese and garnished with sautéed red peppers for a sophisticated brunch. Serve with fruit compote and a Blanc de Noir sparkling wine.

1 cup yellow cornmeal

½ teaspoon baking soda

1 teaspoon salt

1 egg, lightly beaten

1¼ cups buttermilk

¼ cup chopped fresh cilantro

3 tablespoons canola oil

RED PEPPER SAUCE AND GARNISH:

2 red bell peppers, roasted and peeled (see page 17)

1 cup crème fraîche

Salt and freshly ground pepper to taste

8 ounces fresh white goat cheese cut into ½-inch rounds

1 cup fresh corn kernels, cooked (about 2 ears)

1 tablespoon minced fresh flat-leaf parsley

1. Preheat the oven to 200°F. In large bowl, mix the cornmeal, baking soda, and salt together. Add the egg, buttermilk, cilantro, and 1 tablespoon of the oil and stir until just moistened. Let the batter stand for 5 minutes. In a large skillet over medium heat, heat the remaining 2 tablespoons oil. Pour ⅛-cup portions of batter into the hot pan. Cook for 3 minutes, or until browned on the bottom. Turn and cook on the second aide side until browned, about 2 minutes. Transfer to a low oven to keep warm.

2. TO MAKE THE SAUCE: Finely chop 1½ of the peppers. In a small saucepan, cook the chopped peppers over low heat for 5 minutes, or until heated through. Stir in the crème fraîche, salt, and pepper and simmer over low heat for 10 minutes. Cut the remaining pepper half into thin slices and set aside.

3. Arrange 3 pancakes in the center of each warm plate. Overlap 2 slices of goat cheese on the pancakes. Scatter some corn and parsley over each serving. Return the plates to the oven and heat for 4 minutes, or until the cheese and corn are warmed through. Spoon some red pepper sauce around the pancakes. Garnish each serving with some of the sliced red peppers.

Potato Pancakes with Bacon and Chives

SERVES 2

A delicious accompaniment to eggs, or serve with sour cream and smoked salmon.

1. Immediately prior to cooking, shred the potato, using the large holes of a box grater. Press the potato between several thicknesses of paper towels to remove any excess moisture. In a medium bowl, combine the potato, bacon, chives or scallion, salt, and pepper.

2. In a large, heavy skillet over medium-high heat, heat the oil until almost smoking. Form the potato mixture into 4 patties and cook the patties, tapping them down with a spatula, for 5 to 7 minutes on each side, or until golden brown and cooked through. Serve at once, with sour cream.

1 large russet potato, peeled

2 slices lean bacon, cooked and crumbled fine

2 tablespoons snipped fresh chives or scallion tops

¼ teaspoon salt

Freshly ground pepper to taste

2 tablespoons olive oil

Sour cream for serving

Chicken and Pancetta Crêpes with Apples, Leeks, and Shiitakes

SERVES 6

The mixture of sweet, earthy, and smoky flavors creates an appealing brunch entrée. This dish can be assembled at least 1 day in advance. The crêpes can be made several days in advance or even frozen ahead.

WINE SUGGESTION BY DEBBIE ZACHAREAS: QUPE SYRAH

CRÊPES:

1 cup all-purpose flour

⅔ cup milk

⅔ cup water

3 eggs at room temperature

¼ teaspoon salt

6 tablespoons butter, melted

FILLING:

11 tablespoons butter

2 small leeks, white part only, sliced and washed well

8 ounces shiitake mushrooms, stemmed and sliced, or cremini mushrooms, sliced

4 ounces chanterelle mushrooms, sliced (optional)

Salt and freshly ground pepper to taste

1 Fuji or Granny Smith apple, peeled, cored, and diced

½ cup all-purpose flour

4 boneless, skinless chicken breast halves, cut into ½-inch dice

1. TO MAKE THE CRÊPES: In a medium bowl, combine the flour, milk, and water and beat until smooth. Whisk in the eggs, salt, and 3 tablespoons of the melted butter. Let rest for at least 10 minutes or up to 1 hour.

2. Heat a 7-inch crêpe pan or nonstick skillet over medium heat. Brush the pan with melted butter. Pour ¼ cup batter into the pan and tilt the pan to coat it evenly. Cook for 30 to 45 seconds, or until the bottom of the crêpe is lightly browned. Turn and cook the other side until lightly browned. Transfer to a plate. Continue making the crêpes until all the batter is gone, stacking the cooked crêpes. To make ahead, cover and refrigerate for up to 2 days, or freeze for up to 1 month.

3. TO MAKE THE FILLING: In a large skillet, melt 6 tablespoons of the butter over medium-high heat. Add the leeks and cook until soft. Add the mushrooms, salt, and pepper and cook until lightly browned, about 8 minutes. Pour into a bowl and set aside.

4. In the same saucepan, melt 1 tablespoon of the butter over high heat. Add the apples and cook, stirring frequently, until soft, about 4 minutes. Add the apples to the mushroom mixture. In a medium bowl, mix the flour with salt and pepper to taste. Add the chicken and toss to coat the pieces evenly.

5. In the same skillet, melt the remaining 4 tablespoons butter over medium-high heat. Shake off the excess flour from the chicken, add the chicken to the skillet, and cook until lightly browned on all sides, about 8 minutes. Add the wine and cook for 2 minutes. Add the stock or broth, stir until the mixture comes to a boil, then lower heat to a simmer. Add the leeks, mushrooms, pancetta or bacon, sage, and parsley. Simmer for 10 minutes and season with salt and pepper to taste. Add the apples and stir. The sauce should be slightly thickened but not runny. Let the mixture cool. Use the filling now, or refrigerate until ready to assemble the crêpes.

6. TO ASSEMBLE THE CRÊPES: Preheat the oven to 350°F. Spoon 3 to 4 tablespoons of the filling mixture into each crêpe. Roll and place, seam-side down, in a baking dish. Top with the cheese and bake, uncovered, for 20 to 30 minutes, or until the cheese is bubbly and golden brown. Serve at once.

1 cup Chardonnay or other dry white wine

1 cup Chicken Stock (page 61) or canned low-salt chicken broth

5 slices pancetta or bacon, fried crisp, drained of excess fat, and crumbled

1 tablespoon minced fresh sage, or 1 teaspoon dried sage

2 tablespoons minced fresh flat-leaf parsley

½ cup (2 ounces) grated aged Asiago cheese

Asian Pork with Chive-Ginger Crêpes

SERVES 8

Many of San Francisco's best restaurants and caterers include Asian appetizers and entrées on their menus. In this brunch entrée, the pork strips are gently rolled in warm crêpes made with fresh ginger and chives. Make the crêpes in advance and keep wrapped in the refrigerator.

WINE SUGGESTION BY KRIS HARRIMAN: CHATEAU MONTELENA ST. VINCENT

8 ounces pork tenderloin, trimmed
  of excess fat

Salt and freshly ground pepper to
  taste

1 tablespoon peanut oil or olive
  oil

3 tablespoons hoisin sauce

1 tablespoon clover honey

¼ cup Asian plum sauce

4 radishes, cut into thin strips

10 fresh chives, cut into 1-inch-
  long diagonal pieces

2 scallions, cut into 1-inch-long
  diagonal pieces and cut again
  into thin strips

4 carrots, peeled and cut into
  matchsticks

1 small jicama, peeled and cut
  into matchsticks

Crêpes (recipe follows)

1. Preheat the oven to 350°F. Pat the pork dry with paper towels and season with salt and pepper. In a large ovenproof skillet over medium-high heat, heat the oil until almost smoking and brown the pork on all sides. Transfer the skillet to a rack in the center of the oven and bake the pork until a meat thermometer inserted into the center registers 155°F, about 20 minutes. Transfer the pork to a cutting board and let cool completely. Cut the pork into 1-inch-long strips and put in a small bowl. Add the hoisin sauce and honey, stir to combine, and season with salt and pepper to taste.

2. TO ASSEMBLE THE CRÊPES: Brush a crêpe lightly with plum sauce. Arrange 12 to 15 pork strips on the crêpe and top with radish strips, chive pieces, scallion strips, carrots, and jicama. Roll the crêpe around the filling into a cone, tucking in the pointed end while rolling. Repeat to fill and roll the remaining crêpes. Serve at once.

chive-ginger crêpes

1. In a blender or food processor, combine all the ingredients except the chives and butter. Blend until smooth and transfer to a bowl. Let the batter stand at room temperature, covered, for about 1 hour. Add the chives to the batter and stir well. Heat a 7-inch skillet over medium heat until hot. Brush the skillet lightly with melted butter. Pour ⅛ cup crêpe batter into the pan and tilt the pan to coat it evenly. Cook for 30 to 45 seconds, or until lightly browned on the bottom. Turn and cook on the second side until lightly browned. Transfer to a plate. Repeat to use the remaining batter. Stack the crêpes as they are cooked and keep warm in a low oven. To make ahead, let cool, wrap in plastic, and store in the refrigerator. Reheat in a skillet over medium heat for 2 minutes. Or, heat in a preheated 300°F oven for 5 to 7 minutes.

½ cup all-purpose flour

½ teaspoon salt

1 egg at room temperature

⅓ cup milk

½ cup club soda

2 teaspoons canola oil

1 teaspoon grated fresh ginger

Freshly ground pepper to taste

¼ cup snipped fresh chives

2 tablespoons butter, melted

Banana-Stuffed French Toast with Streusel Topping

SERVES 6

This breakfast treat begins with rich egg bread, adds ripe bananas and toasted almonds, and finishes with a cinnamon streusel. Use pure maple syrup to top off this hearty morning meal.

2 tablespoons unsalted butter

2 tablespoons plus ½ cup sugar

2 tablespoons water

2 large ripe bananas, peeled and
    cut into ½-inch rounds

Six 1 ½-inch-thick slices challah
    or egg bread

2 cups milk

6 large eggs at room temperature

½ teaspoon ground cinnamon

4 tablespoons pure vanilla extract

2 cups thinly sliced almonds

STREUSEL TOPPING:

¼ cup packed light brown sugar

¼ cup quick-cooking oats

2 tablespoons all-purpose flour

2 teaspoons ground cinnamon

4 tablespoons unsalted butter at
    room temperature

Maple syrup for serving

1. In a large, heavy skillet, melt the butter over medium heat. Add the 2 tablespoons sugar and the water and stir until the sugar dissolves. Continue stirring until the mixture is foamy, about 2 minutes. Add the bananas. Cook until the bananas are tender, stirring occasionally, about 5 minutes. Transfer to a small bowl and let cool. The bananas can be prepared up to 4 hours ahead. Cover and refrigerate for up to 4 hours.

2. Preheat the oven to 350°F. Using a sharp knife, cut a 2-inch-long slit in one side of each bread slice, cutting three-fourths of the way through the bread to make a pocket. Divide the banana mixture equally among the pockets in the bread. In a large bowl, combine the milk, eggs, cinnamon, vanilla, and the ½ cup sugar. Whisk until blended. Pour into a large glass baking dish. Place the bread slices in the egg mixture and soak for 10 minutes, turning several times.

3. Put the almonds in a shallow bowl. Using a slotted metal spatula, transfer a slice of bread to the bowl of almonds and coat both sides with the almonds. Place the bread on a large insulated baking sheet or 2 stacked baking sheets.

4. TO MAKE THE STREUSEL: In a small bowl, mix the brown sugar, oats, flour, and cinnamon together. Add the butter and rub it in with your fingers until moist clumps form.

5. Sprinkle the topping streusel over the bread. Bake until the topping is golden brown and the filling is hot, about 25 minutes. (If you would like to freeze the French toast, let cool, wrap in aluminum foil and freeze. To reheat, place the foil packages on a baking sheet in a preheated 350°F oven and bake for 15 to 20 minutes.) Transfer the toast to warm plates. Serve hot, with syrup.

Baked French Toast with Blueberry Sauce

SERVES 8

This isn't your typical French toast; it's more like a bread pudding with blueberry sauce. Make it the night before and serve it as the centerpiece of a Sunday brunch the next day.

1. Butter a 9-by-13-inch baking dish. Arrange half the bread cubes in the prepared dish. Scatter the cream cheese cubes over the bread and sprinkle 1 cup of the blueberries over the cream cheese. Arrange the remaining bread cubes over the blueberries. In a large bowl, whisk the eggs, syrup, and milk together. Pour the egg mixture evenly over the bread mixture. Cover the baking dish with aluminum foil and refrigerate overnight.

2. Preheat the oven to 350°F. Bake the foil-covered dish of French toast in the oven for 30 minutes. Remove the foil and bake 30 minutes longer, or until puffed and golden.

3. Meanwhile, in a small saucepan, stir the sugar, cornstarch, and water together. Cook the mixture over medium-high heat, stirring occasionally, for 5 minutes, or until thickened. Stir in the remaining blueberries and simmer the mixture, stirring occasionally, for 10 minutes, or until the berries have burst. Add the butter and stir until the butter has melted. Set aside and keep warm. Serve the French toast with the warm blueberry sauce.

12 thick slices firm white bread, crusts trimmed, cut into 2-inch cubes

16 ounces cold cream cheese, cut into 1-inch cubes

2 cups fresh or frozen blueberries

12 eggs at room temperature

⅓ cup maple syrup

2 cups milk

1 cup sugar

2 tablespoons cornstarch

1 cup water

1 tablespoon butter

Grand Marnier Stuffed French Toast

SERVES 6

An elegant twist on the classic, this French toast, made with rich brioche bread, is stuffed with a creamy orange filling before being dipped in egg batter and fried. Lightly dust it with powdered sugar and serve with warm maple syrup. Your family will think they woke up at the Ritz-Carlton!

FILLING:

16 ounces cream cheese at room
   temperature
¼ cup powdered sugar
2 teaspoons pure vanilla extract
1 tablespoon half-and-half
2 teaspoons grated orange zest

1 loaf brioche bread or egg bread
1 cup half-and-half
4 eggs at room temperature
1 teaspoon ground cinnamon
½ teaspoon ground nutmeg
¼ teaspoon ground cloves
1 tablespoon Grand Marnier
4 tablespoons butter
Powdered sugar for dusting
Warm maple syrup for serving

1. TO MAKE THE FILLING: In a medium bowl, combine all the ingredients and beat until smooth. Set aside.

2. Set the loaf of bread on end and use a serrated knife to cut out a 3-inch tunnel down the length of the loaf. Save the cut-out bread for another use. Spoon the filling into the tunnel or pipe it into the loaf using a pastry bag. Wrap the bread in aluminum foil. Refrigerate for 30 minutes.

3. In a medium bowl, whisk the half-and-half, eggs, cinnamon, nutmeg, cloves, and Grand Marnier together just until blended. Pour into a small baking dish.

4. Preheat the oven to 200°F. Remove the foil and cut the bread into 1-inch slices. Dip the bread into the egg mixture, soaking it on both sides for a few minutes. In a large skillet, melt 2 tablespoons of the butter over medium heat. Cook the slices in batches until lightly browned, keeping it warm in a low oven, lightly covered with aluminum foil. Garnish with powdered sugar and serve at once with warm maple syrup.

Vegetable, Cheese, and Sausage Bread Pudding

SERVES 6

Sautéed vegetables, lean sausage, and eggs are baked and topped with Gruyère cheese
to make this savory breakfast casserole. Bruce Aidells of San Francisco offers a variety of fresh
sausages including chicken-apple and pork-fennel. This is a great addition to a buffet luncheon;
make it the night before to allow you more time for last-minute details, like sleeping in!

WINE SUGGESTION BY DEBBIE ZACHAREAS: GROTH CHARDONNAY

1. In a large skillet over medium heat, heat the oil and sauté the onion for 3 to 4 minutes, or until translucent. Add the zucchini, mushrooms, bell pepper, artichoke hearts, salt, and pepper. Cook for 3 to 4 minutes. Add the garlic and cook for 1 minute. Remove from heat.

2. Remove the sausage meat from the casings. In a medium skillet, cook the sausage over medium-high heat until browned, about 5 minutes. Drain off the fat and add the sausage to the vegetables.

3. In a large bowl, combine the eggs, milk, ¾ cup of the Gruyère cheese, the Parmesan, oregano, rosemary, mustard, and salt and pepper to taste. Whisk until thoroughly blended.

4. Preheat the oven to 350°F. Coat a 9-by-13-inch baking dish with vegetable-oil cooking spray or butter. Add the bread cubes and gently stir in the vegetable mixture. Pour the egg mixture over the vegetables. Cover with the remaining cheese, or cover and refrigerate overnight before adding the remaining cheese. Bake for 45 minutes, or until lightly browned and bubbly.

1 teaspoon olive oil

1 yellow onion, finely diced

2 cups sliced zucchini

10 ounces wild or white
    mushrooms, sliced

1 cup finely diced red bell pepper

¾ cup fresh or frozen canned
    artichoke hearts, diced

Salt and freshly ground pepper to
    taste

3 garlic cloves, minced

4 fresh chicken, turkey, or pork
    sausages

5 eggs at room temperature

4 cups milk or half-and-half

1 cup (4 ounces) shredded
    Gruyère or sharp Cheddar
    cheese

¼ cup grated Parmesan cheese

1 tablespoon minced fresh
    oregano, or 1 teaspoon dried
    oregano

2 teaspoons minced fresh chopped
    rosemary, or ¾ teaspoon dried
    rosemary

½ teaspoon dry mustard

1 large day-old loaf Italian
    bread, cut into 1-inch cubes

San Francisco—Style Eggs Benedict

SERVES 4

In this rendition of Eggs Benedict, poached eggs top fresh asparagus and a pancetta waffle.
However, tradition isn't totally abandoned. Lemon hollandaise smothers it all.
Look for Meyer lemons to enhance the sauce further. (See photograph, page 273.)

WINE SUGGESTION BY KRIS HARRIMAN: IRON HORSE VRAIS AMIS SPARKLING WINE

PANCETTA WAFFLES:

4 slices pancetta or bacon, cut
    into 1-inch pieces

1 cup cake flour

1 teaspoon baking powder

½ teaspoon salt

1 cup heavy cream

2 eggs at room temperature

HOLLANDAISE SAUCE:

3 egg yolks at room temperature

Salt and ground white pepper to
    taste

1½ cups (3 sticks) unsalted butter

2 teaspoons grated lemon zest,
    preferably Meyer lemon

2 tablespoons fresh lemon juice,
    preferably Meyer lemon

1 tablespoon snipped fresh chives

12 asparagus stalks, trimmed

1 tablespoon Chardonnay or
    white wine vinegar

8 eggs

1. TO MAKE THE WAFFLES: In a small skillet, cook the pancetta or bacon over medium high heat until lightly browned. Using a slotted spoon, transfer to paper towels to drain.

2. Preheat a waffle iron. In a blender or food processor, combine the flour, baking powder, and salt. Pulse quickly to blend. Add the pancetta or bacon, cream, and eggs and process for 6 seconds. Scrape the sides of the container. Pulse for 3 seconds to fully mix.

3. Pour ½ cup of the batter onto the hot waffle iron and cook for about 5 minutes, or until golden brown. Keep warm in a low oven. Repeat to cook the remaining batter. (To make ahead, let the waffles cool, then wrap in plastic wrap, place in a freezer bag, and freeze. To thaw, place in the toaster or 350°F oven and cook until heated through.)

4. TO MAKE THE SAUCE: In a blender or food processor, combine the egg yolks, salt, and pepper and process for 10 seconds. In a small saucepan, melt the butter until it foams. With the machine running, pour the melted butter in a thin stream into the blender or processor. Add the zest and lemon juice and pulse to incorporate. Pour the sauce into a bowl and place over a pan filled with 2 inches of hot water to keep the sauce warm. Stir in the chives just before serving. (You can also keep the hollandaise warm in a Thermos.)

5. Cook the asparagus in a skillet of salted boiling water for 3 minutes, or until easily pierced with a knife. Drain and reserve.

6. Bring a large skillet of water to a boil. Add the vinegar and reduce heat to a simmer. Break the eggs, one at a time, into a saucer and slide them into the water. With a spoon, gently bring the egg white over the center of each yolk to keep the whites intact. Cook for 4 minutes for soft-centered yolks. With a slotted spoon, transfer the eggs to a clean dish towel. (To make the eggs ahead of time: Cook the eggs for 3 minutes. Place them in a bowl of ice water to stop the cooking. Before serving, cook the poached eggs in simmering water for 1 minute to reheat.)

7. To serve place a hot waffle on each of 4 warm plates and top with 3 asparagus stalks, 1 poached egg, and some hollandaise.

 THOMAS KELLER, THE FRENCH LAUNDRY RESTAURANT:
Add a few tablespoons of white vinegar to the poaching water. The vinegar will keep the egg whites from falling apart in the water and keep the egg whole. You won't be able to taste the vinegar.

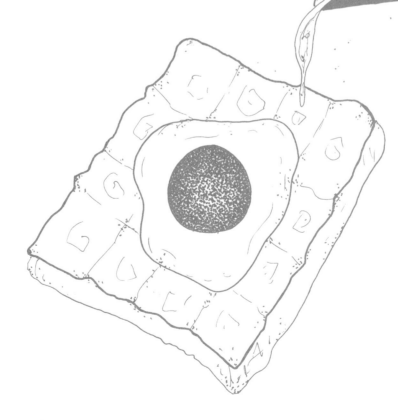

Escarole Torta with a Sweet Potato Crust

SERVES 4

This tart is an updated version of a rich and creamy quiche, and
the delicious crust makes it an elegant brunch entrée.

WINE SUGGESTION BY DAVID PAULEY: SABON FAMILY VINEYARD SANGIOVESE

SWEET POTATO CRUST:

4 pounds sweet potatoes, peeled

1 small onion, grated

½ teaspoon salt

2½ tablespoons flour

Freshly ground pepper to taste

Olive oil for brushing

1 tablespoon olive oil

1 large onion, finely chopped

2 garlic cloves, minced

4 cups escarole leaves

1 tablespoon balsamic vinegar

6 eggs at room temperature,
   lightly beaten

½ cup (2 ounces) grated
   Parmesan cheese

1 cup (4 ounces) grated provolone
   cheese

1 cup milk

2 tablespoons minced fresh
   oregano, or 2 teaspoons dried
   oregano

1 teaspoon red pepper flakes
   (optional)

Salt and freshly ground pepper to
   taste

1. TO MAKE THE CRUST: Preheat the oven to 400°F. Shred the sweet potatoes on the large holes of a box grater. In a colander set in the sink, combine the sweet potato, onion, and salt. Let drain for 15 minutes, then squeeze out the excess liquid. Transfer to a medium bowl, add the flour and pepper, and mix well. Press the mixture evenly into a 10-inch pie pan and push it up the sides of the pan to form a crust. Brush olive oil over the entire crust. Bake for 25 minutes, or until golden brown.

2. Meanwhile, in a large skillet over medium-high heat, heat the olive oil. Add the onion and cook for 5 minutes, or until translucent. Add the garlic and cook for 1 minute. Add the escarole and cook for 3 minutes. Add the balsamic vinegar and cook for 2 minutes. Transfer to a colander and press out any liquid. Let cool.

3. In a medium bowl, beat the eggs until blended. In a small bowl, mix the cheeses together. Add 1 cup of the mixed cheeses, the milk, oregano, and pepper flakes to the eggs. Add the escarole mixture and salt and pepper to taste. Pour the mixture into the sweet potato crust and sprinkle the remaining mixed cheeses on top.

4. Reduce the oven temperature to 375°F and bake the tart for 45 minutes, or until the center is set and the top is lightly browned. Let sit for 5 to 10 minutes before cutting into wedges to serve.

Wine Country B.L.T.

SERVES 4

This is a great rendition of the B.L.T. we all know. San Franciscans might pack this in a picnic to take to the wine country or have it at home while watching the 49ers play. It also makes an excellent addition to a brunch buffet.

1. TO MAKE THE MAYONNAISE: In a blender or food processor, combine the basil, pine nuts, and garlic. Puree until smooth. Add the mayonnaise and process until incorporated. Stir in the salt and pepper.

2. Sprinkle a few pinches of salt over the chopped tomatoes. In a medium bowl, toss the bacon, tomatoes, and onion together. Add the basil mayonnaise to the bowl and mix well.

3. Cut the loaf of bread in half lengthwise. Spread the bacon mixture on the bottom half. Loosely arrange the arugula over the mixture. Cover with the top loaf and cut into 8 pieces.

BASIL MAYONNAISE:

2 tablespoons fresh basil leaves

2 tablespoons pine nuts, toasted (see page 18)

2 garlic cloves, chopped

½ cup good-quality mayonnaise

Salt and freshly ground pepper to taste

Salt for sprinkling

2 red tomatoes, chopped

2 yellow tomatoes, chopped

10 slices apple-wood smoked bacon, cooked crisp and crumbled

1 small red onion, finely chopped

1 loaf pugliese or ciabatta bread (a long loaf not more than 1½ inches high)

2 cups arugula

Greek Salad Sandwich with Oregano Vinaigrette

SERVES 6

This picnic sandwich is loaded with crunchy vegetables. Pick the freshest available to ensure the best color and flavor. The oregano vinaigrette adds a nice punch. There are different types of feta available, such as the traditional drier Greek feta, or the creamier version from France.

One 10-inch round bread loaf

½ cup Oregano Vinaigrette
   (recipe follows)

2 cups mixed salad greens

1 cup (5 ounces) crumbled feta
   cheese

1 English (hothouse) cucumber,
   thinly sliced

2 large tomatoes, thinly sliced

1 small red onion, thinly sliced

1 small yellow bell pepper, seeded,
   deveined, and thinly sliced
   (optional)

¼ cup oil-cured black olives,
   pitted and coarsely chopped

¼ cup minced fresh oregano

1. Cut the bread in half and scoop out some of the soft center. Brush each half generously with the oregano vinaigrette. In the bottom half of the bread, arrange the greens, cheese, cucumber, tomatoes, onion, bell pepper, olives, and oregano. Place the remaining bread half on top, wrap in plastic wrap, and place on a baking sheet. Set a plate on top of the loaf and top with some canned food or another weight to compress the loaf. Refrigerate for 1 hour. Cut into 6 wedges to serve.

oregano vinaigrette

MAKES 1 CUP

1. Combine all the ingredients in a blender or food processor and puree until smooth. Store in an airtight container in the refrigerator for up to 1 week.

1 tablespoon chopped fresh oregano

¼ cup fresh lemon juice

¼ cup lemon-infused olive oil or extra-virgin olive oil

2 garlic cloves, chopped

1 tablespoon capers, drained

1 teaspoon salt

1 teaspoon ground pepper

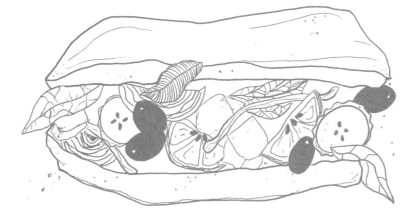

Crab Salad Niçoise

SERVES 6

The beginning of Dungeness crab season is a big event in San Francisco,
often making the front page.San Franciscans often substitute crab for other fish in recipes.
Here crab claws its way into the famous salade niçoise, ousting the traditional tuna.
The result is a sweet and satisfying salad all will enjoy. (See photograph, page 274.)

WINE SUGGESTION BY DAVID PAULEY: LATCHAM ZINFANDEL

8 ounces haricots verts or baby
    Blue Lake green beans, trimmed

12 asparagus stalks, trimmed

1 pound Yukon Gold, Yellow Finn,
    or baby red potatoes

VINAIGRETTE:

3 anchovy fillets

2 tablespoons capers, rinsed and
    drained

3 tablespoons fresh lemon juice

3 teaspoons tarragon mustard or
    Dijon mustard

2 tablespoons minced fresh
    tarragon

1 tablespoon minced fresh
    flat-leaf parsley

1 shallot, coarsely chopped

2 garlic cloves, chopped

3 tablespoons Cabernet or other
    red wine vinegar

1 tablespoon balsamic vinegar

1 teaspoon salt

1 teaspoon ground pepper

1 cup extra-virgin olive oil

1. Cook the beans in a pot of salted boiling water until crisp-tender, 2 to 3 minutes. Transfer to a bowl of ice water to stop the cooking. Bring the water in the pot back to a boil and add the asparagus. Cook for 2 to 3 minutes, or until a knife can easily pierce the stalk. Transfer to a bowl of ice water. Drain the beans and asparagus in a colander.

2. Meanwhile, cook the potatoes in salted boiling water until tender, about 15 minutes. Transfer to a bowl of ice water. Drain in a colander. Cut into quarters or in halves.

3. TO MAKE THE VINAIGRETTE: In a blender or food processor, combine all the ingredients except the oil and puree until smooth. With the machine running, gradually add the olive oil. Taste for seasoning. Store in an airtight container in the refrigerator for up to 3 days.

4. On a large serving platter or 6 individual serving plates, place the lettuce and arrange the beans, asparagus, potatoes, crab, eggs, olives, tomatoes, and onion on top. Drizzle the vinaigrette over the salad and garnish with lemon wedges.

HUBERT KELLER, FLEUR DE LYS RESTAURANT: *To cook perfect hard-cooked eggs, start with eggs that are at least a day old and at room temperature. In a pot large enough to hold the eggs in a single layer, bring salted water to a boil. Place the eggs in the pot and boil for 10 minutes. Cool immediately in several changes of cold water.*

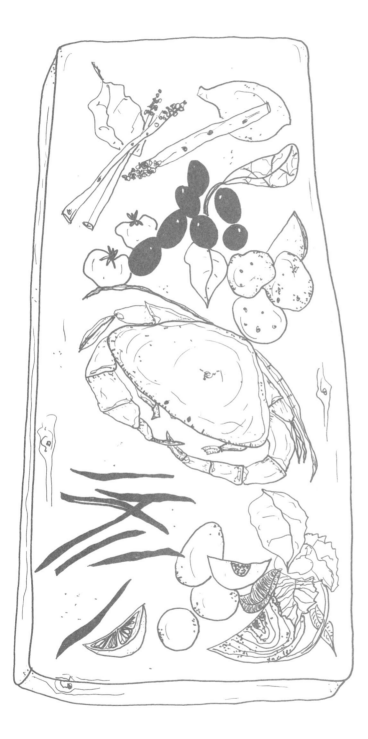

4 cups mixed salad greens

2 cups fresh lump Dungeness
    crabmeat

18 hard cooked quail eggs,
    halved, or 6 hard cooked eggs,
    quartered

4 ounces niçoise olives, pitted and
    halved

2 cups mixed red and yellow
    cherry tomatoes, stemmed

1 small red onion, thinly sliced

1 Meyer lemon, cut into wedges
    (optional)

Salmon Hash with Horseradish-Dill Sauce

SERVES 4

Yellow Finn and Yukon Gold are buttery varieties of potatoes that lend an extra creaminess to hash. Pick some up at the farmers' market or look for them in your supermarket. This dish can be made the day before serving and is also delicious topped with poached eggs.

WINE SUGGESTION BY DAVID PAULEY: SCHUG CELLARS NORTH COAST PINOT NOIR

One 12-ounce salmon fillet

Salt and freshly ground pepper to taste

10 Yellow Finn or Yukon Gold potatoes, halved and scrubbed

7 tablespoons heavy cream

4 tablespoons prepared horseradish, or more to taste

3 tablespoons snipped fresh dill

1 teaspoon white wine vinegar

½ cup chopped scallions

4 tablespoons unsalted butter

1. Preheat the oven to 350°F. Place the salmon in a small baking pan and season with salt and pepper. Bake until opaque on the outside and just barely translucent in the center, about 18 minutes. Transfer to a plate and refrigerate until cold, about 1 hour. Remove any skin and bones, and flake the salmon into ½-inch pieces.

2. Meanwhile, cook the potatoes in salted boiling water until tender, about 15 minutes. Drain, let cool, and cut into quarters.

3. In a small bowl, whisk 5 tablespoons of the cream, 2 tablespoons of the horseradish, and 2 tablespoons of the dill until stiff peaks form. Whisk in the vinegar. Season with salt and pepper to taste. Cover and refrigerate.

4. In a medium bowl, mash ¾ cup of the diced potatoes, the remaining 2 tablespoons cream, the remaining 2 tablespoons horseradish, and the remaining dill until almost smooth. Gently fold in the salmon, onions, and remaining potatoes. Season with salt and pepper to taste.

5. In a medium, heavy nonstick skillet, melt the butter over high heat. Add the hash and press to compact. Reduce heat to medium and cook until the bottom is brown and crusty, about 10 minutes. Using a large spatula, turn the hash over in sections. Press lightly and cook until the bottom is browned, about 5 minutes. Turn the hash out onto a serving plate. Serve with the horseradish sauce.

Panfried Trout with Bacon and Sage

SERVES 8

Bacon and sage infuse the subtle flavor of trout. The cornmeal allows the fish
to fry up nicely, while adding some crunch. (See photograph, page 275.)

WINE SUGGESTION BY DAVID PAULEY: GUNDLACH BUNDSCHU CABERNET FRANC

1. Preheat the oven to 400°F. In a large, heavy skillet, cook 8 of the bacon slices over medium heat, turning occasionally, until crisp. Transfer to paper towels to drain. Pour the fat from the pan. Crumble the cooked bacon into a small bowl and stir in the minced sage. In the same skillet, cook the remaining bacon slices in 2 batches until the fat is rendered but the bacon is not crisp. Transfer to paper towels to drain. Pour the fat from the pan.

2. Evenly stuff each trout with the crumbled bacon mixture. Sprinkle with salt and pepper to taste. Wrap 2 of the whole bacon slices around each trout. Secure the bacon with toothpicks and close the cavities. In a shallow bowl, combine the cornmeal, 1 teaspoon salt, and 1 teaspoon pepper, and stir to blend. Coat each trout evenly in the cornmeal mixture and gently shake off the excess.

3. In the same skillet over medium-high heat, heat the oil until almost smoking. Fry the trout, not touching each other, in batches for 3 minutes on each side, or until they are just firm and the bacon is golden. Using a long spatula, transfer the trout, as they are fried, to a baking pan. Bake the trout for 5 minutes, or until opaque throughout. Remove and discard the wooden picks. Arrange the trout carefully on a platter. Garnish with lemon wedges and sage leaves.

24 slices bacon

3 tablespoons minced fresh sage, plus sage leaves for garnish

8 boned whole trout, 10 ounces each

Salt to taste, plus 1 teaspoon salt

Freshly ground pepper to taste, plus 1 teaspoon ground pepper

2 cups yellow cornmeal

⅓ cup olive oil

Lemon wedges for garnish

Pecan-Crusted Trout with Orange-Rosemary Sauce

SERVES 4

Fresh trout is a delicious brunch entrée. Here, coated in toasted pecans
and panfried in butter, it cooks up with a scrumptious crust and is finished in a sweet
citrus butter sauce. Serve with fresh orange juice and offer a topper of champagne.

2 cups (8 ounces) pecans, toasted
    (see page 18)

1 cup all-purpose flour

Salt and freshly ground pepper to
    taste

4 large boneless trout fillets

3 egg whites, beaten

1 tablespoon unsalted butter

1 tablespoon olive oil

Orange-Rosemary Sauce (recipe
    follows)

Orange segments and fresh chives
    for garnish

1. In a blender or food processor, finely grind the pecans with 1 table-spoon of the flour. Transfer to a plate. Place the remaining flour on another plate. Wash the trout and pat dry with paper towels. Sprinkle the trout with salt and pepper and place in the flour. With a pastry brush, brush the flesh side with the egg whites. Place the fillet, egg-white-side down, onto the pecan mixture and press to coat. Transfer to a parchment paper-lined baking sheet, pecan side down. Repeat with the remaining fillets and refrigerate for 1 hour.

2. In a large skillet over medium-high heat, melt the butter with the oil until the butter begins to brown slightly. Place the fillets, pecan-side down, in the pan and cook until crust is golden brown and crisp on the bottom, about 2 minutes. Turn fillets over and cook until browned on the second side and opaque throughout, about 2 minutes.

3. To serve, reheat the sauce over low heat. Do not boil. Place the fish on individual serving plates and spoon some sauce over each fish. Garnish the plates with orange segments and chives.

orange-rosemary sauce

1. In a small saucepan, combine the orange juice, wine, shallots, vinegar, parsley, lemon juice, and thyme and boil for 10 minutes. Add the rosemary and continue to boil until the liquid is reduced to ½ cup, about 10 minutes. Strain the mixture into another saucepan and discard the solids. Place the saucepan over medium-low heat. Slowly whisk in the butter pieces until thoroughly incorporated. Taste for seasoning. This sauce can stand at room temperature for up to 2 hours.

1 ½ cups fresh orange juice

1 cup Chardonnay or other dry
    white wine

4 shallots, minced

¼ cup champagne or other white
    wine vinegar

6 fresh flat-leaf parsley sprigs

2 tablespoons fresh lemon juice

2 tablespoons minced fresh thyme,
    or 2 teaspoons dried thyme

2 sprigs fresh rosemary, or 2
    teaspoons dried rosemary

1 cup (2 sticks) cold unsalted
    butter, cut into small pieces

BEVERAGES

SPARKLING FRUIT PUNCH

Rum and Fruit Punch

RED RUM PUNCH

Pink Lady

RUSSIAN HILL MARTINI

Sangría

WATERMELON AGUA FRESCA

San Francisco Coffee

HOT BUTTERED RUM

Lemon-Ginger Iced Tea

GRAPEFRUIT SMOOTHIE

Iced Sun Tea

MANGO-ORANGE LASSI

Sparkling Fruit Punch

SERVES 30

You don't have to use French Champagne to get good results in this crowd-pleasing punch, as California produces some fine sparkling wines, including Gloria Ferrer, Domain Chandon, and Iron Horse. Serve this for a spring or summertime luncheon.

3 cups unsweetened pineapple
    juice, chilled

1 cup guava juice, chilled

1 bottle Riesling wine, chilled

¼ cup Cognac

¼ cup Grand Marnier or other
    orange-flavored liqueur

1 lemon, sliced

1 orange, sliced

2 cups fresh raspberries

Ice cubes

2 bottles sparkling wine, chilled

1. In a large punch bowl, combine all the ingredients except the ice and sparkling wine. Stir. Keep refrigerated until ready to serve. Just before serving, add the ice and sparkling wine.

Rum and Fruit Punch

Tropical nectars and fresh mint leaves make this a refreshing punch. For a beautiful presentation, add fresh slices of lemon and orange and mint leaves to a bundt cake pan, fill it with cold water, and freeze until ready to serve. Place the ice ring in the punch bowl at the last minute.

1. In a blender or food processor, puree the mint leaves and boiling water until smooth. In a large punch bowl, combine all the remaining ingredients except the ice and mix. Add the mint puree and stir. Refrigerate until ready to serve.

30 fresh mint leaves

¼ cup boiling water

2 cups papaya nectar

2 cups passion fruit nectar

1½ cups lemon-lime soda

1 cup dark rum

1 cup light rum

1 cup fresh orange juice

¼ cup fresh lemon juice

¼ cup superfine sugar

1 teaspoon vanilla extract

Ice for serving

Red Rum Punch

SERVES 1

This potent punch is made with REDRUM, a deep red rum produced in the Bay Area.

1. Fill a tall glass with ice and add all the remaining ingredients.

1 ounce REDRUM, Meyer's, or other dark rum

½ cup pineapple juice

½ cup cranberry juice

Ice cubes

Pink Lady

SERVES 4

A refreshing drink after a day in the sun. The blood orange juice
gives this drink extra fruit flavor and a slight red tinge.

6 ounces frozen pink lemonade
   concentrate

6 ounces half-and-half

6 ounces vodka

Juice of ½ blood orange

6 ice cubes

1. In a blender, combine all the ingredients and blend until smooth. Pour into 4 flute glasses and serve immediately.

Russian Hill Martini

SERVES 2

Traditional martinis are made with gin; in San Francisco, however, vodka is quite popular.
Ideally, these martinis should be enjoyed from a penthouse with a 180-degree view of San Francisco Bay.

4 ounces vodka

1 ounce dry vermouth

2 pimiento-stuffed green olives

1. Pour the vodka and vermouth into a cocktail shaker filled half full of ice. Shake. Strain into Martini glasses and garnish each with an olive.

Sangría

SERVES 12 TO 16

This is one time when the best wine isn't needed to get the best result. Use an inexpensive fruity Merlot.

1. In a large punch bowl, combine all the ingredients except the ice cubes. Refrigerate for 4 to 6 hours. Taste for sweetness, then add the ice.

4 cups fresh blood orange or
  regular orange juice
3 bottles dry red wine, preferably
  Merlot
4 oranges, thinly sliced
6 lemons, thinly sliced
8 limes, thinly sliced
¾ cup sugar, or more to taste
Ice cubes

Watermelon Agua Fresca

SERVES 2

The taquerias in San Francisco's Mission District serve the best burritos and soft tacos. Fresh fruit drinks made from papaya, guava, strawberry, and watermelon sit on the counters in huge glass containers. This recipe uses fresh watermelon for a refreshing sweet drink the entire family will enjoy.

1. In a blender, combine all the ingredients and blend until smooth. Pour into tall glasses and serve immediately.

2 cups chopped watermelon,
  seeded
¼ cup sugar
1 cup water
1 cup ice cubes

San Francisco Coffee

SERVES 6

Peet's coffee, a Berkeley brand, is known for its intense French roast flavor. The most ardent coffee-lovers drink it black, but this drink is guaranteed to take the chill out of a foggy day.

4 cups hot strong coffee

⅔ cup whiskey

3 tablespoons packed brown sugar

6 cinnamon sticks

1. In a tall heatproof pitcher, pour the hot coffee over the whiskey and sugar and stir until the sugar has dissolved. Pour into warmed mugs and add a cinnamon stick to each serving.

Hot Buttered Rum

SERVES 4

This drink will really warm you up!

½ cup packed brown sugar

½ cup (1 stick) unsalted butter,
   cut into pieces

1 teaspoon ground cinnamon

1 teaspoon freshly grated nutmeg

¼ teaspoon ground cloves

2 cups water

⅔ cup dark rum

1. In a small saucepan, combine the sugar, butter, cinnamon, nutmeg, and cloves. Add the water. Bring to a boil over medium-high heat, stirring constantly. Reduce heat and simmer for 5 minutes. Add the rum and ladle into heated cups.

Lemon-Ginger Iced Tea

SERVES 8

This "tea" is really a tisane, or herb tea. Fresh ginger and lemon juice make a spicy drink with a sweet finish.

1. In a medium saucepan, combine the ginger, honey, lemon juice, and water. Bring to a boil. Let cool. Serve over ice in tall glasses, with a lemon wedge and a sprig of lemon verbena.

One 4-inch piece of fresh ginger, peeled and cut into paper-thin slices

⅓ cup orange blossom or other mild flavored honey

Juice of 2 lemons, plus 8 lemon wedges

8 cups cold water

Ice cubes

Sprig of lemon verbena for garnish (optional)

Grapefruit Smoothie

SERVES 4

A delicious low-calorie smoothie to serve before brunch or as a nutritious afternoon snack.

1. In a blender, combine all the ingredients and blend until smooth. Serve in tall glasses.

3½ cups fresh pink grapefruit juice

3 ripe bananas, peeled and chopped

2 cups crushed ice

1 tablespoon orange blossom honey

Iced Sun Tea

SERVES 4

When you don't want to heat up the house but want a refreshing pitcher of tea,
steep the tea in the sun, at room temperature, or in the refrigerator.
Tea and Company, of San Francisco, offers a wide variety of imported teas.

3 tablespoons loose Russian,
orange pekoe, or other black tea
leaves

4 cups cold water

Juice of 2 lemons

Juice of 1 blood orange or Valencia
orange

¼ to ½ cup superfine sugar

Ice cubes

Lemon or orange slices for garnish

1. In a 6-cup glass container, combine the tea and water. Cover and let sit in strong sunlight for 2 to 3 hours, at room temperature for 6 hours, or in the refrigerator overnight. Add the lemon and orange juices. Stir in the sugar to taste. Pour through a strainer into ice-filled glasses. Garnish with lemon or orange slices.

Mango-Orange Lassi

SERVES 2

An Indian favorite, this yogurt-based drink is light and refreshing.
Cardamom seeds are very potent so use a smaller amount, if desired.

1½ cups plain yogurt

1 ripe mango, peeled and cut from
the pit

2 teaspoons grated orange zest

2 tablespoons fresh orange juice

3 tablespoons sugar

¼ teaspoon ground cardamom

10 ice cubes

1. In a blender, combine all the ingredients and process until well pureed. Pour into tall glasses and serve.

DESSERTS

ROSE GERANIUM POUND CAKE

Toasted Coconut–Lemon Angel Food Cake

WARM CHOCOLATE-BROWNIE CUPS

Apple Cake with Hot Caramel Sauce

CHOCOLATE FUDGE CAKE

Warm Upside-Down Pear Cake with Tangerine Custard Sauce

PUMPKIN CHEESECAKE IN A GINGERSNAP CRUST

North Beach Tiramisù

BLACKBERRY COBBLER

Strawberry-Mango Cobbler

Peach-Almond Cobbler

Cranapple-Currant Pie

Raspberry-Fig Galette

Caramelized Pears with Ginger Crisp

Lavender-Essence Lemon Tart in a Shortbread Crust

Crustless Santa Rosa Plum and Almond Tart

Baked Banana Tart with Macadamia Nuts and Caramel Sauce

Aprico t and Olallieberry Tart in a Cornmeal Crust

Chocolate-Espresso Cookies

Meyer Lemon Cookies

Chocolate-Walnut Biscotti

Molasses Sugar Cookies

Coconut and Oatmeal with Chocolate Chip and Raisin Cookies

Mocha Meringue Kisses

Oatmeal-Cherry Cookies

Perfect Chocolate Chip Cookies

Strawberry Granita

Blueberry-Banana Brûlée

Summer-Berry Pudding

Crystallized Ginger and Citrus-Rice Pudding

Ginger and Green Tea Sorbet

Rose Geranium Pound Cake

SERVES 10

This old-fashioned pound cake is subtly perfumed with rose geranium leaves.
Be sure to use unsprayed leaves. If you like, substitute 1 tablespoon grated lemon zest
for the geranium leaves. For an elaborate presentation, decorate the cake with edible flowers
that have been painted with an egg white wash, dipped in superfine sugar, and dried.

WINE SUGGESTION BY KRIS HARRIMAN: TRIA LATE-HARVEST PINOT NOIR

20 small rose geranium leaves

2 cups (4 sticks) unsalted butter
   at room temperature

2 cups granulated sugar

6 eggs at room temperature

1 teaspoon rosewater

2 teaspoons pure vanilla extract

1 teaspoon salt

4 cups cake flour

¾ cup half-and-half

1. Preheat the oven to 325°F. Butter and flour a 9-inch round spring-form pan or a 10-inch bundt or tube pan. Arrange the rose geranium leaves around the bottom of the pan, undersides up.

2. In a large bowl, cream the butter and sugar together until light and fluffy. Beat in the eggs one at a time. Add the rosewater, vanilla, and salt and beat well. Alternately add the flour and half-and-half in thirds, mixing well after each addition. Carefully spoon some of the batter onto the leaves to anchor them in place, and then pour the rest of batter into the pan.

3. Bake for 50 to 60 minutes, or until a toothpick inserted in the center comes out clean. Remove from the oven and let cool for 10 minutes. Unmold the cake onto a serving plate and let cool completely.

Toasted Coconut—Lemon Angel Food Cake

This light lemony angel food cake with the added touch of coconut
is perfect with your afternoon tea. (See photograph, page 276.)

WINE SUGGESTION BY KRIS HARRIMAN: NAVARRO LATE HARVEST GEWÜRZTRAMINER

1. Preheat the oven to 325°F. Sift the cake flour, powdered sugar, and salt onto a sheet of waxed paper and set aside. In a large bowl, beat the egg whites until foamy. Add the cream of tartar and beat until soft peaks form. Gradually beat in the granulated sugar, until stiff glossy peaks form. Finally, blend in the vanilla and lemon zest.

2. Sprinkle one-fourth of the flour mixture over the whites and, using a rubber spatula, gently fold the dry ingredients into the whites. Fold the shredded coconut into the whites, then fold in the flour mixture in fourths.

3. Carefully pour the batter into an ungreased 10-inch tube pan. Bake in the bottom third of the oven until the top is light golden and the cake springs back when touched, 45 to 50 minutes. Invert the pan and let the cake cool completely. To remove the cake from the pan, tilt the pan on its side and tap the bottom against the counter to loosen the cake. Rotate the pan, tapping a few more times as you turn it, until the cake comes free.

4. TO MAKE ICING: Preheat the oven to 325°F. Spread the coconut shavings on a baking sheet and toast in the oven for 3 to 5 minutes, or until light golden. Remove and set aside. Sift the powdered sugar into a small saucepan and stir in the lemon juice and rum to make a smooth paste. Heat the glaze over medium-high heat until just warm to the touch. Pour over the top of the cake or individually sliced pieces, then sprinkle with the toasted coconut.

1 cup sifted cake flour

1⅓ cups powdered sugar

¼ teaspoon salt

12 egg whites at room temperature

1½ teaspoons cream of tartar

1 cup granulated sugar

1 teaspoon pure vanilla extract

2 teaspoons finely grated lemon zest

½ cup unsweetened shredded coconut

LEMON-RUM ICING:

2 cups sweetened coconut shavings

2 cups powdered sugar

3 tablespoons strained fresh lemon juice

1 tablespoon dark rum

Warm Chocolate-Brownie Cups

These individual cakes with an oozing, velvety chocolate center
will delight the child in everyone. They can be made ahead of time and
refrigerated until the next day, or frozen. (See photograph, page 277.)

6 ounces bittersweet chocolate,
    chopped, preferably Scharffen
    Berger

¾ cup (1½ sticks) unsalted butter

3 eggs at room temperature

3 egg yolks at room temperature

6 tablespoons sugar

1 tablespoon pure vanilla extract

½ teaspoon salt

5 tablespoons flour

¼ cup ground pecans (optional)

Crème fraîche, fresh raspberries,
    and fresh mint sprigs for
    garnish

1. Preheat the oven to 375°F. Butter and flour six 6-ounce custard cups
or ramekins. Set aside. In a medium saucepan, melt the chocolate with
the butter over low heat. Let cool slightly.

2. In a medium bowl, combine the eggs, egg yolks, and sugar. Beat until
the mixture is pale and a slowly dissolving ribbon forms on the surface
when beaters are lifted, about 10 minutes. Mix in the vanilla and salt.
Beat in the flour and optional pecans. Add the chocolate mixture and
beat until thick and glossy, about 5 minutes. Pour the batter equally
into the cups or ramekins. (At this point, the cups or ramekins can be
covered with plastic wrap and refrigerated or frozen until future use.)

3. TO BAKE: Remove the cups or ramekins from the refrigerator or
freezer and place immediately in the preheated oven. Bake until each
cake is set around the edges but moves slightly in the center, about 10
minutes, or 15 minutes if frozen; do not over bake. Let cool slightly. Run
a knife around the edges and invert onto dessert plates. Garnish each
with a dollop of crème fraîche, fresh raspberries, and a mint sprig.

MARIA HELM, PLUMPJACK CAFÉ: *You can melt chocolate in
your microwave oven by placing the chocolate in a microwave-
safe bowl and slowly melting the chocolate on low for several minutes.*

Apple Cake with Hot Caramel Sauce

SERVES 8

A trip north on Highway 101 leads to the orchards of Sonoma County. Bring home fresh apples for this wonderful dessert. Cakes with warm sauces have made a comeback on restaurant menus, and your family and friends will be delighted to be served this old-fashioned dessert at home.

1. Preheat the oven to 350°F. Grease a 9-inch round cake pan. In a blender or food processor, grind the pecans until fine.

2. In a large bowl, cream the butter and sugar together until fluffy. Add the eggs and beat until well blended. In a medium bowl, stir the flour, baking soda, salt, cinnamon, and nutmeg together. Stir the dry mixture into the wet mixture just until blended. Fold the apples and nuts in until blended.

3. Pour the batter into the prepared pan and smooth the top. Bake for 50 minutes, or until a toothpick inserted in the center comes out clean. Let cool on a wire rack for 15 minutes, then remove from the pan. The center may sink a bit.

4. TO MAKE THE SAUCE: In a small saucepan, melt the butter with the brown sugar and salt over medium heat. Bring to a boil, whisking constantly. Remove from heat and whisk in the vanilla and milk. Set aside and keep warm. To make ahead, let cool and store in an airtight container in the refrigerator for up to 3 days. Reheat over barely simmering water.

5. To serve, cut the cake into 8 wedges. Ladle a large spoonful of the hot caramel sauce onto each of 8 dessert plates. Place a wedge of cake on top of the sauce. Garnish with a spoonful of whipped cream and 2 apple slices.

DARCY TIZIO, FARALLON RESTAURANT: *Use red Jonathan apples for baking, Granny Smiths or pippins for pies and tarts, and Pink Ladies for sorbets and granitas.*

½ cup pecans

½ cup (1 stick) butter at room temperature

1 cup sugar

2 eggs at room temperature

1 cup all-purpose flour

1 teaspoon baking soda

1 teaspoon salt

1 teaspoon ground cinnamon

1 teaspoon freshly ground nutmeg

3 McIntosh, Gravenstein, or Granny Smith apples, peeled, cored and finely chopped, plus 16 apple slices for garnish

HOT CARAMEL SAUCE:

½ cup (1 stick) unsalted butter

1 cup packed light brown sugar

½ teaspoon salt

1½ teaspoons pure vanilla extract

½ cup evaporated milk

Whipped cream for garnish

Chocolate Fudge Cake

A wonderful, old-fashioned, moist chocolate cake to serve on special occasions. Scharffen Berger chocolate is an indulgence worth seeking out. Made by a small local company, Scharffen Berger has quickly become the chocolate choice of many connoisseurs. (See photograph, page 278.)

WINE SUGGESTION BY DAVID PAULEY: ROEDERER ESTATE SPARKLING WINE

2½ ounces unsweetened chocolate, preferably Scharffen Berger or Ghirardelli, chopped

⅔ cup (1⅓ sticks) unsalted butter, at room temperature

1¾ cups sugar

2 eggs at room temperature

2 teaspoons pure vanilla extract

2¼ cups all-purpose flour

1¼ teaspoons baking soda

1 teaspoon salt

1¼ cups ice water

CHOCOLATE FROSTING:

5 ounces unsweetened chocolate, preferably Scharffen Berger or Ghirardelli, chopped

4 cups powdered sugar

6 tablespoons hot water

2 eggs at room temperature

⅔ cup (1⅓ sticks) butter at room temperature

2 teaspoons pure vanilla extract

1 teaspoon salt

1. Preheat the oven to 350°F. Butter and lightly flour two 8-inch round cake pans. In a double boiler over barely simmering water, melt the chocolate. Set aside to cool.

2. In a large bowl, cream the butter and sugar together until fluffy. Beat in the eggs one at a time. Add the vanilla and blend. Beat for 5 minutes, or until light and fluffy. Add the cooled melted chocolate and mix until well incorporated.

3. In a small bowl, stir the flour, baking soda, and salt together. Add one fourth of the flour mixture to the butter mixture and mix thoroughly. Alternately add the remaining ice water and remaining flour mixture in thirds to the butter mixture, mixing well after each addition and scraping down the sides of the bowl.

4. Pour the batter into the prepared pans and bake in the center of the oven for 25 minutes, or until a toothpick inserted in the center still has a few moist crumbs. Let cool on wire racks for 3 minutes, then invert the cakes onto the wire racks, unmold, and let cool completely before frosting.

5. TO MAKE THE FROSTING: In a double boiler over barely simmering water, melt the chocolate. Set aside and let cool.

6. Prepare a pan of ice water large enough for you to set a large bowl in the center, and put in enough ice water to come at least 3 inches up the side of the bowl.

7. In a large bowl, combine the powdered sugar, hot water, eggs, butter, vanilla, salt, and melted chocolate. Beat until thoroughly incorporated. Place the bowl in the pan of ice water and continue beating the frosting until it becomes lighter and forms a ribbon on the surface of the frosting when you pick the beaters up. Do not overbeat, the frosting should just be spreadable. Remove the bowl from the ice water.

8. Place one cake layer on a serving plate and spread the top with some frosting. Place the second layer on top. Frost the top and sides of the cake. Let the icing set before serving.

DARCY TIZIO, FARALLON RESTAURANT: *My favorite way to melt chocolate is to bring a pot of water to a boil, turn heat off, then place a bowl of chopped chocolate over the steaming water. This should be enough heat to melt the chocolate. Also, be careful not to get water drops in your chocolate because it will make the chocolate become gritty.*

Warm Upside-Down Pear Cake
with Tangerine Custard Sauce

SERVES 8

An old-fashioned dessert, updated with a tangy, smooth sauce.
If tangerines are not in season, substitute oranges.

WINE SUGGESTION BY KRIS HARRIMAN: QUADY ESSENCIA (ORANGE MUSCAT)

TOPPING:

¾ cup sugar

3 tablespoons water

3 large Bartlett or Bosc pears,
  peeled, cored, and cut into thin
  slices

CAKE:

1½ cups all-purpose flour

1 tablespoon baking powder

1 teaspoon salt

½ cup (1 stick) plus 1 tablespoon
  unsalted butter at room
  temperature

1 cup plus 2 tablespoons sugar

2 large eggs at room temperature

2 teaspoons grated tangerine zest

3 tablespoons milk

3 tablespoons heavy cream

3 tablespoons Cognac

½ cup (2 ounces) chopped pecans

Tangerine Custard Sauce
  (recipe follows)

1. TO MAKE THE TOPPING: Preheat the oven to 350°F. Butter a 9-inch round cake pan. In a small saucepan, stir sugar and water over low heat until the sugar dissolves. Increase heat and simmer, without stirring, until the color is a deep amber, about 10 minutes, swirling the pan occasionally and brushing down the sides with a wet pastry brush. Pour the caramel into the prepared pan, tilting to coat the bottom. Overlap the pears in concentric circles on top of the caramel.

2. TO MAKE THE CAKE: In a small bowl, stir the flour, baking powder, and salt together. In a large bowl, cream the butter and sugar together until fluffy. Add the eggs and zest and beat until light and fluffy. In a small bowl, combine the milk, cream, and Cognac. Alternately add the flour mixture and milk mixture to the batter in thirds, stirring to blend after each addition. Stir in the nuts. Pour the batter over the pears.

3. Bake until the cake is golden and a tester inserted in the center comes out clean, about 1 hour. Let cool in pan for 5 minutes. Run a knife around the edges, place a platter over the cake, and invert. Let rest for 1 minute, then remove the pan. Serve the cake warm, with the cold sauce on the side.

tangerine custard sauce

1. In a medium bowl, whisk the sugar and egg yolks together. In a small, heavy saucepan, bring the half-and-half and zest just to a simmer; do not boil. Gradually whisk half the hot mixture into the yolk mixture. Return to the saucepan. Cook over medium heat, stirring constantly, until the custard thickens and coats a spoon, about 5 minutes; do not boil. Strain the custard into a clean bowl. Whisk in the tangerine juice and vanilla. Refrigerate for at least 2 hours or up to 2 days.

¼ cup sugar

2 egg yolks at room temperature

1 cup half-and-half

Grated zest of 2 tangerines

1 teaspoon fresh tangerine juice

1 teaspoon pure vanilla extract

Pumpkin Cheesecake in a Gingersnap Crust

SERVES 12

This cheesecake could replace pumpkin pie at your Thanksgiving feast. The gingersnap crust is enhanced with hazelnuts and crystallized ginger. You can find crystallized ginger at most supermarkets, or order it from Williams-Sonoma (see Resources, page 311).

GINGERSNAP CRUST:

1½ cups ground crushed ginger-snap cookies or crisp-baked Molasses Sugar Cookies (page 296), broken up

¾ cup hazelnuts, toasted and skinned (see page 18)

3 tablespoons packed brown sugar

1 tablespoon crystallized ginger, finely chopped

6 tablespoons butter, melted

FILLING:

Three 8-ounce packages cream cheese at room temperature

1 cup firmly packed brown sugar

1½ cups canned pumpkin puree

½ cup heavy cream

⅓ cup pure maple syrup

1 tablespoon pure vanilla extract

1 teaspoon ground cinnamon

½ teaspoon ground allspice

1 teaspoon salt

4 large eggs at room temperature

1. TO MAKE THE CRUST: Preheat the oven to 325°F. In a blender or food processor, grind the cookies until finely ground. Add the hazelnuts, brown sugar, and ginger and pulse until ground. Pour into a bowl, add the butter, and mix until well combined. Press the mixture into the bottom and 2 inches up the sides of a 9-inch round springform pan. Bake for 8 minutes, or until lightly browned. Let cool.

2. TO MAKE THE FILLING: In a large bowl, beat the cream cheese and brown sugar together until smooth. Add the pumpkin and mix well. Add the cream, maple syrup, vanilla, cinnamon, allspice, and salt, and beat until smooth and fluffy. Beat in the eggs, one at a time, until just combined.

3. Pour the batter into the prepared crust. Bake the cheesecake in the center of the oven until it is puffed and the center is set, 1 to 1½ hours. Transfer to a wire rack and let cool for 30 minutes. Run a knife around the sides to loosen the cheesecake. Let cool completely. Cover and refrigerate overnight. Unmold the cake before serving.

SAN FRANCISCO—STYLE EGGS BENEDICT, *page 240*

CRAB SALAD NIÇOISE, *page 246*

PANFRIED TROUT WITH BACON AND SAGE, *page 249*

TOASTED COCONUT–LEMON ANGEL FOOD CAKE, *page 265*

WARM CHOCOLATE-BROWNIE CUPS, *page 266*

CHOCOLATE FUDGE CAKE, *pages 268–269*

LAVENDER-ESSENCE LEMON TART IN A SHORTBREAD CRUST, *page 288*

BAKED BANANA TART WITH MACADAMIA NUTS
AND CARAMEL SAUCE, *pages 290–291*

280

North Beach Tiramisù

SERVES 10

The Italian enclave in San Francisco, North Beach bustles with sidewalk cafés, coffeehouses, and Italian restaurants. Tiramisù is a traditional espresso-soaked dessert layered with a rich mascarpone cheese filling. Buy good-quality ladyfingers or pound cake from a bakery, or make your own.

WINE SUGGESTION BY DAVID PAULEY: HONIG NAPA CABERNET

1. Preheat the oven to 325°F. Place the ladyfingers or pound cake slices on a baking sheet and bake for 2 to 3 minutes. Remove from the oven and let cool. In a small bowl, combine the espresso, 1 tablespoon sugar, and hot water. Stir in 3 tablespoons of the rum or Marsala and set aside.

2. In a large bowl, beat the egg yolks and ¼ cup sugar until the mixture forms a slowly dissolving ribbon on the surface when the beaters are lifted. With a wooden spoon, blend in the cheese until smooth. Add the remaining 1 tablespoon rum the lemon juice, and vanilla. In a deep bowl, beat the cream with the powdered sugar until soft peaks form. Fold into the egg mixture. In a large bowl, beat the egg whites until stiff, glossy peaks form. Fold into the cream mixture.

3. To assemble, dip the ladyfingers, one at a time, into the espresso (do not soak) and place in a 9-by-13-inch glass baking dish. Sprinkle half of the grated chocolate over the ladyfingers. Spread half the cream mixture over the fingers. Add another layer of ladyfingers dipped in the espresso mixture and the remaining grated chocolate. Spread the remaining cream mixture over. Dust the top with cocoa powder. Place in the refrigerator for 4 hours. Serve.

48 small ladyfingers or finger-sized slices of pound cake

2 tablespoons instant espresso powder

1 tablespoon plus ¼ cup sugar

1 cup hot water

2 eggs, separated

4 tablespoons light rum or Marsala wine

6 ounces mascarpone cheese or natural cream cheese at room temperature

1 tablespoon fresh lemon juice

1 teaspoon pure vanilla extract

2 cups heavy cream

1 tablespoon powdered sugar

12 ounces bittersweet chocolate, grated

¼ cup unsweetened cocoa powder for dusting

Blackberry Cobbler

SERVES 12

Summer is a pastry chef's favorite season and it's difficult to pass up any
fruit dessert featured on a menu. This cobbler is a simple and delicious summer
dessert. Try it also with a combination of sliced fresh peaches and berries.

8 cups fresh blackberries

3 tablespoons sugar

1 tablespoon flour

COBBLER TOPPING:

2 cups all-purpose flour

2 cups sugar

1 teaspoon salt

3 eggs at room temperature,
    beaten

¾ cup (1½ sticks) unsalted
    butter, melted

1. Preheat the oven to 375°F. Put the blackberries, sugar, and flour in a
9-by-13-inch baking dish and gently mix together.

2. TO MAKE THE TOPPING: In a large bowl, stir the flour, sugar, and salt
together. Mix in the beaten eggs; the dough will be very sticky. Spread
the dough evenly over the berries. Pour the melted butter evenly over
the dough. Bake for 45 minutes, or until lightly browned. Serve warm.

DARCY TIZIO, FARALLON RESTAURANT: *When cooking or
baking with butter, always use unsalted butter. This will enable
you to have better control over the salt content of your dish.*

Strawberry-Mango Cobbler

SERVES 12

Strawberries and mangos make a luscious cobbler that will remind you of a tropical sunset.

1. Preheat the oven to 375°F. Cut the strawberries into halves or quarters, depending on their size. Cut the mango flesh into pieces about the size of the strawberries. In a bowl, gently mix the fruit together with the sugar, cinnamon, cardamom, and flour. Pour into a 9-by-13-inch baking pan. Add the cobbler topping. Bake for 45 minutes, or until golden brown.

4 cups fresh strawberries, hulled

3 mangoes, peeled and cut away
   from the pit

½ cup sugar

½ teaspoon ground cinnamon

½ teaspoon ground cardamom

2 tablespoons flour

Cobbler Topping (page 282)

Peach-Almond Cobbler

SERVES 12

Peaches and almonds are a delicious combination. Use yellow peaches at their peak
of ripeness. Finish ripening the peaches in a paper bag overnight, if necessary.

3 tablespoons butter, melted

½ cup (2 ounces) slivered
almonds

4 pounds ripe peaches, peeled,
pitted, and sliced

2 tablespoons amaretto

Cobbler Topping (page 282)

1. Preheat the oven to 375°F. In a small skillet, melt the butter over
medium-high heat, and sauté the almonds, stirring constantly, for about
5 minutes, or until lightly browned. In a large bowl, gently mix the
peaches, amaretto, and the almonds.

2. Pour the fruit into a 9-by-13-inch glass baking dish. Add the cobbler
topping. Bake for 45 minutes, or until lightly browned. Serve warm.

Cranapple-Currant Pie

SERVES 8

A tangy combination of fruits makes this pie a favorite.
Serve it slightly warm, with vanilla bean ice cream.

1. TO MAKE THE DOUGH: In a food processor, pulse the flour, salt and sugar together quickly to mix. Add the butter and shortening and quickly pulse until the butter resembles small peas. Add the ice water and pulse until dough almost forms a ball. Or to make by hand, stir the flour, salt, and sugar together in a medium bowl. Cut in the butter and shortening with a pastry cutter or 2 knives until mixture resembles coarse meal. Stir in the water with a fork until all the ingredients are moistened. Form the dough into a ball with your hands. Remove and flatten dough into a disk and wrap in plastic wrap. Place in refrigerator for 30 minutes. Remove from refrigerator, and on a floured surface, roll pie crust to fit a 9-inch pie pan and keep in refrigerator until ready to use.

2. Preheat oven to 375°F. In a small bowl, combine the currants and water and let soak for 10 minutes.

3. Meanwhile, in a large saucepan, stir the sugar, flour, citrus zests, and cardamom or cinnamon together until blended. Stir in the cranberries, apples, lemon juice, currants, and any unabsorbed water. Bring to a boil, stirring, over medium heat. Reduce heat to a simmer and cook, stirring constantly, until the sugar dissolves and the filling thickens slightly, about 5 minutes. Stir in the butter and vanilla until blended.

4. On a lightly floured surface, roll out the dough to an 11-inch circle. Fit into a 9-inch pie pan. Trim the edges to a 1-inch overhang, fold dough under, and flute the edges. Pour in the filling, mounding it slightly in the center. Place on a baking sheet to catch any overflow and bake in the center of the oven for 45 to 50 minutes, or until the crust is nicely browned and the filling is bubbly. Transfer to a wire rack and let cool until warm.

PASTRY DOUGH:

1½ cups all-purpose flour

1 teaspoon salt

1 tablespoon sugar

8 tablespoons cold butter, cut into chunks

3 tablespoons shortening, frozen

¼ cup ice water

FILLING:

1¼ cups dried currants

¼ cup hot water

1½ cups sugar

3 tablespoons flour

½ teaspoon grated lemon zest

½ teaspoon grated orange zest

¼ teaspoon ground cardamom or cinnamon

3 cups fresh or frozen cranberries, coarsely chopped

3 tart apples, such as Granny Smith, peeled, cored, and finely chopped

½ teaspoon fresh lemon juice

1½ teaspoons unsalted butter

1 teaspoon pure vanilla extract

Raspberry-Fig Galette

SERVES 4

The combination of raspberries and figs makes this free-form tart a
beautiful centerpiece. Ripe figs should be soft and slightly wrinkled. Try Adriatic figs,
which have bright pink flesh inside a pale green skin, or Black Mission figs.

WINE SUGGESTIONS BY DEBBIE ZACHAREAS: HUSCH LATE HARVEST GEWÜRZTRAMINER,
BONNY DOON MUSCAT, SAUCELITO CANYON LATE HARVEST ZINFANDEL,
OR GREENWOOD RIDGE LATE HARVEST WHITE RIESLING

CRUST:

2 cups white pastry flour

1 tablespoon granulated sugar

1 teaspoon packed brown sugar

1 teaspoon salt

4 tablespoons cold unsalted
butter, cut into small pieces

¼ cup ice water

2½ cups fresh raspberries

¼ cup granulated sugar, plus
more for sprinkling

4 teaspoons packed brown sugar

3 tablespoons orange blossom or
other mild honey

1½ cups fresh figs, diced

4 tablespoons butter, melted

1. TO MAKE THE CRUST: In a medium bowl, stir the flour, sugars, and salt together. Using a pastry cutter or 2 knives, cut the butter into the flour until it resembles small peas. Sprinkle the cold water into the butter mixture and stir with a fork to combine. Gather the dough into a ball, wrap in plastic wrap, and refrigerate for at least 20 minutes or overnight.

2. Preheat the oven to 400°F. In a large bowl, combine the berries, sugars, and honey. On a lightly floured board, roll the dough into a 10-inch circle. Sprinkle the berry mixture in the center of the dough, leaving a 2-inch border. Top with the figs. Fold over the edges of the circle, pleating as you go. Brush melted butter over the dough and figs. Sprinkle with granulated sugar. Bake for 30 to 40 minutes, or until golden brown.

Caramelized Pears with Ginger Crisp

Make this dessert in early fall when winter pears are coming to market. Firm Bosc pears are good for caramelizing without breaking down. Asian pears are a nice alternative. Molasses Sugar Cookies (page 296), baked longer until crisp, can be used in place of gingersnaps.

1. Preheat the oven to 325°F. In a medium bowl, combine the pears, sugar, corn syrup, vanilla, apple brandy, and lemon juice and mix until evenly coated. Divide the pear mixture among six 4-inch ramekins.

2. TO MAKE THE TOPPING: In a small bowl, cut the butter into pea-sized pieces and mix with the cookies until blended. Stir in the orange juice. Top each ramekin with the topping. Bake for about 25 minutes, or until the top is slightly browned and the pear mixture bubbles slightly around edges. Let cool slightly and serve warm.

4 firm but ripe Bosc pears, peeled, cored, and cut into 1-inch pieces

½ cup sugar

1½ tablespoons corn syrup

1 teaspoon pure vanilla extract

1 tablespoon Calvados or applejack (apple brandy)

1 teaspoon fresh lemon juice

GINGER CRISP TOPPING:

2 tablespoons unsalted butter

2½ cups crushed gingersnaps (about 12 cookies)

1 tablespoon orange juice

Lavender-Essence Lemon Tart in a Shortbread Crust

SERVES 8

The unique pairing and subtle addition of fresh lavender blossoms
makes this lemon tart special. Choose an organic lavender, free of pesticides.
Serve with English tea for an afternoon treat. (See photograph, page 279.)

SHORTBREAD CRUST:

¾ cup (1½ sticks) cold unsalted
   butter
¼ cup granulated sugar
1 tablespoon powdered sugar
2 cups all-purpose flour

FILLING:

1 cup granulated sugar
2 tablespoons flour
½ teaspoon baking powder
½ teaspoon salt
2 eggs at room temperature, beaten
1 teaspoon grated Meyer lemon or
   regular lemon zest
2 tablespoons fresh Meyer lemon or
   regular lemon juice
2 tablespoons fresh lavender
   blossoms, minced

LEMON GLAZE:

½ cup powdered sugar, sifted
1 tablespoon fresh lemon juice,
   preferably Meyer lemon
1 tablespoon melted butter

Fresh lavender blossoms for garnish

1. TO MAKE THE CRUST: Preheat oven to 325°F. In a medium saucepan, melt the butter over low heat. Remove from heat, add both sugars, and stir to combine. Stir in the flour. Let cool for 15 minutes. The dough will still be warm. Press the dough onto the bottom and up the sides of a 9-inch tart pan with a removable bottom. Bake for 15 minutes, or until light golden. Let cool.

2. TO MAKE THE FILLING: In a medium bowl, stir the sugar, flour, baking powder, and salt together. Add the remaining ingredients and stir to blend. Pour into the partially baked crust. Bake for 25 minutes, or until the crust is golden. Let cool.

3. TO MAKE THE GLAZE: Combine all the ingredients and spread over the cooled tart. Decorate the tart with lavender blossoms.

Crustless Santa Rosa Plum and Almond Tart

SERVES 8

Tree-ripened plums are your best bet, so venture to your farmers' market to get the freshest available. This dessert is easy to prepare and is good hot or cold. Use other fruits in season like pears, peaches, apricots, or apples.

WINE SUGGESTION BY DAVID PAULEY: LIVINGSTON STANLEY'S SELECTION CABERNET

1. Preheat the oven to 350°F. Butter a fluted 9-by-1-inch round ceramic baking dish or tart pan.

2. In a blender or food processor, process the almonds and the ½ cup of sugar until finely ground. In a medium bowl, stir the almond mixture, flour, and salt together. Stir in the eggs, milk, melted butter, and vanilla until smooth. Pour batter into the prepared dish.

3. Place the plums, cut-side down, on a cutting board and cut into ¼-inch-thick slices without cutting through at one end, to make a fan. Slide each plum half onto a metal spatula and set it on top of the batter skin side up. Gently press each plum down into the batter to fan it out so only the surface of the fruit is showing. Sprinkle the 2 tablespoons sugar evenly over the tart. Scatter the butter pieces over the tart.

4. Bake in the upper third of the oven until golden brown and slightly puffed, 40 to 45 minutes. Serve warm, garnished with whipped cream or crème fraîche.

GERALD HIRIGOYEN, FRINGALE RESTAURANT AND PASTIS RESTAURANT: *To sweeten whipping cream, try adding powdered sugar instead of granulated sugar. It not only dissolves easier and more uniformly, but it also helps to stabilize the whipped cream because it contains cornstarch. Often, however, I prefer serving whipped cream without any added sugar. Unsweetened whipped cream has its own natural sweetness and is a striking counterbalance to very sweet desserts. The same goes for crème fraîche.*

1 ¼ cups (7 ounces) whole
  blanched almonds

½ cup plus 2 tablespoons
  granulated sugar

⅓ cup all-purpose flour

½ teaspoon salt

2 eggs at room temperature,
  slightly beaten

¼ cup milk

4 tablespoons butter, melted, plus
  2 tablespoons cut into small
  chunks

1 teaspoon pure vanilla extract

5 Santa Rosa or other large
  plums, halved and pitted

Whipped cream or crème fraîche
  for garnish

Baked Banana Tart with Macadamia Nuts and Caramel Sauce

SERVES 6 TO 8

A spectacular finalé for a special dinner, this rich tart is topped with a warm caramel sauce. For true indulgence, serve with chocolate ice cream. (See photograph, page 280)

WINE SUGGESTION BY KRIS HARRIMAN: DOLCE LATE HARVEST TABLE WINE

CRUST:

1 cup all-purpose flour

¼ cup sugar

½ teaspoon salt

6 tablespoons cold unsalted
   butter, cut into pieces

2 tablespoons frozen chilled
   vegetable shortening

1 teaspoon pure vanilla extract

1 egg yolk at room temperature

BANANA FILLING:

4 large ripe bananas, peeled

1 cup macadamia nuts, lightly
   toasted and coarsely chopped
   (see page 18)

1 tablespoon butter, melted

1 tablespoon sugar

1. TO MAKE THE CRUST: In a food processor, combine the flour, sugar, and salt and process until blended. Add the butter and shortening and quickly pulse until mixture resembles small peas. Add vanilla and the egg yolk and process until mixture almost forms a ball. Remove from processor, gather in a ball, and form a disk. Cover with plastic wrap and refrigerate for 30 minutes. Or, to make by hand, stir the flour, sugar, and salt together in a medium bowl. Cut in the butter and shortening with a pastry blender or two knives until mixture resembles coarse meal. Stir in the vanilla and egg yolk until all the dry ingredients are moistened. Remove from processor or bowl and gather in a ball. Flatten into a disk, cover with plastic wrap, and refrigerate for 30 minutes.

2. Preheat the oven to 450°F. Remove the dough from the refrigerator, and on a lightly floured surface, roll out dough to a 9-inch circle and press into the bottom of a 9-inch springform pan. Bake for 12 to 14 minutes, or until lightly browned. Remove from oven and let cool.

3. Slice bananas through on the diagonal. Lay the slices, overlapping slightly, onto the pastry round in concentric circles until the pastry is completely covered in banana slices. Sprinkle the macadamia nuts over the tart. Brush the top of the bananas with the melted butter, and sprinkle sugar over the tart. Place in the oven and bake for 10 minutes, or until lightly browned. Remove from the oven.

4. TO MAKE THE SAUCE: In a small, heavy saucepan, over medium-high heat, stir sugar and water until the sugar dissolves. Boil the sugar until the syrup is amber colored, stirring occasionally, about 8 minutes. Remove from heat and quickly add the cream, butter, vanilla, and salt, and stir with a whisk to combine. Return the pan to low heat, and stir until the caramel is smooth and the color deepens, about 5 minutes. The caramel can be refrigerated for up to 2 days and reheated gently over low heat. Set aside and keep warm until serving. To make ahead, let cool, cover, and refrigerate.

5. TO SERVE: Cut the tart into 6 or 8 wedges and place on individual serving plates with a scoop of chocolate ice cream, if you like. Pass warmed caramel sauce.

CARAMEL SAUCE:

¾ *cup sugar*

⅓ *cup water*

⅓ *cup heavy cream*

5 tablespoons unsalted butter

1 teaspoon pure vanilla extract

½ *teaspoon salt*

Chocolate ice cream for serving
  (optional)

Apricot and Olallieberry Tart in a Cornmeal Crust

SERVES 6

A subtle hint of cornmeal adds a slight crunch to the crust of this tart. You can use
fresh peaches or nectarines in place of the apricots, and raspberries and or blueberries in place
of the olallieberries. This is a quick tart because the crust doesn't need to be rolled out!

6 ripe apricots, pitted and cut
  into eighths
1 cup olallieberries or blackberries
¼ cup granulated sugar

CORNMEAL CRUST:

1 cup all-purpose flour
¼ cup cornmeal
¼ cup sugar
½ teaspoon salt
½ cup (1 stick) cold unsalted
  butter, cut into pieces
1 egg yolk at room temperature
1 teaspoon pure vanilla extract

⅓ cup apricot preserves (optional)
Crème fraîche or mascarpone
  cheese for garnish (optional)

1. Preheat the oven to 400°F. In a medium bowl, combine the fruit and
sugar. Mix and set aside.

2. TO MAKE THE CRUST: In a food processor, combine the flour, cornmeal, sugar, and salt and quickly pulse. Add the butter, egg yolk, and
vanilla and pulse until mixture starts to form a ball. Or to make by hand,
stir the flour, cornmeal, and salt together in a medium bowl. Have the
butter at room temperature. Stir the butter, egg yolk, and vanilla into
the flour mixture until blended.

3. Press the dough into an ungreased 8-inch tart pan with removable
bottom. Place the tart in refrigerator for 30 minutes, or in the freezer
for 10 minutes. Remove from the refrigerator and bake for 15 minutes,
or until lightly browned. Remove from the oven.

4. Reduce the oven temperature to 350°F. Arrange the fruit in the crust.
Bake for 15 to 20 minutes, or until the apricots are tender. Remove from
the oven and let cool on a wire rack. To glaze the tart, if you like, in a
small saucepan, heat the apricot preserves until almost bubbling. With a
pastry brush, brush preserves over the entire tart. Serve dolloped with
crème fraîche or mascarpone, if you like.

Chocolate-Espresso Cookies

MAKES 30 COOKIES

San Franciscans have had a long love affair with Italian coffee.
These mocha flavored cookies will give you a lift, whether
dipped in a steaming cup of java or an ice-cold glass of milk.

1. Preheat the oven to 350°F. In a small bowl, stir the flour, baking powder, and salt together. In a heavy saucepan, melt the bittersweet chocolate and butter together over low heat. In a medium bowl, beat the eggs, sugar, espresso powder, and vanilla together. Stir in the warm chocolate mixture. Add the flour mixture and stir until blended. Fold in the chocolate chips and nuts. Refrigerate the dough for 1 hour.

2. Drop the dough in generous tablespoonfuls 1½ inches apart on non-stick or greased baking sheets. Bake until the tops crack but the cookies are still soft inside, about 12 minutes. Let cool on the pan for 5 minutes, then transfer to wire racks.

HUBERT KELLER, FLEUR DE LYS RESTAURANT: *To skin hazelnuts, preheat the oven to 375°F. Place the hazelnuts in a single layer on a baking sheet. Using a spray bottle, mist them with water, and place them in the oven. Toast for 7 to 8 minutes. This small amount of water sprayed on the hazelnuts creates enough steam to loosen the skins so that they slip right off the nuts.*

6 tablespoons flour

¼ teaspoon baking powder

¼ teaspoon salt

8 ounces bittersweet chocolate, preferably Scharffen Berger, chopped

½ cup (1 stick) unsalted butter

2 eggs at room temperature

¾ cup sugar

3 tablespoons instant espresso powder

2¼ teaspoons vanilla extract

1 cup semisweet chocolate chips

1 cup hazelnuts, toasted, skinned, and chopped (see Chef's Tip)

Meyer Lemon Cookies

MAKES 2 ½ DOZEN COOKIES

Meyer lemons have a thin skin and a delicate flavor. These shortbread-like
cookies take minutes to make, and the dough can be made ahead
and frozen in a log form to bake for unexpected guests. Serve them with
your favorite ice cream or Ginger and Green Tea Sorbet (page 305).

1 Meyer lemon or regular lemon

1 cup sugar

1 cup (2 sticks) cold unsalted
*   butter, cut into small pieces*

2⅓ cups all purpose flour

½ teaspoon baking soda

½ teaspoon salt

Colored sugar for sprinkling
*   (optional)*

1. Using a paring knife, cut the yellow zest from the lemon in strips, leaving the white pith. In a food processor, combine the lemon zest and sugar and process for 1 minute, or until the zest is the size of the sugar granules. Add the butter and process until fluffy. Add the flour, baking soda, and salt and process for 25 seconds. Form the dough into a log and cover with plastic wrap and chill the dough for 2 hours. (Or, cover with aluminum foil and freeze for up to 1 month. Cut into slices and bake in a preheated oven for 10 minutes.)

2. Or to make by hand, grind the zest and sugar together in a blender. Have the butter at room temperature. In a medium bowl, cream the butter and the sugar mixture together until light and fluffy. In another medium bowl, stir the flour, baking soda, and salt together. Stir the flour mixture into the butter mixture until blended. Form the dough into a log and cover with plastic wrap and chill for 2 hours.

3. Preheat the oven to 350°F. Cut the log into ¼-inch slices and place on ungreased baking sheets. Sprinkle with colored sugars, if you like. Bake for 8 to 10 minutes, or until lightly golden. Transfer to wire racks and let cool.

MARIA HELM, PLUMPJACK CAFÉ: *When Meyer lemons are in season, zest, juice, and freeze them so that when the season is over so you can keep on enjoying their flavor.*

Chocolate-Walnut Biscotti

MAKES 24 BISCOTTI

A great dipping cookie that goes well with cappuccino or Vin Santo
as a pick-me-up or after-dinner treat. For an authentic San Francisco note,
use Ghirardelli Chocolate, manufactured in the Bay Area since 1852.

1. Preheat the oven to 350°F. In a medium bowl, stir the flour, cocoa,
baking soda, and salt together. In a large bowl, beat the butter and sugar
together until fluffy. Add the eggs and beat until combined. Stir in the
flour mixture to form a stiff dough. Stir in the nuts and chocolate chips.
2. Form the dough into 2 flattened logs, 12 inches by 2 inches, and
sprinkle with the powdered sugar. Place the logs on a baking sheet and
bake for 35 minutes, or until lightly browned. Let cool on the pan for 5
minutes. Cut the logs into ¾-inch slices. Arrange the slices cut-side down
on baking sheets and bake for 5 minutes on each side. Let cool on
wire racks.

2 cups all-purpose flour

*⅓ cup unsweetened cocoa powder,
preferably Ghirardelli*

1 teaspoon baking soda

1 teaspoon salt

*6 tablespoons (¾ stick) butter at
room temperature*

1 cup granulated sugar

2 large eggs at room temperature

*1 cup (4 ounces) walnuts or
almonds, toasted and chopped
coarsely*

*¾ cup semisweet chocolate chips,
preferably Ghirardelli*

*2 tablespoons powdered sugar,
sifted*

Molasses Sugar Cookies

MAKES ABOUT 4 DOZEN COOKIES

These old-fashioned cookies are moist and chewy and conjure up images of
fall weather and Halloween. Serve these delicious autumn treats with hot apple cider.

¾ cup (1½ sticks) unsalted
    butter, melted and cooled

1 cup sugar, plus ½ cup sugar for
    coating

¼ cup light molasses

1 egg at room temperature

2 cups all-purpose flour

2 teaspoons baking soda

1 teaspoon ground cloves

1 teaspoon ground ginger

1 teaspoon ground cinnamon

1 teaspoon salt

1. In a large bowl, combine the melted butter, the 1 cup sugar, the molasses, and egg. Beat well. In a medium bowl, stir the flour, baking soda, cloves, ginger, cinnamon, and salt together. Add to the butter mixture and beat well. Refrigerate for 30 minutes.

2. Preheat the oven to 375°F. Pour the ½ cup sugar into a shallow dish. Form tablespoons of chilled batter into 1-inch balls. Roll the balls in the sugar to coat evenly and place 2 inches apart on greased baking sheets. Bake for 8 to 10 minutes, or until lightly browned for soft cookies, and 10 to 12 minutes, or until golden brown, for crisper cookies.

Coconut and Oatmeal with Chocolate Chip and Raisin Cookies

MAKES 24 3-INCH COOKIES

These cookies are wonderfully moist with the addition of molasses. Make a double batch and freeze to have fresh cookies on hand at a moment's notice.

1. In a large bowl, cream the butter and the sugars together until fluffy. Add the eggs and beat well. Stir in the vanilla, molasses, and milk. In a medium bowl, stir the flour, baking soda, salt, and optional cinnamon together. Add to the wet ingredients and mix well to thoroughly incorporate. Add the oats and coconut and mix well. Add the chocolate chips, raisins, and optional nuts and mix until well incorporated. Refrigerate the dough for 1 hour.

2. Preheat the oven to 350°F. Drop the dough by large tablespoonfuls (or use a 3-inch ice cream scoop) onto ungreased baking sheets, 3 inches apart. Bake for 13 to 14 minutes, or until lightly browned, for soft, chewy cookies. Bake for 15 to 16 minutes for crisper cookies. Remove from the oven and let cool on the pans for 2 minutes then transfer to a wire rack to cool completely.

¾ cup (1½ sticks) unsalted butter
   at room temperature

1 cup packed brown sugar

½ cup granulated sugar

2 eggs at room temperature

2 teaspoons pure vanilla extract

2 tablespoons light molasses

¼ cup milk

1½ cups all-purpose flour

1 teaspoon baking soda

1 teaspoon salt

1 teaspoon ground cinnamon
   (optional)

2 cups old-fashioned oats

1 cup shredded unsweetened
   coconut

2 cups semisweet chocolate chips,
   preferably Ghirardelli

1 cup raisins

¼ cup walnuts (optional)

Mocha Meringue Kisses

MAKES 30 KISSES

Another sweet treat that combines two favorite flavors, chocolate and coffee.
These cookies will keep in an airtight container for up to 3 days.

½ ounce unsweetened chocolate,
    grated

¼ cup unsweetened cocoa powder

3 tablespoons cornstarch

½ cup powdered sugar, sifted

½ teaspoon instant coffee or
    espresso powder

½ teaspoon hot water

1 teaspoon pure vanilla extract

⅛ teaspoon almond extract

3 large egg whites at room
    temperature

⅛ teaspoon salt

⅔ cup granulated sugar

1. Preheat the oven to 275°F. Line several large baking sheets with parchment paper. In a small bowl, stir the chocolate, cocoa powder, cornstarch, and powdered sugar together until well blended. In a cup, stir the coffee powder, hot water, and vanilla and almond extracts together until the coffee dissolves.

2. In a large bowl, beat the egg whites until foamy. Add the salt and beat until soft peaks form. Immediately begin adding the granulated sugar, 2 tablespoons at a time, continuing to beat until all the sugar is incorporated and stiff, glossy peaks form. Beat the coffee mixture into the meringue until smooth and well incorporated. Using a rubber spatula, fold in the cocoa mixture just until evenly incorporated; do not overmix. Spoon the mixture into a pastry bag fitted with a ½-inch-diameter plain tip. Pipe quarter-sized portions 1½ inches apart onto the prepared pans. Alternatively, drop the mixture by small rounded teaspoonfuls.

3. Bake the cookies in the center of the oven for 17 to 20 minutes, or until crisp on the outside and lightly browned. Remove from the oven and let cool completely still attached to the paper, until completely cooled. Carefully peel the kisses from the paper. Store in an airtight container for up to 3 days.

Oatmeal-Cherry Cookies

MAKES ABOUT 1½ DOZEN COOKIES

Oatmeal cookies bring warm thoughts of home, hearth, and happiness. In this recipe, dried cherries are a tangy alternative to raisins. They also add a nice accent color to the cookies.

1. Preheat the oven to 350°F. In a small bowl, combine the oats, flour, salt, baking soda, and spices and mix. In a large bowl, cream the butter and sugars together until light and fluffy. Beat in the egg yolks and vanilla. Blend in the dry ingredients until thoroughly incorporated. Fold in the cherries or raisins. Drop tablespoon-sized portions of the dough 3 inches apart on a parchment-lined or nonstick baking sheet. Bake for about 12 minutes, or until lightly browned. Let cool on the pan for 3 minutes, then transfer to wire racks.

MARIA HELM, PLUMPJACK CAFÉ: *To soften brown sugar, place it in the microwave for 1 to 2 minutes. Use immediately.*

1 cup old-fashioned oats

1¼ cups all-purpose flour

½ teaspoon salt

1 teaspoon baking soda

½ teaspoon ground cinnamon

½ teaspoon ground cardamom

½ teaspoon ground nutmeg

½ cup (1 stick) butter at room temperature

½ cup packed brown sugar

½ cup granulated sugar

2 egg yolks at room temperature

1 teaspoon pure vanilla extract

½ cup dried cherries or raisins

Perfect Chocolate Chip Cookies

MAKES ABOUT 2 ½ DOZEN COOKIES

This is one of the best versions of an old favorite. Also try
peanut butter or butterscotch chips in place of the chocolate chips.

*1 cup (2 sticks) butter at room
temperature*

¾ cup packed brown sugar

¾ cup granulated sugar

2 eggs at room temperature

2 teaspoons pure vanilla extract

2½ cups all purpose flour

1 teaspoon salt

1 teaspoon baking soda

*2 cups semisweet chocolate chips,
preferably Ghirardelli*

*½ cup walnuts, chopped
(optional)*

1. Preheat the oven to 350°F. In a large bowl, beat the butter and sugars together until light and fluffy. Beat in the eggs and vanilla. Add the flour, salt, and baking soda and mix well. Fold in the chocolate chips and walnuts. Refrigerate the dough for 1 hour. Using an ice cream scoop or a tablespoon, drop the dough 2 inches apart onto parchment-lined or nonstick baking sheets. Bake for about 12 minutes, or until lightly browned. Let cool on the pan for 2 minutes, then transfer to wire racks.

FLO BRAKER, COOKBOOK AUTHOR: *Use ice cream scoops for measuring food consistently, quickly, and easily. They're great for scooping vegetable shortening, peanut butter, cookie dough, cupcakes, and muffin batter.*

Strawberry Granita

MAKES ABOUT 1 ½ QUARTS

A refreshing summertime snack or dessert, this granita is bursting with strawberry flavor.
It can also be frozen in popsicle molds. Fresh raspberries or blackberries can be
substituted for the strawberries. Adjust the amount of sugar to the sweetness of the fruit.

1. In a small saucepan, combine the water and sugar. Bring to a boil, then reduce heat to medium and cook until the sugar is completely dissolved, about 5 minutes. Let cool slightly, then cover and refrigerate until cold.
2. In a blender or food processor, puree the strawberries until smooth. Add the chilled sugar syrup, orange juice, lemon juice, and liqueur. Puree until thoroughly blended. Let sit for 5 minutes, or until most of the seeds have sunk to the bottom of the bowl.
3. Pour all but the sediment of the mixture into a metal pan or a metal baking bowl. Freeze until ice crystals form around the edges, about 30 minutes. Stir well and return to the freezer. Continue freezing, stirring every 30 minutes, until the granita is thoroughly frozen, about 2½ hours. Serve, or transfer to a covered container to store in the freezer until needed.

3 cups water

1 cup sugar

2 cups fresh strawberries, hulled

½ cup fresh orange juice

¼ cup fresh lemon juice

1 tablespoon crème de cassis or kirsch liqueur

CHEF'S TIP

DARCY TIZIO, FARALLON RESTAURANT: *To wash strawberries, place them in a bowl of cold water, gently lift the berries out of the water, and place them on a baking sheet lined with a clean lint-free towel. Pat dry and use as needed.*

Blueberry-Banana Brûlée

SERVES 6

Crème brûlée is a popular dessert on many menus in San Francisco.
Here, tart blueberries and sweet ripe bananas hide beneath the creamy
custard and golden sugary crust. Williams-Sonoma sells a propane blow torch
for carmelizing the sugar, or you can also melt it under the broiler.

5 large egg yolks at room
temperature

½ cup granulated sugar

2 cups half-and-half

1 vanilla bean, split halved
lengthwise

3-inch cinnamon stick

4 ripe bananas, peeled and cut
into sliced ¼-inch-thick slices

2 cups fresh or frozen blueberries

½ cup packed dark brown sugar

1. Preheat the oven to 325°F. In a bowl, beat the egg yolks and granulated sugar together. In a heavy saucepan, combine the half-and-half, vanilla bean, and cinnamon stick. Heat over medium-high heat until bubbles appear around the edges of the pan. Gradually whisk half of the hot liquid into the yolks. Return the mixture to the saucepan and cook over low heat, stirring constantly with a wooden spoon, until the custard is thick enough to coat the spoon, about 5 minutes; do not boil.

2. In a bowl, combine the bananas and blueberries and divide among individual ramekins. Strain the custard over the fruit and set the ramekins in a pan. Pour 1 inch of boiling water into the pan and place in oven. Bake for 35 to 40 minutes, or until the custards are set in the center. Refrigerate for 4 hours.

3. Preheat the broiler. Remove the ramekins from the refrigerator. Put the brown sugar in a small sieve and push through the sieve with a spoon to evenly top the custards. Place the custards under the broiler for 1 to 2 minutes, or until sugar is melted and golden brown.

HUBERT KELLER, FLEUR DE LYS RESTAURANT: *To get a crisp, thin layer of caramelized sugar on top of the brûlée — buy a propane torch. Sprinkle a thin dusting of sugar over the top of the brûlée. Apply the lighted torch, keeping it several inches above the dish, and move the flame quickly back and forth to melt the sugar into a thin, glassy crust.*

Summer-Berry Pudding

Make this dessert when berries are abundant in summer. Visit your farmers' market to find the best combination of berries. You may come across golden raspberries or olallieberries. Look for large, mature berries; they have more flavor.

1. In a large saucepan, combine the strawberries and sugar and cook over medium heat for 10 minutes, or until the strawberries give up some of their juice. Add the blackberries and raspberries and cook for 5 minutes. Let cool. Add the Chambord and salt and stir.

2. Spoon 1 cup of the berry mixture into a 10-inch soufflé dish. Add a layer of bread cubes. Continue to alternate the berry mixture and bread cubes, ending with the bread. Cover the pudding with a round of parchment paper. Place the dish on a baking sheet and place another, slightly smaller dish or pan on top of the pudding. Add a 3-pound weight or several cans of food to the smaller dish or pan to compress the pudding. Refrigerate overnight.

3. To unmold, remove the weighted dish or pan. Place a serving plate with a broad rim on top of the bread pudding dish and invert. Top each serving of pudding with a dollop of crème fraîche.

3 cups fresh strawberries, hulled and quartered

½ cup sugar

2 cups fresh blackberries

2 cups fresh golden or red raspberries

2 tablespoons Chambord (raspberry liqueur)

Pinch of salt

1 loaf brioche or egg bread, crust removed, cut into 2-inch cubes

Crème fraîche for serving

Crystallized Ginger and Citrus-Rice Pudding

SERVES 8

In San Francisco you can take a stroll through Chinatown or along
Clement Street to get in the mood for this Asian-influenced dessert. Jasmine
rice, crystallized ginger, and tangerine zest give this a fabulous flavor.

1 cup jasmine rice

5 cups whole milk

3 tablespoons butter

¾ cup plus 2 tablespoons
granulated sugar

1 vanilla bean, split lengthwise

Zest of 1 tangerine or orange

2 teaspoons crystallized ginger,
minced

6 yolks at room temperature

1 cup crème fraîche

2 tablespoons packed brown sugar

1. Preheat the oven to 350°F. In a medium saucepan, combine the rice, milk, butter, ¾ cup granulated sugar, vanilla bean, zest, and ginger. Bring almost to a boil, reduce heat to a simmer, cover, and cook until the rice is creamy and has absorbed all the liquid, about 20 minutes. Let cool slightly.
2. In a medium bowl, whisk the egg yolks and crème fraîche together. Stir into the rice. Pour the mixture into a buttered 8-cup baking dish. In a small bowl, blend the 2 tablespoons granulated sugar and the brown sugar together. Sprinkle the sugar mixture over the rice pudding. Bake, uncovered, for about 20 minutes, or until lightly browned and bubbly. Remove from the oven, turn on the broiler, and broil for 1 to 3 minutes to caramelize the sugar on top.

DARCY TIZIO, FARALLON RESTAURANT: *Vanilla beans can be reused over and over again as many as 10 times. After using one, rinse off with hot water and place in an airtight container in your freezer. After the final use, dry the beans in a 200°F oven, then place in a food processor or coffee grinder with some sugar and grind to a powder. Place in an airtight container. Use vanilla sugar in cakes, cookies, or even to flavor your morning coffee. You can also soak used vanilla beans in a little brandy, and in a few months you will have homemade vanilla extract.*

Ginger and Green Tea Sorbet

SERVES 6

This refreshing sorbet blends green tea with honey and crystallized ginger to clean the palette between courses or to serve as a light dessert. Serve with Meyer Lemon Cookies (page 294).

1. In a large saucepan, bring the water to a boil. Put the tea leaves in a tea ball. Remove the pan from heat, add the tea ball, and steep for 8 minutes. Remove the tea ball. Add the sugar, honey, and corn syrup to the liquid and stir until dissolved. Add the lemon juice and crystallized ginger. Transfer the hot liquid to a shallow glass dish. Let cool, then cover with aluminum foil and freeze for 2 hours.

2. Remove the sorbet from the freezer and transfer to a blender or food processor. Pulse the mixture until smooth. Return the sorbet to the dish and freeze for at least 2 hours.

3½ cups water

1 tablespoon loose green tea leaves, such as Jasmine Jazz by Republic of Tea

½ cup sugar

¼ cup lavender honey or other mild honey

¼ cup light corn syrup

¼ cup fresh lemon juice

⅓ cup crystallized ginger, finely chopped

ARBORIO RICE: A medium-grain rice traditionally used in risotto. Its high starch content produces the creamy texture associated with risotto.

ASIAN SESAME OIL: This dark, rich Asian oil tastes like toasted sesame seeds. Used in small amounts to impart a nutty flavor in marinades, dressings and stir-fries, it can be found in most supermarkets.

BASMATI RICE: A long-grain rice with a fine texture. Grown in the foothills of the Himalayas for thousands of years, it is a staple of Indian and Middle Eastern foods. The aging process of this grain reduces its moisture content and produces a nutty flavor. It can be found in most supermarkets.

CANNELLINI BEAN: Large white Italian kidney beans available both dried and canned.

CHANTERELLE MUSHROOMS: Bright yellow to orange trumpet-shaped mushrooms with a nutty flavor and chewy texture. Available fresh in summer and fall, and dried year-round in specialty food markets.

CHEVRIL: A member of the parsley family, this herb has fragile, curly leaves with an elusive anise flavor.

CHILI OIL: Vegetable oil in which hot red chilies have been steeped to release their heat and flavor. Popular in Chinese cooking, this spicy red oil can be found in Asian markets and most supermarkets.

CHINESE FERMENTED BLACK BEANS: Small black soybeans preserved in salt. These have an extremely salty, pungent flavor and usually must be soaked in water for about 30 minutes before using.

CHINESE CHILI GARLIC SAUCE: A sauce made from Chinese red chili peppers and garlic. It is widely used in Chinese cooking and as a spicy table condiment. It can be found bottled in most supermarkets and Asian markets.

CHINESE FIVE-SPICE POWDER: A pungent mixture of equal parts of cinnamon, cloves, fennel seed, star anise, and Szechuan peppercorns. Packaged five-spice powder is available in Asian markets and most supermarkets.

CHINESE PLUM SAUCE: A thick, reddish brown sweet-sour sauce that is most often used as a condiment in Chinese cuisine. Made from plums, apricots, sugar and seasonings, it can be found in most supermarkets and Asian markets.

CHIPOTLE CHILIES: Smoked, dried jalapeños. Chipotles have a wrinkled, dark brown skin and a smoky, sweet-hot flavor. They are available dried, pickled, or canned in adobo sauce.

CORIANDER: A plant related to the parsley family. The green lacy leaves of this plant are known as cilantro, or Chinese parsley, or fresh coriander, and can be found in the produce section of most markets. Tiny, yellow-tan coriander seeds, the dried, ripe fruit of the plant, have a flavor akin to a combination of lemon, sage, and caraway. Available whole or ground in the spice aisle of your most local markets.

COUSCOUS: These tiny pellets are not grains, but pasta made from rolled coarse and fine semolina wheat flour. A staple in North African cuisine, it is quick to prepare.

CRÈME FRAÎCHE: A thickened cream with a slightly tangy flavor and a velvety rich texture. It can be found in most gourmet supermarkets, or a similar version can be made at home: Combine 1 cup heavy cream and 2 tablespoons buttermilk in a glass container. Cover and let stand at room temperature for 8 to 24 hours. Stir well, cover and refrigerate for up to 10 days. Makes 1 cup.

CREMINI MUSHROOMS: A smaller version of portobellos, these dark brown mushrooms are slightly firmer in texture and have a fuller flavor than cultivated white mushrooms.

CRYSTALLIZED GINGER: Fresh ginger that has been sliced and cooked in a sugar syrup and coated with sugar to preserve it. The sweet-hot taste combination makes crystallized ginger a wonderful accompaniment to many desserts. Some people eat it like candy!

FAVA BEANS: Popular in Mediterranean dishes, these flat tan beans are shaped like large lima beans. Once removed from the inedible pod, larger fava beans are usually peeled before cooking. To do so, drop the beans into boiling water for 2 minutes, drain, and plunge into ice water. When cool enough to handle, pinch the beans between fingers to remove skin. Favas are also available dried.

FISH SAUCE: A salty fermented sauce with an extremely pungent odor. Known as *nam pla* in Thailand and *nuoc mam* in Vietnam, fish sauce is available in Asian markets and some supermarkets.

FUYU PERSIMMONS: Small tomato-shaped fruits that, when ripe, have a red-orange skin and flesh. Unlike the larger Hachiya persimmon, which is very soft when ripe, a ripe Fuyu is quite firm, with a smooth and glossy skin. Available during fall and winter months.

GARAM MASALA SPICE: An Indian blend of ground dry-roasted spices that can include black pepper, cinnamon, cloves, coriander, cumin, cardamom, dried chilies, fennel, mace, nutmeg, and other spices. Available in Indian markets, and most supermarkets.

HEIRLOOM VEGETABLES AND FRUITS: Produce grown from "heirloom seeds," that were saved from the few remaining varieties of vegetables and fruits produced without human manipulation. Most fruits and vegetables today are produced from seeds that are intended for mass production because they are the heartiest varieties, not necessarily the best-tasting. As people are becoming more aware of better-tasting alternative varieties, these are becoming more and more available in specialty produce markets and at farmers' markets.

JASMINE RICE: A fragrant long-grain white rice from Thailand. Its flavor and aroma are similar to those of its cousin Basmati rice.

HOISIN SAUCE: A slightly sweet sauce made from soybeans, garlic, chili peppers, and various spices. It is widely used in Chinese cooking and as a table condiment. It can be found in supermarkets and Asian markets.

KAFFIR LIME LEAVES: The glossy dark green leaves of the kaffir lime, a small pear-shaped citrus fruit grown in Southeast Asia and Hawaii, are imbued with a mysterious floral-citrus aroma. Dried or frozen kaffir lime leaves can be found in Asian markets. Fresh leaves, which have a more intense aroma, are available through mail order (try Smith & Hawken or Gardener's Eden) and sometimes in Southeast Asian markets. There is no substitute for these leaves, but if you must, try using grated lime zest mixed with finely chopped fresh lemongrass.

KALAMATA OLIVES: Almond-shaped Greek olives with a dark eggplant color and a rich and fruity flavor. Kalamata olives come packed in either olive oil or vinegar.

LAVENDER: A relative of mint, this aromatic plant has violet flowers and green or pale gray leaves, both of which have a bitter pungency.

LEMONGRASS: One of the most important herbs in Thai cooking, lemongrass has long, thin gray-green leaves, a scallionlike bulb base, and a sour lemon flavor and fragrance.

MEYER LEMONS: Thin-skinned rounded lemons with a deep yellow to orange color. Sweeter than a regular lemon, it has a low-acid juice that makes it ideal for use in many dishes. Try to find Meyer lemons at your local farmers' market, or ask your grocer to order them. To order a Meyer lemon tree, see the Smith & Hawken or Gardener's Eden entries in Resources (page 311). Regular Eureka lemons may be substituted if necessaary.

MISO PASTE: A Japanese fermented soybean paste with the consistency of peanut butter. Miso is available in three forms: white, yellow, and red. This Japanese culinary mainstay can be found in Asian markets and many natural food stores.

MOREL MUSHROOMS: Edible wild mushrooms of the same fungus species as the truffle. They have a spongy, honeycombed, cone-shaped cap, a smoky and earthy flavor, and range in color from a rich tan to dark brown. Fresh morels can be found in early spring in gourmet markets. Dried morels, which have a more intense flavor than fresh ones, are available year-round in many markets.

ORZO: A tiny, rice-shaped pasta.

PANCETTA: An Italian bacon that is cured with salt and spices but not smoked. It is used in Italian cooking to flavor sauces, meats, and vegetables. It is available in Italian delicatessens and some gourmet markets.

QUINOA: A staple in Latin American cuisine, this small round grain cooks up like rice, but in half the time and at four times its original volume. It has more protein than any other grain, containing all eight of the essential amino acids.

ROSEWATER: A distillation of rose petals with the intense perfume of its source. It is a popular flavoring in the cuisines of the Middle East and India.

SHIITAKE MUSHROOMS: Also known as black mushrooms, their caps are dark brown, sometimes with tan striations, and are typically 3 to 6 inches in diameter. The stems are quite tough and are usually discarded or reserved to flavor stocks and sauces. Shiitakes are available year-round in many supermarkets, but are most plentiful and least expensive in spring and autumn.

TAMARIND PASTE: A paste made from the fruit of a small tree native to India, Asia, and Northern Africa. The paste has a sweet-sour taste and is used to flavor foods such as chutneys and curry dishes. It can be found in Indian, Latino, and Asian markets.

THAI CHILIES: This tiny red chili produces a fiery heat that does not dissipate when cooked. It is a popular seasoning in many Asian cuisines and can be found in most Asian markets. Some cooks remove the chilies from the finished dish because of their intense heat.

TOMATILLOS: A small, green or purple tomatolike fruit that grows in a husk and is native to Mexico. Once the husk is removed, the fruit is usually roasted for use in salsas and other sauces. It can be found in most supermarkets and many Latin American markets.

WASABI: This Japanese version of horseradish comes from the root of an Asian plant and has a sharp, fiery flavor. It is available in Asian and specialty markets in paste and powder form.

Contributing Chefs

We thank the following chefs for their submissions of fabulous tips incorporated throughout the book.

FLO BRAKER
Lives in the Bay Area and is author of *The Simple Art of Baking* and *Sweet Miniatures,* and is a regular contributor to the *San Francisco Chronicle* food section.

REED HEARON
Rose Pistola Restaurant
532 Columbus Avenue
San Francisco
(415) 399-0499

Rose's Café
2298 Union Street
San Francisco
(415) 775-2200

Black Cat Restaurant
501 Broadway
San Francisco
(415) 981-2233

MARIA HELM
PlumpJack Café
3127 Fillmore Street
San Francisco
(415) 563-4755

GERALD HIRIGOYEN
Fringale Restaurant
570 Fourth Street
San Francisco
(415) 543-0573

Pastis Restaurant
1015 Battery Street
San Francisco
(415) 391-2555

HUBERT KELLER
Fleur de Lys
777 Sutter Street
San Francisco
(415) 673-7779

THOMAS KELLER
The French Laundry Restaurant
6640 Washington Street
Yountville
(707) 944-2380

MICHAEL MINA
Aqua Restaurant
252 California Street
San Francisco
(415) 956-9662

DARCY TIZIO
Farallon Restaurant
450 Post Street
San Francisco
(415) 956-6969

ARNOLD WONG
EOS Restaurant and Wine Bar
901 Cole Street
San Francisco
(415) 566-3063

Wine Consultants

We thank the following wine consultants for their suggestions for pairing foods with wine.

KRIS HARRIMAN
Sommelier at PlumpJack Café and wine shop.

PlumpJack Wine Shop
3201 Fillmore Street
San Francisco, CA 94123
(415) 346-9870
Call to order any wines he has suggested.

PlumpJack Café,
3127 Fillmore Street
San Francisco, CA 94123
(415) 563-4755

PlumpJack Squaw Valley Inn
1920 Squaw Valley Road
Olympic Valley, CA 96146
(800) 323-7666

DAVID PAULEY
Wine buyer for London Wine Bar.

London Wine Bar
415 Sansome Street
San Francisco, CA 94111
(415) 788-4811

DEBBIE ZACHAREAS
Wine Director and Buyer for Ashbury Market and EOS Restaurant and Wine Bar.

Ashbury Market
205 Frederick Street
San Francisco, CA 94117
(415) 566-3134
Call to order any wines she has suggested.

EOS Restaurant and Wine Bar
901 Cole Street / 101 Carl Street
San Francisco, CA 94117
(415) 566-3063

Resources

Retail and Mail-Order Sources for Specialty Ingredients

(C) = catalog available for mail order

☎ = *phone orders only*

ASIAN INGREDIENTS

UWAJIMAYA (C)
(206) 624-6248
(800) 889-1928
WEBSITE ADDRESS:
WWW.UWAJIMAYA.COM

Japanese, Thai, Vietnamese, Cambodian, Indian, and Chinese cooking products.

CHEESES

BELLWETHER FARMS
(888) 527-8606 ☎
Handmade cheeses.

BODEGA GOAT CHEESE
(707) 876-3483 ☎
Many varieties of goat cheese.

COWGIRL CREAMERY (C)
(415) 663-9335
WEBSITE ADDRESS:
WWW.COWGIRLCREAMERY.COM

Cheese products from local dairies using organic milk.

CYPRESS GROVE
(707) 839-3168 ☎
A variety of goat cheeses.

DEAN AND DELUCA (C)
607 SOUTH ST. HELENA HIGHWAY
ST. HELENA, CA 94574
(707) 967-9980
WEBSITE ADDRESS:
WWW.DEAN-DELUCA-
NAPAVALLEY.COM

The Napa Valley branch of the famed New York culinary store.

DRAEGER'S MARKET PLACE
222 EAST FOURTH AVENUE
SAN MATEO, CA 94401
(650) 685-3700
WEBSITE ADDRESS:
WWW.DRAEGERS.COM

An extensive gourmet market and cookware store.

OAKVILLE GROCERY (C)
7856 ST. HELENA HIGHWAY
ST. HELENA, CA 94562
(707) 996-4477
(800) 973-6324

An old-fashioned grocery store with fabulous gourmet products and a deli.

ROCKRIDGE MARKET HALL
5655 COLLEGE AVENUE
OAKLAND, CA 94618
(510) 601-8208
WEBSITE ADDRESS:
WWW.MARKETPLACE.COM

A food hall with the Bay Area's finest and freshest food selection.

STRAUS FAMILY CREAMERY (C)
P.O. BOX 768
MARSHALL, CA 94940
(415) 663-5464
WEBSITE ADDRESS:
WWW.STRAUSMILK.COM

Producers of organic milk, butter, and cheese.

WHOLE FOODS (C)
1765 CALIFORNIA STREET
SAN FRANCISCO, CA 94109
415-674-0500

WEBSITE ADDRESS:
WWW.WHOLEFOODS.COM

A food store featuring a wide variety of organic produce, cheese, bread, and bulk items.

WILLIAMS-SONOMA (C)
150 POST STREET
SAN FRANCISCO, CA 94108
(415) 362-6904
(800) 541-2233
WEBSITE ADDRESS:
WWW.WILLIAMS-SONOMA.COM

Cowgirl Creamery and Laura Chenel goat cheeses are available through the catalog.

CHOCOLATES

GHIRARDELLI CHOCOLATE
900 NORTH POINT
SAN FRANCISCO, CA 94109
(888) 402-6262 ☎

The famous 150-year-old San Francisco chocolate factory and shop.

SCHARFFEN BERGER
CHOCOLATE MAKERS (C)
(800) 930-4528
WEBSITE ADDRESS:
WWW.SCHARFFEN-BERGER.COM

The founder of Scharffenberger sparkling wines now makes a remarkable bittersweet and unsweetened chocolate that's great for baking.

WILLIAMS-SONOMA
(SEE ABOVE)

CRYSTALLIZED GINGER, EDIBLE FLOWERS, AND LAVENDER

GARDENER'S EDEN (C)
(800) 822-1214 📞
Mail order catalog for herbs and edible flowers.

HERB LADY
52792 42ND AVENUE
LAWRENCE, MI 49064
(616) 674-3879 📞
Crystallized ginger, edible flowers.

MAXIE FLOWERS A LA CARTE
1015 MARTIN LANE
SEBASTOPOL, CA 95472
(707) 829-0592 📞
Edible flowers.

SMITH & HAWKEN (C)
1330 TENTH STREET
BERKELEY, CA 94710
(510) 527-1076
(800) 776-3336
WEBSITE ADDRESS:
WWW.SMITH-HAWKEN.COM
Potted herbs and seeds for edible flowers. Meyer lemon and kaffir lime trees available through mail order.

STONE FREE FARMS
(831) 726-5111 📞
Edible flowers.

WHOLE FOODS
(SEE ABOVE)
Edible flowers, lavender.

WILLIAMS-SONOMA
(SEE ABOVE)

MEATS

AIDELL'S SAUSAGE COMPANY (C)
(800) 546-5795
WEBSITE ADDRESS:
WWW.AIDELLS.COM
Fresh and pre-cooked sausages including chicken and turkey based sausages.

GINGRASS FAMILY SAUSAGES
HAWTHORNE LANE RESTAURANT
22 HAWTHORNE STREET
SAN FRANCISCO, CA 94105
(415) 777-5667 📞
WEBSITE ADDRESS:
WWW.HAWTHORNELANE.COM
Fresh sausages, including chicken, duck, pork, lamb and salmon.

WILLIAMS-SONOMA
(SEE ABOVE)
Aidell's sausages, Niman beef, applewood smoked bacon are available through mail order.

OILS AND VINEGARS

CONSORZIO (C)
NUMBER 4 FINANCIAL PLAZA
NAPA, CA 94558
(800) 288-1089
WEBSITE ADDRESS:
WWW.CONSORZIO.COM
Infused olive oils and other gourmet products.

DEAN & DELUCA
(SEE ABOVE)

DRAEGER'S MARKET PLACE
(SEE ABOVE)
EVO olive oil produced by Thomas Keller is available here.

O OLIVE OIL COMPANY
(415) 460-6598 📞
Blood Orange olive oil, Meyer Lemon olive oil, Tahitian Lime olive oil, and Zinfandel vinegar.

OAKVILLE GROCERY
(SEE ABOVE)
EVO olive oil produced by Thomas Keller is available here.

VIANSA WINERY (C)
25200 ARNOLD DRIVE
SONOMA, CA 95476
(707) 935-4700
(800) 995-4740

WEBSITE ADDRESS:
WWW.VIANSA.COM
A beautiful winery and gift store carrying a large selection of Napa Valley gourmet foods.

WILLIAMS-SONOMA
(SEE ABOVE)

PASTA AND POLENTA

DEAN & DELUCA
(SEE ABOVE)

PASTA SHOP
1786 FOURTH STREET
BERKELEY, CA 94710
(510) 528-1786

WHOLE FOODS
(SEE ABOVE)

WILLIAMS-SONOMA
(SEE ABOVE)

TEAS

TEA AND COMPANY (C)
2207 FILLMORE STREET
SAN FRANCISCO, CA 94115
(415) 929-TEAS
WEBSITE ADDRESS:
WWW.TEAANDCOMPANY.COM
Specialty teas from around the world.

COOKWARE

DRAEGER'S MARKET PLACE
222 EAST FOURTH AVENUE
SAN MATEO, CA 94401
(650) 685-3700

SUR LA TABLE (C)
77 MAIDEN LANE
SAN FRANCISCO, CA 94108
(415) 732-7900

WILLIAMS-SONOMA (C)
(SEE ABOVE)

INDEX

TABLE OF EQUIVALENTS

The exact equivalents in the following tables have been rounded for convenience.

Liquid/Dry Measures

U.S.	METRIC
¼ teaspoon	1.25 milliliters
½ teaspoon	2.5 milliliters
1 teaspoon	5 milliliters
1 tablespoon (3 teaspoons)	15 milliliters
1 fluid ounce (2 tablespoons)	30 milliliters
¼ cup	60 milliliters
⅓ cup	80 milliliters
½ cup	120 milliliters
1 cup	240 milliliters
1 pint (2 cups)	480 milliliters
1 quart (4 cups, 32 ounces)	960 milliliters
1 gallon (4 quarts)	3.84 liters
1 ounce (by weight)	28 grams
1 pound	454 grams
2.2 pounds	1 kilogram

Length

U.S.	METRIC
⅛ inch	3 millimeters
¼ inch	6 millimeters
½ inch	12 millimeters
1 inch	2.5 centimeters

Oven Temperature

FAHRENHEIT	CELSIUS	GAS
250	120	½
275	140	1
300	150	2
325	160	3
350	180	4
375	190	5
400	200	6
425	220	7
450	230	8
475	240	9
500	260	10